Contributors

Eleanor Bell is Leverhulme Post-Doctora⸻
culture at the Department of English Stu⸻
rently writing a monograph, *Questioning Scotland,*⸻
grave MacMillan.

Kasia Boddy teaches in the Department of English at University College, London. Her book on cultural representations of boxing will be published in 2003 by Reakton Books.

Cairns Craig is Professor in the Department of English Literature at the University of Edinburgh. His publications include *Out of History* (1996) and *The Modern Scottish Novel* (1999). He is also Director of the Centre for the History of Ideas in Scotland.

Thomas Docherty is Professor in the School of English at the University of Kent. His books include *On Modern Authority, After Theory: Postmodernism/Postmarxism* and *Criticism and Modernity*. He is currently engaged in a three-volume study of the conditions of criticism and ethics.

Christopher Harvie is Professor of British and Irish Studies at Tübingen University in Germany. His most recent book is *Scotland: A Short History*, published by Oxford University Press. He is also working on *North Britain: West Britain* for the same publishers.

Ellen-Raïssa Jackson now works for the BBC having completed a PhD in contemporary Scottish and Irish Writing in 1999.

Willy Maley is Professor of Renaissance Studies at the University of Glasgow. His publications include *A Spenser Chronology* (Macmillan, 1994), *Salvaging Spenser: Colonialism, Culture and Identity* (Macmillan, 1997) and *Nation, State and Empire in English Renaissance Literature: Shakespeare to Milton* (Palgrave, 2002).

Gavin Miller has worked for the Departments of English Literature at the Universities of Glasgow, Edinburgh and Dundee. He is currently writing two books: an introduction to R.D. Laing (to be published in the series *Edinburgh Review Introductions*) and a study of Alasdair Gray (contracted to Rodopi).

Tom Nairn is Research Professor at RMIT University, Melbourne. His publications include *The Break-Up of Britain, The Enchanted Glass: Britain and its Monarchy, After Britain* and *Pariah: Misfortunes of the British Kingdom*.

Sarah Neely has written on several areas of film adaptation, including the "teen-pic" and Shakespeare, and has had reviews published in *English*, *SCOPE: an Online Film Journal* and *Textual Practice*. She lectures in film studies at the University of Paisley.

Laurence Nicoll teaches in the Department of English Literature and in the Office of Lifelong Learning at the University of Edinburgh. His primary research interests are James Kelman, Samuel Beckett, Philip Roth, philosophy and the novel, and existentialism.

Berthold Schoene is Lecturer in Contemporary British Literature and Culture at the University of Manchester. His main research interests are in gender theory and masculinity studies, postcolonialism, and contemporary British fiction. He is the author of *Writing Men* (2000) and co-editor of *Posting the Male* (2003). He is currently completing a book on Irvine Welsh.

Anne McManus Scriven is completing her PhD thesis at the Department of English Studies, University of Strathclyde. Her thesis discusses the previously unexamined "Scottishness" of the writings of Margaret Oliphant.

A.J.P. Thomson is Lecturer in English Literature at the University of Glasgow. In addition to a book on Hegel and Critical Theory, he is working on the political theory of deconstruction, and on devolution in contemporary British politics. Other research interests include twentieth-century literature, contemporary Scottish writing and Continental philosophy.

Ronald Turnbull is Editor of *Edinburgh Review*. He is writing a book on John Macmurray to be published in the series *Edinburgh Review Introductions*.

Christopher Whyte is Reader in the Department of Scottish Literature at Glasgow University. His *Modern Scottish Poetry*, a study of twenty poets from the period between 1939 and 1999, will appear in 2003 from Edinburgh University Press. His edition of Sorley MacLean's *Dain do Eimhir* received a Saltire Award in 2002. He is the author of four novels in English and two collections of poetry in Gaelic.

Scotland in Theory

Scottish Cultural Review
of Language and Literature

Volume 1

Series Editors
John Corbett
University of Glasgow

Sarah Dunnigan
University of Edinburgh

James McGonigal
University of Glasgow

Production Editor
Gavin Miller
University of Edinburgh

SCROLL

The Scottish Cultural Review of Language and Literature publishes new work in Scottish Studies, with a focus on analysis and reinterpretation of the literature and languages of Scotland, and the cultural contexts that have shaped them.

Further information on our editorial and production procedures can be found at www.rodopi.nl

Scotland in Theory

Reflections on
Culture & Literature

Edited by

Eleanor Bell & Gavin Miller

Amsterdam – New York, NY 2004

Cover design: Gavin Miller

The paper on which this book is printed meets the requirements of "ISO
9706:1994, Information and documentation - Paper for documents -
Requirements for permanence".

ISBN: 90-420-1028-2
©Editions Rodopi B.V., Amsterdam - New York, NY 2004
Printed in The Netherlands

Contents

Acknowledgements

Eleanor Bell and Gavin Miller would like to thank Professor Cairns Craig of the University of Edinburgh for his support and funding for the Scotland in Theory conference which inspired this collection of essays. We would also like to thank him for his continuing support and encouragement during the preparation of this volume. Our further thanks are due to Professor James McGonigal of the Faculty of Education, University of Glasgow, who has overseen this volume in his role as Series Editor to SCROLL. His support, encouragement and advice have been invaluable. We would also like to thank Marieke Schilling of Rodopi for useful technical and procedural advice throughout the preparation of this book. We also gratefully acknowledge the Scottish Parliament Building Information Centre for permission to photograph the model of the Holyrood Parliament which is pictured on the cover of this volume.

Introduction

Gavin Miller and Eleanor Bell

Questions surrounding communal identity and the future of the nation-state are clearly multi-disciplinary, and may involve issues of post-modernism, postcolonialism, identity politics and postnationalism. *Scotland in Theory*, emerging from a conference held at the University of Edinburgh in 1999, addresses some of these concerns in a Scottish context.

While many Scottish critics recognise the need for plural read-ings of nationhood, there is arguably still a lingering parochialism in Scottish literary studies, where, for example, literature from Scotland must firstly be explained in terms of its Scottishness, rather than in terms of its literary or aesthetic qualities. Although *Scotland in Theory* is clearly concerned with literary and cultural representations of the nation, this book also encourages an awareness of the changing nature of Scottish studies. It draws attention to new types of criticism which are able to challenge the cultural-nationalist paradigm, and which also reflect the sociological and intellectual changes now taking place.

It is time for Scottish studies to take some tentative steps towards the future. While a brief survey of contemporary Irish literary studies will reveal rich theoretical material, in Scottish literary studies there has so far been an absence of, and perhaps resistance to, newer forms of thinking. Where, for example, in Irish studies there are many books on topics such as postmodernism, postcolonialism, and feminist read-ings of nationalism and national identity, from a Scottish-studies per-spective very little exists in print. The editors of this book therefore feel that we are now at a timely moment in the development of Scot-tish studies. Our enterprise, however, is not being carried out in the spirit of an "anything goes" postmodernism where categories such as nationhood can be lightly dismissed. Rather, it is carried out in order to develop a stronger knowledge of the discipline in which we work.

Scotland in Theory begins with Tom Nairn's introduction to a re-cent edition of his classic, *The Break-Up of Britain*. Nairn discusses how the political landscape has changed in the twenty-five years since the book was first published. Scotland now has a devolved parliament: will this contain the energies of nationalism, or is it just another step toward the dissolution of the United Kingdom? Nairn argues firmly for the latter. Although nationalism may seem an irrelevance in a globalised world, it is, he believes, increasingly vital that Scotland should escape from the United Kingdom, a political entity that is now little more than a client state to the USA.

In his article, however, Nairn still tends to see nationalism as a means to such ends as resisting globalisation (or Americanisation, as he would more likely regard it). Ronald Turnbull in "Nairn's Nationalisms" explores this reluctance to admit that nationalism may be an end in itself. Turnbull argues that nationalism is not just an instrument for a higher purpose (such as socialism, or recovery of national "potency"); rather, nationalism has a serious content of philosophical ideas which are debated and discussed within the space of national identity. One should not, therefore, merely dismiss nationalism as (useful) false-consciousness.

Even successful Scottish nationalists, though, would have to use everyday, mundane institutions in order to govern an autonomous nation. Christopher Harvie's article, "The Case of the Postmodernist's Sore Thumb, or the Moral Sentiments of John Rebus" asks how optimistic one can be about such a future state. The Scottish Parliament, he argues, does not seem to have taken Scotland further down the road to a national utopia. Even an independent Scotland would face problems encountered by the devolved parliament: the reactionary tendencies of the popular press and institutional religion, the persistence of political and economic élites, and the threat of a "plutonic" economy based on consumption and leisure. Fictional detectives like Ian Rankin's John Rebus are a vital, sceptical antidote to nationalist optimism.

In his article "Phrasing Scotland and the Postmodern", A.J.P. Thomson also criticises an easy "postmodern" national confidence. He perceives a tendency in sociologists such as David McCrone and critics such as Cairns Craig to legitimate their nationalist concerns by exploiting the fashionability of postmodern ideas. For both, Scotland has a privileged relation to the postmodern, as either an early entrant to the sociological condition of postmodernity, or as a prime example of heterogeneous postmodernist debate and dissent. In either case, argues Thomson, the validity of national politics is presumed, and remains uncriticised throughout these exercises in re-branding Scotland as "postmodern".

In a similar vein, Eleanor Bell discusses the failure of many Scottish theorists to take seriously postnational challenges to conventional politics. In "Postmodernism, Nationalism and the Question of Tradition", she shows how Scottish criticism has neglected the postnational and postmodern ideas of thinkers such as Richard Kearney and Anthony Giddens. Bell challenges Scottish critics to take seriously these ideas – or to face obsolescence and marginalisation within literary studies.

A more sceptical attitude towards postnationalism is presented in Willy Maley and Sarah Neely's "'Almost afraid to know itself': *Macbeth* and Cinematic Scotland". They show how the historical neglect of Scotland in productions of *Macbeth* has continued, and even intensified, in the global cultural market. Film adaptations of *Macbeth* seem incapable of representing the country as anything other a collection of kitsch signifiers (even as Scotland itself gains a surer sense of identity after devolution).

A similar cautionary note is sounded by Ellen-Raïssa Jackson's analysis of recent Scottish film-making in "Dislocating the Nation: Political Devolution and Cultural Identity on Stage and Screen". The Scottish Parliament seems unwilling or unable to protect and nourish a cinema that could combat Hollywood's colonisation of the imagination.

Berthold Schoene, however, is more optimistic about Scotland's potential postnational and postmodern condition. In "Nervous Men, Mobile Nation: Masculinity and Psychopathology in Irvine Welsh's *Filth* and *Glue*", Schoene explores the connections between Scottish nationality and the unemotional, self-contained, nigh-on "autistic" ideals of Scottish masculinity. The newly devolved Scotland must give up these standards, and enter a more fluid condition which is neither rigidly territorial nor stiffly masculine.

Christopher Whyte too points out the gendered and sexualised limits to Scottishness in his article "Queer Readings, Gay Texts: From *Redgauntlet* to *The Prime of Miss Jean Brodie*". At one time, Christian interpreters tried to remove the sexual meaning from even

such unabashedly erotic texts as *The Song of Solomon.* The canon of
Scottish literature operates a similar hermeneutic which banishes
transgendered or homoerotic meanings from its classic texts. Cross-
dressing in *Redgauntlet,* and lesbianism in *The Prime of Miss Jean
Brodie*, are allegorised into comments upon national identity, rather
than simply accepted as the representation of pleasures which are
excluded by "Scottishness".

Anne Scriven's "The Muted Scotswoman and Oliphant's
Kirsteen" further explores such canonical exclusions through an examination of one of Margaret Oliphant's neglected nineteenth-century
novels. *Kirsteen* represents a protagonist who must develop beyond
the rigid and masculine confines of her Scottish identity and upbring-
ing. Through the character of Kirsteen, Oliphant tackles the difficult
combination of Scottishness with womanhood.

The masculinity of Scottish national identity is made even more
apparent by Kasia Boddy's examination of boxing in "Scottish Fighting Men: Big and Wee". From Walter Scott to Thomas Healy and
Hugh McIlvanney, the Scottish "hardman" has been a mascot for his
nation. Boddy, though, shows how this image has been challenged in
recent years: the "Big Man" of McIlvanney's novel must give up his
grand gestures and acquire the practicality and everyday heroism exhibited in feminine solidarity.

The image of Scottishness as raw physicality has an effect on
more than just Scottish popular and folk culture. In "'Persuade without convincing … represent without reasoning': the Inferiorist
Mythology of the Scots Language", Gavin Miller shows how this inferiorist thought-pattern has entered into Scots-language poetry and the
criticism which surrounds it. The myth of "phonaesthesia" preserves
an image of the Scotsman as the speaker of a uniquely sensual, primitive, and magical language.

Ironically, this mythology of the Scots language emerged in opposition to English cultural domination. Laurence Nicoll in his article
"Philosophy, Tradition, Nation" explores another myth created to
counteract perceived English colonialism – that of a distinct and uniform tradition of Scottish philosophy (denoted by George Davie's
phrase "the democratic intellect"). This unfortunate fiction, argues

Nicoll, potentially restricts Scottish intellectual and cultural life, and certainly misrepresents the practice and history of philosophy.

In Thomas Docherty's "The Existence of Scotland", the democratic intellect is again considered as a paradigm for Scottishness. Yet, argues Docherty, Scotland is more "possibility" than "theory". To theorise Scotland, as much as to administer or manage it, risks neglecting the communication of possibility through social bonds. Only such a condition of shared possibility can allow Scotland to be a place of social agency rather than of static reflection.

Docherty's interest in communication and sociability is paralleled by Cairns Craig's argument in "Beyond Reason – Hume, Seth, Macmurray and Scotland's Postmodernity". Craig argues that Scottish literature has been presciently postmodern: this peculiarity, though, is not explicable by reference to conventional postmodern thought. Rather, Scottish literature was formed by a more authentically postmodern philosophical debate in which communication and agency were central ideas.

Taken together, the essays which constitute *Scotland in Theory* both represent and help to create such communication and agency. The new parliament building at Holyrood, depicted in the architect's model on the cover of this volume, stands for this renewed vitality in Scottish culture. From their different perspectives, and with various agendas, the contributors to this collection insightfully analyse the condition and meaning of the society that is "Scotland". Without such debate, the parliament would remain merely an emblem, and Scottish intellectual life would be as "theoretical" – in the pejorative sense of the word – as an architect's plans and wooden models. *Scotland in Theory* is therefore a step towards a new Scotland, a Scotland in practice. The arguments in the following pages deserve to be understood, considered, and opposed (or accepted) by more than an insular élite of writers and academics. That is why this volume exists.

Break-Up: Twenty-Five Years On

Tom Nairn

In the twenty-five years since *The Break-Up of Britain* was published, Scotland has achieved devolution. The Scottish Parliament was intended to prevent the disintegration of the United Kingdom; however, in an era of globalisation, Scottish nationalism may become yet more attractive as a means of resisting US hegemony.
Keywords: nationalism, Eric Hobsbawm, Ernest Gellner, devolution, Margaret Thatcher, Tony Blair, New Labour, globalism, internationalism.

When *The Break-Up of Britain* was first published in 1977, the publisher asked whether a question mark after the title might not be more appropriate. After some argument, it was fortunately left out. Peremptory statements can last better than nervous questions. New Left Books, ancestor of Verso Books, held a reception for the book in London at which the historian Eric Hobsbawm expressed in quite vehement terms his doubts and misgivings about the book's prophecy. Later he published his message as a critique in the *New Left Review* (Hobsbawm 1977).[1] His argument was that on no account should intellectuals try to "paint nationalism red" – that is, present it as an inherently progressive or emancipatory phenomenon. The Soviet, Yugoslav and British multinational states might be in mounting trouble. But troubles may be soluble through the adoption of better policies (communist, civic-liberal, multicultural or other). To anticipate break-ups was therefore to risk hastening them – in effect, a wilful betrayal of enlightened principles.

Such misgivings seemed reasonable at the time. After all, Scottish and Welsh political nationalism were still uncertain and faltering growths, and the renewed "Troubles" in Northern Ireland were in some ways reminiscent of earlier times rather than of new developments. English nationalism remained a curiosity, the fringe interest of

---

[1] For a very different and much more comprehensive critique of the ideas in *Break-Up* I would urge readers to consult Cocks 2002. Although Cocks discerns a defence of "ethnicity" where none exists, she none the less appraises the book in relation to the 1980s and 1990s, rather than to abstract notions of past history.

academics and folklorists. Equivalent symptoms in Belgium, France, Italy, Spain and Eastern Europe could also be dismissed as marginal, or more frankly as a "reactionary" nostalgia either for Fascism, or for nations that never were. Karl Popper's *The Open Society* (1945) was still frequently invoked as philosophical justification for this position. Its mixture of anti-Marxism, anti-Historicism and Liberal empiricism was still popular, and it would go on to enjoy a rebirth twelve years later, after Margaret Thatcher's election in 1979.[2] In general terms, progress was assumed to be a long-range and one-time transition: from the pre-historic condition of "closed" or tribal cultures to one of "open", liberal or social democratic civilisation. Nationalism was automatically suspected of seeking reversion from the latter to the former. It was putting the clock back, therefore, and reopening the door to the blood-politics of irrational communalism, and the atavistic voices of a former age.

The doubts voiced in *The Break-Up of Britain* were of course instinctive rejections of this philosophical perspective, as well as discrete arguments about the political condition of the United Kingdom. On the other hand, they were never endorsements of ethnic nationalism either. With the benefit of one quarter-century's hindsight, I see no reason for disavowing that underlying position. At the same time, revising the philosophical foundations has proved damnably hard.[3] As for the condition of the UK, this has disappointed both parties to the old quarrel. It has been too tenacious of life for nationalists, and yet done extremely little to satisfy protagonists of Union and greatness.

1. Internationalism and Politics

What passed for "internationalism" in the 1970s was in truth an abstract and narrow creed, resting on pious and selective acceptance of

---

[2] For the origins and fate of *The Open Society*, see Jarvie and Pralong 1999.

[3] The author's latest stumbling venture in this direction was an inaugural talk at RMIT University in Melbourne, soon to be published as *Black Pluto's Door: the 'DNA' of Nationalism*. This suggests a general socio-historical explanation for the persistence and contemporary recrudescence of nationality politics, taking social nature as starting point rather than modernity alone.

certain Enlightenment ideas – those that could be made to look favourable to the state authorities of the era, and to some political parties of the moment.[4] Nor has this tendency to travesty lessened since the 1970s. Neo-liberalism would in the 1990s carry it to new heights of absurdity. While proclaiming themselves revolutionary, the orthodox Left movements of 1977 were even then turning into fossilised remnants.

However, ethnic nationality politics had its own narrow piety as well, derived from almost equally old counter-constructions of Romanticism, and from a misconstrued Social Darwinism. The species-differentiation which turned into "nationality" is ancient; but the "ethnic" label is very recent, deriving from colonialism and American dilemmas of the 1960s. The antagonism of these philosophies was to be artificially preserved until the 1990s, within the permafrost of Cold War fear and rigid confrontation.

However, it should be emphasised how long the post-Cold War thawing process is likely to be. The Cold War lasted for longer than a conventional generation; recovery from it could occupy another. And the slowest region to thaw out is, unfortunately, the one where change is now most urgently and obviously needed: politics. Globalisation will be tolerable only via re-constituted democratic polities, in an altered international order; yet politics and culture make up the zone upon which the dead generations weigh most heavily.

The causes of such uneven liberation are very deep-rooted. They probably lie in the symbiosis of two factors, each tenaciously conservative in its own right. On one side is the modern or post-Westphalian state, the characteristic power-structure still evoked by the description, "nation-state". This extruded apparatus of authority is defined by separation from the society that it supposedly "serves", but also controls. Abstraction is inseparable from the modern "Leviathan", as is a resultant rigidity of both human organisation and outlook – the typical traits of formal administration or "bureaucracy". State power looks first of all to precedent and establishment; it looks backwards rather

---

[4] The most important study since then on Enlightenment is surely Rothschild 2001. Rothschild shows how misrepresentation of Adam Smith and David Hume began in the late 18th century, in a style recognisably similar to that of the neo-liberal hysteria two centuries later.

than forwards. This is "How Institutions Think", the justly famous
title of Mary Douglas's anthropological critique of modern bureaucracy (Douglas 1987), but it is also how they survive, above all when
historically successful (as Western institutions were, in the 1980s).

This tendency is automatically reinforced by the second conservative factor involved: that of the "intellectuals". As Antonio Gramsci
observed from the bitter isolation of his prison notebooks in the 1930s,
intellectuals are unavoidably conservative by formation, because
nourished on a humus of accumulated and bygone culture. They may
of course imagine drastic changes and departures from this inheritance
(his own case, and that of the Italian Communist Party he helped
found). Yet the sources of such imagination must lie in well-springs
and traditions themselves inherited. Inherited, and often misunderstood or travestied, above all when a rising educated stratum attains
office by revolution, or even via the representative process. Its self-
justification then becomes allied to that of institutional existence, in
the state-sanctioned compound of "our way" – a national course sanctified by re-written history, and turned into the apparently inevitable
order of things.

2. Break-up to Breakdown

Only two years after *Break-Up* came out, a pseudo-revolutionary
chain of events was launched in Great Britain that exemplified these
characteristics. This was Mrs Thatcher's radical version of conservatism, founded on a "liberation" of socio-economic forces and the roll-
back of state responsibility for civil society. Though almost two centuries old, these neo-liberal formulae were now pitilessly excavated to
suit the conditions of the 1970s and 1980s.[5] Her New Toryism was
accompanied by a reinforcement of the inherited United Kingdom
framework of state. During the Thatcherite 1980s, an uncompromis-
ingly British Union was stressed as never before. The aim was to ex-
tinguish all tendencies towards breakaway, as well as a discredited
socialism. Like the rulers of the Communist East, Thatcherites were

---

[5] See Yergin and Stanislaw 2001.

all for efficient and colourful local government – provided it stayed tame, and offered no political challenge to the imperium.

At the same time, intellectuals were recruited (or recruited themselves) into her altered hegemony, painting hereditary British nationalism in new colours as part of what was in truth a redemption of mildewed tradition. Once socially invisible, or frankly despised, Britain's "thinking reeds" (to borrow Pascal's phrase) now found themselves regimented into bright-eyed Policy Units. The "Unwritten Constitution" was to be revivified by the new entrepreneurial culture, not challenged or replaced by it. A new intelligentsia was needed for this task, ostensibly "radical" but essentially conformist – devoted, in effect, to redeeming British traditions by dazzling conjuring tricks.

Thatcher was deposed by her own party in 1990, when the contradictions of this stance had become electorally intolerable. But her counter-movement had some serious effects. Within a world still generally stultified by the Cold War, the breaking-up process was held back in Britain for eighteen years. Her acceleration of economic change was accompanied by more than plain socio-political conservation: a distinct style of mummification now set in. In 1992, her successor John Major won an election giving further respite to the old state. Five years of further necrosis would be required, before a movement of sheer revulsion gathered strength, and forced a break at the General Election of 1997.

When this moment of rupture did arrive, however, it failed to undo the state. New Toryism gave way to New Labourism. But New Labour was to succeed largely through failure: it refused to undo the Mummy's rags. Indeed it continued, and even intensified Mrs Thatcher's redemptive drive, striving more nimbly and visibly to keep Britain alive and "great". Instead of moving towards a new state and constitution, it plunged swiftly into a still more emphatic ideological campaign of resurrection.[6] But the political terrain was now unavoidable. During the 1979-97 period, the movements for self-government described in the original *Break-Up of Britain* had recovered strength again. They acquired new vitality, both from the absurdities of

---

[6] See Nairn 2002. The last section of this text tries to situate British misfortune within the broader context of political dearth and recession among the Atlantic seaboard states – the misfortunes of the later Enlightenment, as it were.

"Thatcherism" and the obfuscations of neo-liberalism. This recovery led them to an effective re-colonisation of the Labour Party, and simultaneously towards positions clearly to the left of the New formulae of Tony Blair and his Chancellor of the Exchequer, Gordon Brown.

Thus what Thatcherites had perceived as "backward" provinces were borne to centre stage in the post-'97 government. The latter had no choice but to satisfy the demands of Scottish and Welsh Party contingents, by now firmly converted to "home rule". At the same time, the civil warfare in Northern Ireland persisted, and forced the British state towards a quite different version of self-government there as well. Neither the "enterprise culture", the run-down of the welfare state, nor the chest-beating Britishness of the previous years had put a stop to disintegration. It merely slowed it down, forcing it to acquire deeper roots and a wider popular basis.

However, Blair's constitutional "concessions" remained just that. "Devolution" was intended to continue, or even to strengthen, the Union state and its Crown. Just as Thatcher's entrepreneurial Britain was meant to reanimate tradition, Blair's devolved kingdom was now seen as reinforcing its centralising mainspring, the "Unwritten Constitution" of the British Parliament in Westminster, and Britain's remaining world-power pretensions. The latter were destined for a renaissance under his rule. Indeed historians may well record this as the only genuine resurrection of the New Labour period.

In such a context, devolution was no more than enhanced local government, and in no way a prelude to decomposition. Its purpose was restoration, and the safe renewal of British multinational identity. Stability and continuity could not be put at risk by rash or unnecessary reform. A few compromises with political modernity may have become inescapable – for instance, proportional representation in all three new assemblies. But within the prevalent sclerosis these were also sideways steps – Westminster's purpose was that they should weaken and moderate the new authorities. Like other *anciens régimes* before it, the British state was able to bend particular features of a newer political world to its own ends. As I suggested already, the "think-tank" revolution of the 1980s and 1990s had been devoted mainly to clever emasculation in this sense.

In *After Britain* (Nairn 2000), I analysed the New Labour Millennium Dome project in the same light, as a political and ideological farce designed to supplant a vanished Socialism with a rejuvenated British nationalism. There is no need here to recapitulate details of this astonishing disaster. The vision was of a common roof which would house examples of brilliant, forward-looking design – the credentials of a "Cool Britannia" in confident mastery of modernity, at ease with the dawning century. The reality was a costly parade of ineptitude and ambiguity, expressing all too accurately the dilemmas of a faltering realm. The wound to the United Kingdom's dignity and standing ought to have been fatal; but in fact most Britishers shrugged their shoulders at it – as if already too convinced of second-rateness and downfall to be farther affected. The former sense of invincible superiority had become a fatalism of decline, more inclined towards irony and self-mockery, and – again like the old Eastern Europe – towards an exaltation of the private over the public. Hence Blair's New Labour government could persist inertly in his constantly reiterated "Project" – state-maintenance rather than state-renewal or reconstruction.

Other disasters followed upon The Dome. The two years leading up to Blair's second electoral victory in 2001 brought a whole series of them, ranging from crises in the National Health Service, via a rail network breakdown, to the absurd mismanagement of a foot-and-mouth disease epidemic which overshadowed the election itself. New Labourite "triumph" in the subsequent vote now depended upon a novel phenomenon: massive abstention by the entire British electorate. Forty per cent did not participate (and the official figure was almost certainly an under-estimate). Far from being cured by New Labour, the revulsion of the later 1990s had sunk in and grown chronic. Blair's overwhelming Parliamentary mandate was based on less than a quarter of the suffrage. Nationalist campaigners in Scotland, Wales and Northern Ireland had always complained about the UK's "democratic deficit" – the failure of central authority to permit them a voice. But by 2001 the Westminster system itself had become a standing deficit – a desertion of the English voters, as well as of the Celtic fringes. Maintaining "Greatness" now turned out to have its own peculiar cost: the formation of an abyss between state and society, and permanent political malaise.

3. Break-up and Globalisation

Were this the whole story, it would of course be tempting simply to
extrapolate the 1977-2002 narrative forward. Surely "break-up" is
bound to pursue its course via farther stages, amid the debris and contradictions of a collapsing form of state? However, there is now a
great deal more to the tale. Other factors have entered the scene, and a
quite different global narrative now intersects with that of British decline and fragmentation. The break-up of Britain began in one age; but
we can now be certain it will end in another, amid quite different
rules, and disconcerting possibilities undreamt of twenty-five years
ago.
      To perceive the effects of this new conjuncture, one must return
to the old one portrayed in *Break-Up's* earlier editions. The main error
there was a form of historical materialism that reflected both left- and
right-wing preconceptions of the Cold War period. "Uneven development" was the nub of that argument. The intensifying "backwardness"
of a post-imperial and post-industrial Britain was counterposed to the
forward-looking impulses emerging out of its periphery. While nationalism naturally stressed ethnic or cultural motifs, the impulse of
emancipation was also linked to a general idea of being "held back".
And among the Marxists or *marxisant* thinkers active at the theoretical
level (including this author) that idea assumed a primarily economic
form. Nationalism was in this period usually justified as a response to
economic exploitation or imposed retardation – the political mobilisation required to catch up with modernity.[7] It was only one more step to
extend this justification to people and territories being unfairly tied
down by "backward" metropolitan centres: to the Baltic states, for example, escaping from Great-Russian inertia; Catalonia, always eco-
nomically ahead of archaic Castilian centralism; Northern Italy, re-
strained by a central-southern Roman bureaucracy; or Quebec, the
vehicle of a *revolution tranquille* aiming to leave hidebound British
Canada behind.

---

[7] The main culprit here was no Marxist. It was Ernest Gellner's immensely influential
1964 essay, "Nationalism" (Gellner 1964). Gellner was a conservative historical
materialist, much closer to Popper and (later) to George Soros and 1980s neo-
liberalism, than to forces of either the liberal or the socialist left.

Scotland remains the biggest factor in any political breakdown of the United Kingdom, and such convictions were strong there in the 1970s. This followed upon the discovery and exploitation of North Sea oil, mainly in Scottish territorial waters. "It's Scotland's Oil!" was the resultant slogan. Even then, no prophetic insight was needed to see that, unless politically captured, the great windfall would disappear into futile attempts at propping up the British parliamentary imperium.[8] To both nationalists and home-rulers in Scotland and Wales, there seemed at least the possibility of using some of it for economic modernisation – to re-industrialise, and rebuild out-of-date infrastructures, rather than wasting it upon state salvage operations, the "special relationship" with America, and the purely commercial nexus of the City of London.

Such hopes were to be cruelly disappointed. A moribund polity talks new only to prop up the old. In retrospect, it may appear obvious how things might have turned out differently. In theory, a state-led second-stage industrial revolution could have given new life to the island imperium. Could this not have been expressed in drastic constitutional changes, by the formation of a fully federal or confederal British state? Could democracy not have replaced Westminster – rather than the feeble parody of Blair's Devolution?

In practice, no such transformation was remotely possible. Mrs Thatcher's pseudo-revolution of 1979 onwards counted upon what she perceived as the natural bent of the British: an entrepreneurial leap forward, unleashing the potential of a civil society deemed still capable of miracles. Actually, the "natural bent" of Anglo-British identity had long been a specific and historically-consecrated blend of commercialism and conservative hierarchy. "Industrial revolution" had simply been one passing episode in this much longer national trajectory.[9] After 1997, the "regressive modernisation" of the Tories was

---

[8] Harvie 1995 provides a comprehensive indictment of this episode.

[9] This point has been misunderstood in the most important recent reinterpretation of English nationalism (Greenfeld 1992). Greenfeld sees England as the forge of modern national identities, rather than as an archaic template for certain aspects of nationalism. The misunderstanding has been reiterated in her new study (Greenfeld 2001).

taken up, and finally taken much further by Blair's New Labour dispensation (Hall 1983).

So revivalism became the order of the day. The first action of Chancellor Gordon Brown was to relinquish government control of economic interest rates to a City-controlled committee at the Bank of England. Approval of the special relationship with the United States mutated into subservience. Blair's government acted promptly to save the British Crown, and then prop it up, after its foundations were shaken by Princess Diana's strange death in 1997. Not for the first time in twentieth-century history, the Westminster two-party order had become a *de facto* one-party system, devoted to safe modernisation. "Safe" always means conservation of both state and national identity, in some earlier configuration – in this case, the palaeo-modernism of the British early eighteenth century. Hence the contradiction of Blair's rule: a paroxysm of phoney renewal was devoted to enhancing stability – always the most prized virtue of the British evolutionary order. British nationalism rests upon a basic conviction of Providential grace and continuity – not a mentality of risk or societal adventure. Thatcher had hatched a right-wing version of such redemptionism between 1979 and 1997: now Blair and Brown followed with a left-wing one. How weak and slippery the labels of "right" and "left" have become in the unceasing fall of Great Britain!

4. Really Existing Internationalism

But this fall is now also into the much greater abyss of globalisation and a one-world hegemony of capital. Even before leaving their anachronistic kingdom, the components of the archipelago are compelled to face and adapt to a wildly different homeland. Cretinous variants of neo-liberalism continue to dominate the media – in the Celtic fringe as well as in London – and perceive no problems of transition. The strain uppermost in Blairism derives largely from one especially flatulent clamour of the 1990s: "the end of the nation-state". The apotheosis of "economic man" after 1989 was at that time imagined as leaving ideological space only for individuals on the one hand, and a nebulous universal order – or "borderless world" – on the other. Being both ill-defined and inchoately contested, this fog has tended in practice to coalesce around either acceptance or refusal of United States domination. And for a retreating Britain, the parameters of profound acceptance had been established in advance by the mythology of the "special relationship" between London and Washington. From the Suez crisis onwards, the relationship has fossilised into a form of self-colonisation. Under the title of "indirect rule", this abject posture was rather well known to British and other imperialists of the preceding age. Polyvalent dominance – Gramsci's hegemony – is most effective when the suborned have chosen their prostration. Elective subjection is normally founded on apparently sensible economic or career reasons, re-attired as the national interest.

Over nearly half a century, such self-colonisation has become a pillar of Britishness. Indeed it is close to being the heart of the surviving British identity. General de Gaulle thought that Britain would always choose the USA and *les anglo-saxons* if put to the test. Today, this verdict of the 1960s appears sound (even if the General's own alternative French hegemony was to prove equally unacceptable). But here too globalisation makes a profound difference. The UK's dismal prostration has persisted into a post-1989 world of near-universal subservience and collusion. Self-colonisation has become the political norm of neo-liberalism. Most governments strive to align themselves with what they see as "inevitable" global trends. However, this is not because they fear the eruption of American Marines or cruise missiles, or the frown of the Washington court. Uncomfortable as the latter is, we do dwell in post-colonial times, not the old imperialism. Satrapy-leaderships simply believe that "there is no alternative". It was Mrs Thatcher who popularised this phrase in the 1980s. And she has lived to see it become the formative slogan of an emergent world order, that of first-stage globalisation. Marx's "sorcerer" of modernity, capitalist free-market mania, lives like a carrion-crow off the resultant symbiosis.

"Radical" ideologies of transnationalism are sometimes interpreted in the old historical-materialist terms as an emanation of single-market economics and multinational business practices. But one-worldism can also be read more straightforwardly: it expresses an extensive suppression of political nationalism. National identities forged in an earlier modernisation process, above all through revolution and warfare, now compete in an uncanny parody of their former hatreds and jealousies. Veiled abasement and stoutly denied complaisance have become the yardsticks of this transitional age.

The Social Darwinism of the early twentieth century was a struggle for dominance; that of its end has become a competition for wilful curtailment and first-in-line status. Take for example, after 11 September 2001, the swift, assertive and world-wide production of national credentials in President Bush's preposterous "War Against Terrorism". From one week to the next, "cracking down" on all symptoms of subversion became every nation's badge of renewed respectability. Establishment scoundrels of the world hastened to unite, with nothing to lose but their honour (in most cases discarded in advance) – and of course, the active political enthusiasm of their citizens. Like Blair's New Labour after its despicable 2001 general election, the knaves of globalism have been subsequently puzzled by mass apathy and indifference. How can it be that people prefer the honest emotions and colour of the Football World Cup, to playing their part in a world managed by mediocrities, and "led" by a US President unable to fake himself a plausible election, even in Florida?

It seems reasonable to assume that the populations of the globe are approximately as resentful, inchoate, ingenious, ungrateful and potentially rebellious as they were before the "End of History" in 1989 (to use Frances Fukuyama's slogan). But their experience since then has diverged sharply from what zealotic blueprints demanded should occur. Rather than the decline of the nation-state, what they have endured is more like its abnegation and abuse. Post-communism and the closure of socialist short-cuts removed at once the justification and the morale of bourgeois governments. Thus irreproachable mediocrity became the norm. Such are the politics of neo-liberalism: the sanctified misrule of increasingly corrupt hirelings and tenth-rate windbags who, in a world of "no alternatives", feel themselves dispensed even from serious concealment of their delinquency. As in preceding modern epochs, Italy has defined the ideal trend by its anointment of Silvio Berlusconi; but Britain has supplied serious underpinnings with New Labourism and Blair.

Neo-liberal clerics have over the same period constantly proclaimed rising standards and income-levels, and declared the poor to be less absolutely impoverished than previously, even if millions feel themselves worse off. The statements are accurate; but the political conclusions so widely drawn are absurd. The "One-Market-Under-God" brigade surrendered its imagination when it substituted economics for history. Getting better off has always been the trigger of both revolution and nationalism, not its cure. In fact the uneven improvement of conditions is close to being the motor of modern political development. Outside of textbooks, people do not live merely to reproduce themselves in less awful circumstances. Once change is possible, they want to mean something, or to "stand for something" (other than being bottom of the resultant heap).

In the 1970s, when the lineaments of break-up first showed through, the smaller UK countries still imagined themselves as nation-states – that is, frustrated nationalities of the old order. By the year 2000, they were less frustrated, but the old order had largely disappeared. The dominant nation from which they sought political emancipation had become itself a new style of colony – the sergeant-major and cheer-leader of American-led globalisation. Once conceived as a stepping stone towards final independence, devolution now risks turning into a life-sentence as fleas upon the monkey of the Washington organ-grinder. As the subordinates of a subordinate state itself cravenly supine, Scotland and Wales would then be contemplating oblivion in all time coming.

This prospect is less than overwhelmingly popular with the Scottish and Welsh electorates. If there is one thing that the Scots in particular do know all about, it is self-colonisation. They lived with it for three hundred years after the Treaty of Union in 1707. Its pros and cons are second nature in a society that long ago reconfigured itself for mediocre self-management in the absence of politics. The sententious moralism of the marginalised; disregard of democratic deficit for economic opportunity; cultural over-compensation and romantic chest-beating to efface or embellish powerlessness; over-effusive loyalty to a distant cause and metropolis, welcomed and yet somehow never welcome enough – all these tropes of a supposedly post-national world are, alas, tired old family skeletons in Edinburgh and Glasgow.

And after four years of devolved government, they look like being at least temporarily resurrected, rather than disposed of.

This is not a matter of policy. Within their limits, both the Edinburgh Parliament and the Welsh Assembly have argued for more social-democratic positions than those of Westminster, and in Scotland some have been implemented. These achievements have been popular, and outside Ulster there is practically no sign of any longing for return to the once all-powerful centre. In terms of social and economic policy there is no cause for either shame or back-tracking. But at the same time, there appears little appetite for further advance or increased powers of the same sort. In 2001-2 every general survey or commentary revealed something more like fatigue, or general unconcern. A Scottish Council Foundation Report in May 2002 emphasised this sense of disappointment and dearth strongly, and the shrewd conservative columnist Allan Massie summed the matter up in the Scottish edition of *The Sunday Times* newspaper:

The public is not convinced. They see politicians collecting full-time salaries and working part-time. And in the snatches of the parliament in session which TV presents us with, they see a pitifully low level of debate. Then, again, they hear politicians calling for a "national debate" on this or that [... which] never materialises. No wonder so many – and not merely journalists – think things are going wrong, and find their hopes dashed. (Massie 2002)

However, if a political system is accomplishing things voters approve of, like abolishing student tuition fees and improving public care for the elderly and handicapped, and yet still disappointing them, may this be because of things it is not doing? Massie does not miss the point, and concludes ironically:

The parliament has been a resounding success [... It] was devised by the Labour Party precisely to obstruct change, thwart reforms, and shield Scotland from radicalism. So far it has done so triumphantly [...] Devolution was the change Scottish Labour needed to keep things as "they've aye been here". And it is working. (Massie 2002)

In other words, it is preserving the United Kingdom for a time, as Thatcher did, but by more subtle means. It works by a modulation of self-colonisation, rather than by suppression. And of course both the effect and the popular response are quite strongly conditioned by the altered general climate I have described. A particular powerlessness is being consolidated by the universal powerlessness. An emergent nationalism has been partly re-interred by the general paralysis and degradation of politics.

Certainly, the latter derives in part from British constitutional sclerosis; but obeisance to the neo-liberal dogmas of free trade and de-regulation also plays its part. The *Zeitgeist* or faith of the age seeps into the fringes as well. It may even assume crass or caricatured forms there, as if potential reaction has to be repeatedly clubbed at birth. In Cardiff and Edinburgh, for example, a daily overkill is guaranteed by the *Western Mail* and *The Scotsman* respectively. As for popular response, in a political world where self-castration has become the norm of independence, some despondency seems only natural among candidates lining up for the oath. Some nationalists in Scotland and Wales have tended to attribute such uncertainty to moral failings, or to treachery among leaders. But perhaps they should take a wider view.

If they do, then I think there is reassurance as well as warning-signals in this broader perspective. Underneath the present charades of apostasy and self-contempt, those deeper currents that have carried break-up so far are not slackening, but acquiring new force. Just as the tide in favour of home rule built up during the eighteen years of Conservative Unionism, so a new tide seeking real independence is forming itself beneath the facade of Blairism. It will rise into the spaces left by New Labour's collapse, and by the increasing misfortunes of the old Union state. Manfred Steger concluded his recent overview of globalism by pointing out how the "neo-liberal power base" is already losing its grip on the meaning of events, and alternative interpretations of the process are surfacing everywhere. Few wish to turn the clock back. But more and more are certain to seek a say in its ongoing machinery. As a result,

More and more people realize that there is nothing "inevitable" or "irreversible" about the liberalization of markets and the deregulation of the economy [...] However, I fervently hope that new meanings will link "globalization", this central concept of our time, to a progressive political tradition that seeks to give institutional expression to a more democratic and egalitarian international order. (Steger 2002: 150).

And the tradition he refers to is alive and well amongst us. In 2002, as in 1977, it is far better represented by the disrupters than by the old British *status quo*. Through devolution, the deficit in democracy has been partly remedied. But this has in turn unavoidably created a deficit in leadership, largely responsible for the uncertainty of the present moment.

In the political readjustments of the break-up process so far, leadership problems have indeed figured prominently. Northern-Irish, Welsh and Scottish parties and governments have been constantly afflicted by these. However, this is not surprising in new polities attempting separation (or possibly divorce) from such a profoundly conservative form of state. As I mentioned to begin with, "ethnic" motives have had little relevance in this process – and sometimes been counter-productive. Where ethno-nationalism is lacking, civic nationalism is correspondingly more significant – and of course, this returns the argument to that political arena where the palsy of the Cold War and its neo-liberal aftermath remains dominant. It was always unlikely that changes on the fringe of the British-Irish archipelago would find a magical answer to such a global question. Yet they have not done so badly either, by advancing in the right direction and laying some foundations for more independent existence in the future. As the miasma of single-market globalism evaporates, and its British embodiment undergoes further humiliations, then one can be confident that here too new democratic forms will emerge, and engender the national-popular leadership which is needed.

Bibliography

Cocks, Joan. 2002. *Passion and Paradox: Intellectuals Confront the National Question*. Princeton: Princeton University Press.

Douglas, Mary. 1987. *How Institutions Think*. London: Routledge and Kegan Paul.

Gellner, Ernest. 1964. *Thought and Change*. London: Weidenfeld and Nicolson.

Gramsci, Antonio. 1991-1996. *The Prison Notebooks*. New York: Columbia University Press.

Greenfield, Liah. 1992. *Nationalism: Five Roads to Modernity*. Cambridge, Mass. and London: Harvard University Press.

—. 2001. *The Spirit of Capitalism*. Cambridge, Mass.: Harvard University Press.

Hall, Stuart and Martin Jacques (eds). 1983. *The Politics of Thatcherism*. London: Lawrence and Wishart.

Harvie, Christopher. 1995. *Fool's Gold: The Story of North Sea Oil*. London and New York: Penguin.

Hobsbawm, Eric. 1977. "Some Reflections on *The Break-Up of Britain*" in *New Left Review* 105: 3-23.

Jarvie, Ian and Sandra Pralong. 1999. *Popper's Open Society after Fifty Years*. London: Routledge.

Massie, Alan. 2002. "Nothing Happens – Holyrood is Working" in *The Sunday Times* (30 June 2002).

Nairn, Tom. 1977. *The Break-Up of Britain*. London: New Left Books.

—. 2000. *After Britain: New Labour and the Return of Scotland*. London: Granta.

—. 2002. *Pariah: Misfortunes of the British Kingdom*. London and New York: Verso.

Popper, Karl. 1966. *The Open Society*. London: Routledge.

Rothschild, Emma. 2001. *Economic Sentiments: Adam Smith, Condorcet and the Enlightenment*. Cambridge, Mass. and London: Harvard University Press.

Stanislaw, J.A. and D. Yergin. 2001. *The Commanding Heights: the Battle between Government and the Marketplace that is Remaking the Modern World*. London: Touchstone.

Steger, Manfred B. 2002. *Globalism: The New Market Ideology*. Lanham and Oxford: Rowman and Littlefield.

Nairn's Nationalisms

Ronald Turnbull

Tom Nairn has argued for nationalism both as a means to an end and, latterly, as an end in itself. But whether arguing for nationalism as a socialist instrument, or as an antidote to national "impotence", Nairn, like Ernest Gellner, has never taken seriously the content of national ideas. The debates within nationalism, however, have a serious intellectual and philosophical content in themselves.
Keywords: Tom Nairn, nationalism, Ernest Gellner, Scottish independence, Scottish culture.

Tom Nairn is almost a unique figure on the Scottish cultural scene in that he has developed a theory of modern Scottish historical development – a "theory" in the sense of a comprehensive explanatory account, which refers to economics, politics, culture and psychology, and seeks to establish how these domains are connected. The project is exceptional in a number of ways. In its scope and ambition, it goes well beyond normal exercises in academic historiography. Its political seriousness and refusal of (putative) value-freedom are an affront to academic culture in general. These are some of the reasons why his work has largely been disregarded by professional historians. The theory – which has not undergone any substantial modification since the first publication of *The Break-Up of Britain* in 1977 – has also deeply shaped cultural-political discussion in Scotland over the past thirty years or so, not only because it has attracted support, but also, and perhaps more importantly, because it has provoked criticism in the form of reactions which in turn have served to establish new frameworks of debate.

At the same time, and at least since his days as a member – along with Neal Ascherson, Hamish Henderson and other prominent figures – of the Edinburgh branch of the socialist-and-nationalist Scottish Labour Party which was set up by Jim Sillars in December 1975, Nairn has been a consistent supporter of the Scottish nationalist cause, though he is a nationalist with a lower-case "n" who has often been highly critical of the ethos and strategies of the Scottish National Party. However, over the years there has been a radical change –

which, as far as I know, is not explicitly acknowledged in Nairn's published work – in the kind of reasons he provides in justification of his political stance. This paper is a critical discussion of Nairn's theory of Scottish history and culture, his arguments for Scottish independence, his theory of nationalism, and of some of the ways in which these interrelate.

1.

In Nairn's view, and of course not only Nairn's, nationalism has proved to be the dominant political principle of modernity. As political sentiment, it is the root cause of many of the events (in Ireland, Palestine, and elsewhere) to which newspaper columns and TV and radio bulletins are daily dedicated. There is a puzzle here, for as ideology – or so at least it is widely believed – nationalism does not have much to offer. This is the account of the nationalist creed given by the most distinguished student of nationalism, Ernest Gellner:

Nationalism is a political principle which maintains that similarity of culture is the basic social bond. Whatever principles of authority may exist between people depend for their legitimacy on the fact that members of the group concerned are of the same culture (or, in nationalist idiom, of the same "nation"). (Gellner 1997: 3-4)

The (apparent) thinness of nationalist philosophy explains why, in an earlier work, Gellner had felt able to write of nationalist thinkers that

if one of them had fallen, others would have stepped into his place [...] No one was indispensable. The quality of nationalist thought would hardly have been affected much by such substitutions. Their precise doctrines are hardly worth analysing. (Gellner 1983: 124)

But the main point at this stage of our discussion is that the slogan (which is also, according to Gellner, practically the whole philosophy) of nationalism is "one culture, one nation, one state". In Europe – to look no further – in the nineteenth and early twentieth centuries, and then again after the disintegration of Soviet socialism, allegiance to this principle fuelled movements for unification (Germany, Italy), or, more usually, secession (Greece, Poland, Catholic Ireland, Finland, Norway, Latvia, Slovakia, Slovenia, etc.). Nairn's theorisation of modern Scottish history starts from the fact that, in the classic age of European nationalism, 1800-1920, there was no Scottish nationalist movement worthy of the name. Scotland, so to speak, turned its back on the dominant modern political principle.

Nairn's account – at least as set out in some of the essays which comprise *The Break-Up of Britain*, perhaps his best-known and most influential book – will be familiar to many readers, and it is therefore summarised here in the shortest possible way.

Essentially, Nairn argues that Scotland's incorporation into and prolonged acquiescence in membership of the British state, and thus its failure to follow the "normal" trajectory of nations towards development and democracy, have had devastating cultural and psychological consequences. In "normal" modern conditions, peripheries progress by embracing nationalism, of which the cultural correlate is romanticism. In Scotland, the bourgeoisie and institutional élites opted for a non-nationalist route of remunerative impotence and servility. There was thus no political requirement for a Scottish romantic movement, and therefore no such movement arose. Instead, according to Nairn, in the nineteenth century, Scottish high culture – at least beyond the spheres of science and technology – simply disintegrated. And popular culture, unleavened by any high-cultural movement, became singularly mindless and kitsch-ridden. The whole of recent Scottish cultural history, Nairn comes close to saying, can be exhaustively described by reference to the sentimental escapism exemplified by the kailyard school of literature, and to celebration of a fake, show, "highlandist" identity. At the same time, the choice of the non-nationalist route, of the aspiration at most to manage, but not rule, made cringing subservience the dominant national psychological trait. This very bald statement gives little indication of the ferocity of Nairn's account, in which words such as "freakish", "lunatic", "deformed" and "pathological" are liberally applied to describe modern Scottish cultural and psychological conditions.

Of course we need to take into account the standard historical treatments of Scotland on which Nairn's analysis partly relied. He was writing at a time when conventional Scottish historiography was still stricken with inferiorism, and Nairn's account was simply, from one point of view, an extreme version, or *reductio ad absurdum*, of generally accepted beliefs and assumptions about the Scottish past (which can be very crudely summarised as the view that, with the exception of a period in the eighteenth century, Scottish high-cultural history is a kind of void).

The notion that David Hume and Adam Smith emerged, so to speak, from nowhere, and that after them Scotland ceased to have any significant intellectual culture, never had any real *a priori* plausibility. Total demolition of this perspective, and a revolutionising of our conceptions of Scottish cultural history, awaited such recent work as that of Alexander Broadie on Duns Scotus and other pre-modern thinkers, of David Allan on connections between the historiographical culture of the seventeenth century and that of the Enlightenment, of Alasdair MacIntyre on Calvinist Aristotelianism, and on what he terms the second Scottish Enlightenment in the nineteenth century (made manifest in the ninth edition of the *Encyclopaedia Britannica*), and of Cairns Craig on modern Scottish literature.[1] Whatever stories about the historical evolution of Scottish culture are accepted by future generations, the inferiorist version will not be one of them. But Nairn, it appears, has taken no interest in these re-appraisals. He does now concede, however, that his early polemics against what he terms "the follies of tartanry" were excessive (Nairn 1997: 207).

Commitment to a nationalist movement is typically bound up with beliefs about the worth of native traditions, and the value of a particular collective identity. No such beliefs are evident in the pages of *The Break-Up of Britain*: the attitude to Scottish culture and identity is here unwaveringly critical and hostile. Nairn had come to lend support to the movement for Scottish autonomy for reasons quite different from those motivating the mass of nationalists. Allegiance to the nationalist cause was justified as one response to "the need of the post-war British left to discover [...] a way out and forward from its peculiar impasse" (Nairn 1981: 5). Nationalism, in more specific terms, represented an escape route from the sclerotic state and politics of "Ukania", a route whose final destination was socialism. The

---

[1] See for example Broadie 1990, 1995; Allan 1993; MacIntyre 1988, 1990; Craig 1996, 1999.

achievement of Scottish sovereignty was not, in this argument, an end in itself, but the means to socialist ends, as this comment implied: "In a Britain dominated by an England in transition to socialism, it goes without saying that (e.g.) Welsh or Scottish separatism would become – at least in their present form – dubious or backward trends" (Nairn 1981: 7). The subordination of nationalism to socialist ends, together with the total absence of sympathy for Scottish cultural traditions which Nairn's writing displayed, made his position unacceptable to many nationalists. Nevertheless, it should be remembered just how radical and courageous a step it was in the kind of far-left milieu of the age. In such circles the orthodox view was that nationalism was but one step away from racism and fascism, and thus to be combated at all costs.

Nairn's nationalism at this time was a form of what Neil Mac-Cormick has called "utilitarian nationalism". In contradistinction to "pure nationalism" (the view that the Scots, or whichever nation, ought to form a separate state simply because they are a nation) utilitarian or instrumental nationalism justifies independence as an instrument for the achievement of other, *moral* goals (in the form of instrumental nationalism endorsed by MacCormick, these are summarised as "the well-being of the Scottish people" (Storrar 1990: 146-47)). Nairn's political argument, however, was soon to change in a significant way.

2.

Most of the essays comprising *Faces of Nationalism*, the other major collection of Nairn's essays on Scotland and Scottish nationalism, were written after 1989, and in this work the prospect of any "transition to socialism" understandably disappears. "Socialism", Nairn now writes, "has to find new, post-1989 bearings, although some will find this a charitable description of its plight" (Nairn 1997: 163). He even declares, in a slightly less Delphic mode, that uneven development is "the only kind which capitalism allows", and adds that this is "the kind which has finally, definitively established itself since 1989 as the sole matrix of future evolution", which seems to suggest, without quite wholly implying, that capitalism is now inevitable (Nairn 1997: 66).

At the same time, Nairn's commitment to the cause of Scottish nationalism persists. But if the socialist argument for nationalism can no longer be plausibly invoked, on what grounds does Nairn now justify his political position? It is certainly not the case that Nairn's theory and assessment of modern Scotland and its culture have changed. About his unremittingly negative interpretation of modern Scotland, Nairn is unrepentant: on this front no revisionism is to be entertained. He refers to those who want to dispel what he calls "the familiar notion of Scotland's being deformed or deeply defective in some way – a cripple or half-wit among the nations", and continues (in a remark which modestly understates Nairn's own role in making this notion familiar): "Speaking as one guilty of disseminating this libel in times past, I feel obliged to utter a few words in its defence" (Nairn 1997: 205).

Echoing the case made in *The Break-Up of Britain*, Nairn insists on the "freak" nature of modern Scottish historical development, and writes, for example, that the choice of modernisation without nation-alism makes Scotland an "oddity in the zoo" (Nairn 1997: 207). Divorced from the world of high politics, Scottish civil society became "a kind of ailment, a practically pathological condition of claustrophobic, cringing parochialism and dismal self-absorption" (Nairn 1997: 88). Special contempt is reserved for the Scottish insti-tutional élites who are responsible for Scotland's being a "decapi-tated" nation (Nairn 1997: 190). They form, Nairn thunders, "the unique Scots phenomenon of a national sub-mandarin class cringingly proud of its 'responsible' addiction to political *coitus interruptus*" (Nairn 1997: 190). Not only has this "stupefied provincial sub-estab-lishment" failed to exercise proper leadership; its "craintive [i.e. tim-orous] moderation" and "caution" have "permeated the nation" (Nairn 1997: 187).

One implicit challenge to Nairn's reading which has received considerable attention is the argument presented by Lindsay Paterson in *The Autonomy of Modern Scotland*. Once an enthusiastic anti-tartanry crusader, Paterson has since absconded from the Nairnite camp, and in the text cited contends that the political plight of modern

Scotland may not have been as lamentable, after all, as nationalists believe. It is true, his argument goes, that since 1707 Scotland has not been in legal terms a sovereign state, but it has in practice in most important areas been run by Scots through institutions which are themselves distinctively Scottish. After comparing Scotland with other European nations in this regard, he concludes that "by European standards Scottish autonomy was at worst normal, at best actually quite privileged" (Paterson 1994: 203). It is therefore erroneous to regard Scotland's institutional bourgeoisie as a collection of "abject", "timid" "dupes", who well deserve their "reputation for cravenness"; they are to be seen, rather, on Paterson's account, as sage political operators, or, in his own words, practitioners of "sensible *Realpolitik*" (Paterson 1994: 203). This is in Nairn's eyes true and unpardonable heresy. Paterson's defence of a national leadership class content to merely manage rather than actually *rule* Scotland is hounded mercilessly, and depicted as a eulogy to self-inflicted political castration, and acceptance of the "unavowable curse" of an identity definable by the reflex of "doing as you're telt" (Paterson 1994: 205-6).

No-one familiar with Scotland could in honesty deny that Nairn's analysis here captures an important and uncomfortable truth about the national psychology. However, the argument against Nairn's theorisation of Scottish history was never that it fails to describe and account for aspects of Scottish reality, but that it leaves out so many other aspects of that reality.

The reader of *Faces of Nationalism* cannot fail to note the prominence in the text of Nairn's sexual metaphors, or fail to grasp what they signify. The achievement of sovereignty would represent release from the condition of political emasculation, impotence and eunuchdom that Scotland has endured since 1707: the ability, at last, to experience political climax. It is all a question, in the end, of attaining virility, potency – of power.[2]

Nairn has little patience with arguments that national identity is being rapidly superseded by sub- and supra-national (or local and

---

[2] Discussion of the question whether Nairn's politics and his account of national identity are "gendered" in an unacceptable way should perhaps be left to feminist critics.

cosmopolitan) identities. Nor does he have any sympathy for the postmodernist emphasis on identity as a matter of choice, or the notion that in the self "there are multiple or equivalently valid identities existing in no special order of significance", an idea he dismisses as "a form of cant" (Nairn 1997: 206). Here he surely has a point: intellectual modishness notwithstanding, some form of "essentialism" is unavoidable, since the realities of language and *habitus* cannot be escaped. The phenomenon of sovereign statehood continues to be an integral part of the functioning of real politics, he insists, and as long as other nations possess it, so should the Scots. The argument is thus simple, and, as Nairn states, does not resort to the "familiar motifs and incantations" of "standard-issue" false-consciousness nationalism (Nairn 1997: 223). Nairn has arrived, in fact, at an idiosyncratic form of what MacCormick calls pure nationalism. The Scots are a nation; *ergo*, they should possess a state, and exercise the same kind of power as other nation-states do. That is all. ("Idiosyncratic" since pure nationalisms typically invoke former national achievement and greatness to support the case for independent statehood.)

Although it may seem strange for a supporter of Scottish independence to have such a negative view of the national culture as Nairn does, the theorisation of Scottish history and his political stance have never in reality been in tension, because "standard-issue" nationalism (or national trumpet-blowing) has always been eschewed. In *The Break-Up of Britain*, the nationalist stance was adopted as an instrument of socialist strategy, not a matter of asserting one nation's culture, or some aspects of that culture. And in the position presented in *Faces of Nationalism*, the historical theory and the political argument have in fact been brought into alignment. Power as a nation rather than socialism is now the goal, and it is by achieving such power that Scots will overcome that curse of self-inflicted impotence which the theory has revealed to be at the heart of their modern identity.

It is necessary to enter a qualification at this point to pre-empt the charge that Nairn's view is here being caricatured. It is in fact doubtful whether Nairn would dissent from the kind of view expressed by Paul Gilbert when he writes that "the moral character of some groups is worse than that of others, and the worse it is the less their political claims for independence or autonomy will stand scrutiny" (Gilbert

2000: 36); and it is more than doubtful whether Nairn would support a movement for Scottish autonomy not deeply imbued with the liberal and democratic values or strictly bound by the "civic nationalist" discourse which characterise mainstream Scottish nationalism. Nairn's position is of course not "sovereignty no matter what". But this does not invalidate the point that the nature of Nairn's argument for Scottish independence has changed in a significant way: sovereignty is no longer being justified as a means to other ends, but is now seen as itself (granted a background of liberal-democratic circumstances) an end worth pursuing.

What Nairn's instrumental and pure nationalist positions have in common is one unfortunate feature – a form of élitism, for want of a better word – to which an American commentator has alluded in these terms:

> Nairn brings nationalism to centre-stage, explains it and defends it – but he does not believe in it. To see nationalism as intellectually false but historically right has convoluted political implications for the seer; the ability to be a nationalist is not one of them. (Cocks 2002: 152)

On the political ground, effective nationalism requires meaty fare, its characteristic "motifs and incantations". As Nairn insists, common-or-garden nationalism is Janus-like: it looks to an idealised national past, invokes a mythical history, in its task of forging a better future, and thus involves "cults of a particular past and tradition" (Nairn 1997: 71). But Nairn himself of course is above such things as (to use Nairn's vocabulary) ancestor-worship and veneration of tribal custom. He is therefore in much the same position as those who, while not themselves believers, have thought it a good thing that others believe in God. Nairn, we might say, does not believe in the nation, but at the same time he is in favour of belief in the nation. False consciousness is good for you.

3.

Nairn has referred more than once in his published work to W.J.M. Mackenzie's book *Political Identity*, and borrows from it the

idea that national identity is to be defined in terms of communal action
(Nairn 1991: 2). More recently, Cairns Craig, adapting John
Macmurray's definition of the self as agent, has proposed a similar,
"performative" definition of a nation: it is an agent, it is what it does
(Craig 1999: 10). There is in fact nothing new about such conceptions:
the doctrine that the tree is known by its fruit was taught by Matthew,
and Augustine provides a performative definition of nationality when
he writes that "to understand the character of a particular people we
must examine the objects of its love" (Augustine 1998: 24).

Mackenzie actually puts forward two ways of making sense of
the existence of collective identity. The first equates it with the presence of common purpose and action: "A discussion of political identity is perhaps primarily a discussion of the conditions in which it is
possible to realize 'common purpose'"; he also writes that "the
classics of political theory are about communality, about social entities, but only to the extent that they are or may be capable of pur-
posive collective action" (Mackenzie 1978: 109). So, it follows,
statements about strong or weak identity, or about the breakdown of
identity can be translated into equivalent statements about strong or
weak common purpose and collaboration, or the breakdown of common purpose.

But Mackenzie is aware that as an account of national identity
this is still too thin. His second approach appeals to language, but language in a very extended sense. It includes what he terms "myth,
symbol, ritual and ideology" (Mackenzie 1978: 163), the latter term
covering also what he terms "doctrine", or "the attempt to ground
logically and to expound systematically the meaning of a complex of
myth, ritual and symbol" (Mackenzie 1978: 162). These things are, he
says, "of extreme importance in the attempt to give a workable meaning to talk about social and political 'identity'" (Mackenzie 1978:
152).

The relationship between practical identity and what we might
call discoursal identity is of course that, since action is informed by
belief, the former presupposes the latter. Or as Mackenzie writes,
"conscious concerted action is not conceivable without channels of
communication" (Mackenzie 1978: 151). On this aspect of Mackenzie's discussion Nairn does not elaborate: he is understandably

reticent about this stress on the importance of myth, symbol, ideology and doctrine in identity – understandably, since this looks dangerously like the territory occupied by standard-issue false-consciousness nationalism (which, as we have seen, is for Nairn politically neces-sary, but of course specious). One question which Mackenzie's dis-cussion raises for us is whether Nairn's view of nationalism and nationalist debates rests on a serious misapprehension.

Nairn says that he has been "permanently influenced" by the essay on nationalism in Ernest Gellner's *Thought and Change* (1964) – this piece is in Nairn's view "the most important thing written about the subject in recent times (which actually means 'ever')".[3] Gellner's theory – which has been criticised as a form of functionalism – stresses the exclusively modern character of nationhood, and the role of uneven economic development in the origination of nationalisms. The theory that nationalisms invent nations, rather than the other way round, readily fed into the "invention of tradition" discourse which for a time was in vogue, and served as a useful tool to ridicule nationalism in the hands of those (like for instance the historian Lord Dacre) intent on propping up the disintegrating Ukanian empire.[4] It is true also that Gellner greatly enjoyed indulging a caustic wit at the expense of populist or vulgar-nationalist scribblers – though he generously ac-cepted that their enthusiasm, even if it was the fruit of delusion, was sincere, and not consciously driven by the material motive which, at least according to Gellner and Nairn, is the "real", essential logic of nationalism. It is therefore all too easy to overlook or forget that not only did Gellner challenge what had been a kind of liberal intellectual consensus that nationalism was a mode of political atavism, but also that he was in fact arguing that nationalism on the whole is a good thing. (This statement requires qualification, particularly in the light of remarks made in his last book on the subject, but this is not the place to pursue the point. These remarks do not in any case concern the Scottish context.) Marxist-socialist fantasies notwithstanding, it is evident that nation is dominant over class identity and loyalty (the ef-fective political weakness of "internationalism" is another Gellnerian

---

[3] Tom Nairn, personal communication, November 2001.
[4] See, for example, Hobsbawm and Ranger 1992.

theme which is echoed in Nairn's work); so the dispossessed in the peripheries would do well not to expect solidarity from the proletariat in the core, and should attempt to exercise what political control they can over the forces of development. Nationalism also serves to guarantee "cultural diversification" (Gellner's rather cursory argument as to why this is desirable is that "pluralism is some kind of insurance against both tyranny and political folly" (Gellner 1964: 178)).

Nevertheless, according to this theory, as we have seen, the actual content of nationalist arguments – the passionate outpourings of the sincere but deluded propagandists who know not what they do – is of little or no intellectual interest (and of little or no political moment): as Gellner says, "Their precise doctrines are hardly worth analysing" (Gellner 1964: 178). Nairn's theory of Scottish history, which finds nothing of value in modern Scottish culture, is reinforced by the theory of nationalism he adapts from Gellner in the conclusion that "standard-issue" nationalist discourse (which takes this culture as its object), though it is functionally essential – some set of myths and delusions is required to fire the masses – is unworthy of serious intellectual engagement.

Gellner wrote that a grave underestimation of nationalism was one of Marxism's two main errors (the other being the thesis of increasing proletarian immiseration). But perhaps Gellner and Gellnerians like Nairn are also guilty of seriously underestimating nationalism in their view that the content of nationalist discourse is of no import. This suggestion is made in a fascinating recent contribution to nationalism theory by Roman Szporluk (Hall 1998: 35). Briefly, Szporluk's main argument is that nationalist movements are not in reality, as the Gellner theory simply seems to assume, monolithic, homogeneous, unified, and controversy-free. Within nationalist movements there are, typically, debates and disputes about the nature of national identity. Such movements involve a dispute or set of disputes about which aspects of national identity (which will include conflicting and contradictory elements) are to play key roles in the definitions of identity and of policies. In this process some conceptions of national identity, or "visions of the nation", become dominant, others are marginalised or discarded. "National identity is a subject of intranational contestation", says Szporluk, and nationalist debates form "a battlefield in the struggle for hegemony within the nation". And to understand this is also, obviously, to understand that nationalist ideas and nationalist thinkers, *pace* Gellner and Nairn, do after all matter. Indeed, what Szporluk's discussion implies is that it is hard to think of what could matter more. Or, in Szporluk's wonderful ellipsis, "philosophy equals nationalism" (Hall 1998: 36).

One influential "vision of the nation" which has been propagated and contested in recent intellectual debates that concern nationalism is of course Nairn's own. An allied view is presented in a well-known study by Colin Kidd, in which the Scottish past is depicted as ideologically bankrupt, useless as a source of ideas and values that could have relevance to present and future politics (Kidd: 1993). Certain other contributions can be read as critical responses to this position, and elaborations of alternative visions (which does not of course mean that their authors are to be necessarily identified as supporters of Scottish nationalism). We might mention as an example MacIntyre's sympathetic treatment, or, we could perhaps say, defence, of pre-Enlightenment Scotland, a type of community, as he writes,

which is understood by most of those who inhabit it as exemplifying in its social and political order principles independent of and antecedent to the passions and interests of the individuals and groups who compose that society. (MacIntyre 1988: 222-23)

Allied to this view are the attempts by William Storrar, Duncan Forrester and others to argue for the retrieval of a socially radical strain in the history of Scottish Christianity (Storrar 2001; Forrester 2001).[5] It is worth noting, in this connection, that in his study of Scottish nationalism the American scholar Jonathan Hearn emphasises that in much Scottish nationalist discourse there is an invocation of "a national identity historically rooted in egalitarian values and opposed [...] to the values of [...] the unbridled free market", and a re-affirmation of the "social bonds of common membership in a community" (Hearn 2000: 155). Hearn, here echoing the main point made by Szporluk, therefore takes nationalism (or at least Scottish nationalism) to be centrally concerned with what beliefs and values should base and shape the life of the nation.

---

[5] See also Graham 2001.

What "doctrines", to use MacKenzie's word, are the Scots to hold, and what common purposes are their ideas to inform? Or, to put this in other words, borrowing from Augustine, what are to be the objects of the Scottish nation's love? To such questions, Nairn's contentless nationalism provides no answers; but they are the questions that nationalism is – dare this be said? – "really" about.[6]

---

[6] I would like to thank Tom Nairn for his kind co-operation, and also Dr Ellen-Raïssa Jackson and Dr Innes Kennedy for reading and commenting on drafts of this article.

Bibliography

Allan, David. 1993. *Virtue, Learning and the Scottish Enlightenment.* Edinburgh: Edinburgh University Press.

Augustine. 1998. *The City of God Against the Pagans.* Cambridge: Cambridge University Press.

Broadie, Alexander. 1990. *The Tradition of Scottish Philosophy.* Edinburgh: Polygon.

—. 1995. *The Shadow of Scotus.* Edinburgh: T. and T. Clark.

Cocks, Joan. 2002. *Passion and Paradox: Intellectuals Confront the National Question.* Princeton: Princeton University Press.

Craig, Cairns. 1996. *Out of History.* Edinburgh: Polygon.

—. 1999. *The Modern Scottish Novel.* Edinburgh: Edinburgh University Press.

Forrester, Duncan B. 2001. "John the Common-Weal: John Knox and the Radical Tradition in Scottish Christianity" in *Edinburgh Review* 107: 14-28.

Gellner, Ernest. 1964. *Thought and Change.* London: Weidenfeld and Nicolson.

—. 1983. *Nations and Nationalism.* Oxford: Blackwell.

—. 1997. *Nationalism.* London: Phoenix.

Gilbert, Paul. 2000. *Peoples, Cultures and Nations in Political Philosophy.* Edinburgh: Edinburgh University Press.

Graham, Roderick. 2001. *John Knox: Democrat.* London: Robert Hale.

Hall, John A. (ed.). 1998. *The State of the Nation: Ernest Gellner and the Theory of Nationalism.* Cambridge: Cambridge University Press.

Hearn, Jonathan. 2000. *Claiming Scotland: National Identity and Liberal Culture.* Edinburgh: Polygon, 2000.

Hobsbawm, Eric and Terence Ranger (eds). 1992. *The Invention of Tradition.* Cambridge: Cambridge University Press.

Kidd, Colin. 1993. *Subverting Scotland's Past: Scottish Whig Historians and the Creation of an Anglo-British Identity, 1689-c.1830.* Cambridge: Cambridge University Press.

MacIntyre, Alasdair. 1988. *Whose Justice? Which Rationality?* London: Duckworth.

—. 1990. *Three Rival Versions of Moral Inquiry.* London: Duckworth.

Mackenzie, W.J.M. 1978. *Political Identity.* Harmondsworth: Penguin.

Nairn, Tom. 1981. *The Break-Up of Britain.* London: Verso.

—. 1991. "Scottish Identity: a Cause Unwon" in *Chapman* 67: 2-12.

—. 1997. *Faces of Nationalism: Janus Revisited.* London: Verso.

Paterson, Lindsay. 1994. *The Autonomy of Modern Scotland.* Edinburgh: Edinburgh University Press.

Storrar, William. 1990. *Scottish Identity: A Christian Vision.* Edinburgh: Handsel Press.

The Case of the Postmodernist's Sore Thumb, or the Moral Sentiments of John Rebus

Christopher Harvie

Scottish devolution and its consequences have challenged conventional political theorisation. In a postmodern age, why should Scotland remain so nationalist? In the absence of an adequate theorisation of Scottish society, literary detectives such as John Rebus explore the interconnections of power in a devolved Scotland. Keywords: play ethic, postmodernism, devolution, nationalism, civil society.

1. Cheshire-Cat Federalism

In the early 1850s the Pre-Raphaelites set out to decorate the walls and roof of the Oxford University Union with Arthurian scenes. This was more than a symbolic act of dissent from the material world of the Crystal Palace and the Northcote-Trevelyan Report on the Civil Service; it was a calculated bid by an arts-and-crafts, religious and proto-socialist group to influence the politics of the élite of Young England. A caricature in Max Beerbohm's *Dante Gabriel Rossetti and his Circle* (1922) imagined Rossetti banging up against Benjamin Jowett of Balliol, wheeler-dealer in chief to the University and architect of competitive examination in the Civil Service. The latter inquires, "What were they going to do with the Grail when they found it, Mr Rossetti?" (Beerbohm 1922: plate 4). This encounter of the idealistic and the mundane, viewed by a sharp, knowing, metropolitan dandy, has a certain relevance to post-devolution Scotland. The Scottish political élite, or "chattering classes" (depending on your position) had magicked the grail of constitutional change out of the downfall of the Tory party and a diffuse political discontent, while an otherwise manically centralist New Labour government, which hadn't given the matter much thought, played along.

But what were the élite going to do with the Grail? And what did the whole devolution business do for political and social theory?

Did devolution signal the end of the self-confidence of the British Union State? Coming after half a decade of quite spectacular moral collapse, its enactment in 1997-99 appeared to some – Tom Nairn, David Marquand, and others – to reflect the limitations of the academic empiricism of the British behaviourist tradition. Representatives of the latter – such as David Butler, Jean Blondel and Robert McKenzie – departed for the shades only slightly behind their Oxford *doppelgänger* "logical positivism". Also scorched was a Westminster Parliament whose custom was to define and dominate the agenda of subordinate bodies. Decentralist euphoria, however, wasn't shared by the government. After the devolution referenda were over, it was evident that Tony Blair had been persuaded to act in 1997 because he saw devolution as an *event*. In constitutional terms he was preoccupied by the "international" issue of the future of Northern Ireland, and believed that on settling it the Scots would be satisfied with a subordinate legislature – unwisely compared to a parish council – and the Welsh would be bought off with enough autonomy to keep some notion of semi-federalism in being, and nationalism under restraint. This reading was borne out by such political theory as emanated from "sources close to Downing Street" whose valuation of parliamentary democracy was not high. From Conservative Scottish Secretary Ian Lang's memoirs it's evident that the previous British Prime Minister John Major also wanted to organise a referendum, and was prevented from so doing by the fear that Margaret Thatcher and her allies would press for another poll on Britain's membership of the European Union (Lang 2002).

Tony Blair's shadow Scottish Secretary, George Robertson, believed that such measures would deliver "the death blow" to the SNP (the Scottish National Party), by removing independence from the agenda. However, Robertson's successor and Scottish First Minister Donald Dewar defined devolution at the opening of the Scottish Parliament as "a journey begun long ago and which has no end". This somewhat risky phrase echoed (presumably unwittingly) the declaration in 1885 by the Irish Nationalist Charles Stewart Parnell that "no man can set a boundary to the march of a nation". Dewar's speech also seconded the Welsh Secretary Ron Davies' view of the Welsh experience: devolution was in fact a *process* whose goal was somewhere else.

The outcome was unpredictable. For a time in early 1999 a substantial SNP success looked possible, until it was countered by the consequences of a foreign-policy initiative by the party leader Alex Salmond, who criticised the US bombing of Serbia. This line (ironically in accordance with the traditional Foreign Office Balkan policy) gave the Foreign Secretary Robin Cook and Chancellor Gordon Brown, the tabloid press behind them, the chance to "take a baseball bat to the SNP". In the 6 June election it ended up with only 35 seats against Labour's 56. Still, it polled about 70% better for the Scottish parliament than for Westminster.

It was, to say the least, difficult to feed this string of fact into any theory and get a satisfactory outcome. There was, moreover, no political theory of federalism on hand to replace the parliamentary sovereignty broadcast by A.V. Dicey in *The Law of the Constitution* (1885) and finessed in a thoroughly "modernist" way – with due regard to sociology and psychology – by Graham Wallas in his *Human Nature in Politics* (1912), the first great text of the British behaviourist tradition. John Major in 1992-97 still believed in Dicey. So too did the SNP. Much of its programme, predicated on oil revenues, inhibited any conventional political challenge. Yet the dissolving effect of devolution on the institutions of the Union State in Scotland has meant that the party remains in contention; and so long as a new state is a possibility the notion of a market-driven post-modern equilibrium is deferred.

It is thus perhaps a pity that the subtitle of David McCrone's *Understanding Scotland* has so effortlessly made the transition from *The Sociology of a Stateless Nation* (1992) to *The Sociology of a Nation* (2001). The saga of Robertson and Brown indicates the instability of the "neo-nationalism" which is McCrone's terminus. Mature nation-states operate in a diplomacy-driven constellation quite different from the ambiguity of a formerly "stateless" entity whose culture *had to become* its politics. Scotland might be hovering on the verge of nation-status, but the irony was that in *British* politics leading Scots MPs exerted a power quite disproportionate to their numbers. The dominance of this élite contradicted the neo-nationalist thesis, but depended on its British policies holding up. If they fell to bits, they could again trigger a Scots drive to independence.

This was the "old politics" whose number had been chalked up by the postmodern cash-nexus. The politics/state nexus of modernism would be supplanted, not by the old industrial monster feeding on wage-slavery, but by a new technology-enabled pluralism whereby the citizen, individually equipped with the necessary technology, disposed of choices within the producer-consumer continuum which is the service-industry society. Variants on this could be found among the Scottish Executive and surfaced in the SNP. Even the great organising force of the intellectual revival of the 1980s, Professor Cairns Craig, seemed in his study of the twentieth-century Scottish novel to evict historical direction from the literary landscape (Craig 1999).

The problems, however ramified, were found to boil down to a series of unheralded and unadvertised compacts with the metropolitan business élite. This was visible by 11 September 2001, when the instability of the globalised postmodern became palpably apparent. Scottish opinion – or at least civic opinion – hadn't thought about this kind of phenomenon.

2. Statelessness and Theory

Speaking very broadly, social theory comes in two varieties. There is an overreaching theory of the state – what the US political philosopher Walter Lippmann called "the public philosophy" – embodied in a constitution and governing the relationship of state bodies to subordinate authorities and individual rights (Lippmann 1955). This is surrounded by an "official" sociology empirically derived from the classical economics canon and its critics, which links the constitution via its political culture to economic and social institutions. In Lippmann's case this chain of being would stretch back through James Bryce's *American Commonwealth* and Alexis de Tocqueville's *Democracy in America* to the *Federalist Papers*. State theory enables political actors to predict (within limits) the reactions of other parts of the social system to changes in any one part. The public philosophy in a mixed economy with an effective governmental system is a self-trimming mechanism: one of formal commentary in a "rigid" constitution. It can be much more cultural and enterprising when surrounding a "flexible" constitution. I tried to describe this myself in a study of the political novel in Britain interpreted as a treasury of political conventions, from Disraeli onwards, in *The Centre of Things* (Harvie 1991).

Secondly, there is theory in the service of a "profession", something whose social function goes much further back: to guilds and priesthoods, in which the "composure" of the larger society is upheld by a corpus of theory which patrols the institutional bounds of the corporations which compose it and inducts its younger members. Theory in this context is a book of rules by which entry to the professions or "Estates" is regulated: whether the tribalism of the English public schools, the wandering year of the German apprentice, or the micropolitics of the anthropologist Emanuel Todd's "authoritarian family" (Todd 1985).

Anyone who has taught in the German or Germano-American academic world will be aware of the moat – procedural rather than theoretical – which guards the core of any academic thesis: that obligation to catalogue every approach to a subject that has ever been made, in most cases, alas, without any critical faculty being brought into play. Homage to "Science" matters more than understanding the subject itself. "Theory as ritual" is often a means towards professional "composure" at best rather than dynamic comprehension (though the fragments of it that make their way into public ideology can, given the right market conditions, have considerable effect).

In a pure postmodern context the professional sort of model extends itself into interdisciplinary theory (often itself derived from precise political/intellectual structures) and less confidently into social fact, thereby preserving a sort of intra-professional devolution in which an élite can run its own affairs without troubling the central state too much. This has a radical aspect, in that members of a school or persuasion come together to seek a sort of autonomy; but it's also conservative in that the outcome is often an abstention from uncomfortable political intervention, or contact with unpleasant public reality. In a "stateless nation" this academic élite can continue undisturbed, fairly autonomous in its choice of research concerns.

But, given sweeping constitutional change, this equilibrium will give way to something quite different: the transactions of cabinets, parties and individual politicians. Transactional politics establishes its own priorities, often near-impenetrable to the outside view because they depend on secrecy, personal ambition, the technicalities of parliamentary procedure, or downright tedium. Secondly, such theoretical constructs as "policy communities" are disrupted by this. In place of a broadly predictable bureaucracy-advisor approach we have a minister who has to be a cabinet actor, living off competence and charisma, which may make him/her alarmingly flexible in terms of policy. Maybe in due course imaginative categories will evolve to give reality and purpose to the transactions: only then will a political culture of autonomous government have emerged.

Some theories of the state are no more and no less than an anticipation that practice in one political system will (all other factors being equal) replicate itself when the main elements of that system are introduced elsewhere. This was termed by James Bryce's generation the "comparative method" and seems tautologous, although the underlying notion remains lively in our present mania for "benchmarking". Real learning takes time, and Scotland's politicians have been less than prescient in such matters.

To take one example. The system of proportional representation chosen for the Scottish Parliament at Holyrood comes closest in general structure to that of federal Germany. There, parties which are dependent on winning constituencies will organise themselves in a decentralised fashion, and those dependent on a list will be centralised. The Scottish Labour Party in 1999 adopted a centralised appraisal of candidates, despite its strength in constituency contests. This narrowed its social base – Holyrood MSPs (Members of Scottish Parliament) are said to be six times more middle-class than Westminster MPs – and exposed it to continual erosion through the activities of the Scottish Socialist Party. The SNP was no more skilful. Famed for its opportunism, it required a (genuinely) democratic-centralist constitution, but preserved its old and hitherto highly nominal confederal structure. This meant that it lurched to the other extreme and allowed local oligarchies to marginalise senior members of the party.

By the run-up to the 2003 elections, the Scottish party landscape came to look particularly dysfunctional. Small groups of activists and office-bearers exercised disproportionate influence in selecting candidates; on the other hand, they increased the possibility of an electoral rebellion, a breakout into a far more variegated political system. Nothing of this could have been predicted from the conditions appertaining prior to September 1997.

3. Marching Backwards?

Post-1989, we were informed by the likes of Francis Fukuyama in his *The End of History and the Last Man* that the institutions of politics and the state would ebb, and deserved to do so (Fukuyama 1992). The attempt to transform Scotland *into* a nation-state thus stood out in this postmodern context like a sore thumb. Was this wilful swimming-against-the-tide the cause of the recurrent problems of the first Holyrood years? The Section 28 affair over the supposed "promotion" of homosexuality in schools saw the confrontation of the Scottish Executive with the Catholic hierarchy *and* the tabloid press. Even when the Parliament proved effective at unearthing the breakdowns of the *ancien régime* – in school exams, in health care, in the world's worst recycling record, in menacing drug and alcohol consumption – action on them could rarely be slotted into the timetable. Matters were made worse by a gerrymandered local government system. Local authorities, properly organised, could have expanded the parliament's capability. Unreformed, they became a centre of opposition to those councillors who had made it to Holyrood. Others, particularly in the media, could not conceal their delight at having a custom-made target to hand in the Scottish Parliament.

The postmodern notion assumed that the grand perspectives and great traditions of the nation-state were at an end, and with it the ideological confrontation of the Cold War, and its grim predecessors: Marxism versus liberal constitutionalism, the French Revolution versus the organicism of Burke, and so on. The German *Bundesrepublik* – whose member regions furnished some models for a devolved Scotland – *was* the first postmodern state, rather than the explicitly ahistorical USA. German history was sidelined as the class and economic confrontations which destroyed the institutions of Weimar, and projected the Nazis into power, were dissolved in favour of decentralised *nexi* of power governed by the free market, the constitution, and the internal politics and hierarchy of such institutions as the judiciary, universities and municipal councils. Along with an industrial establishment which was, for the first time, competitive rather than cartelised, this meant a radical break with the German past. So while the *Bundesrepublik* produced a state, it was one which proved almost alarmingly plastic: able to be expanded and, simultaneously, merged into Europe. Nationalism was, for obvious reasons, only thinly present, in the sociologist and philosopher Jürgen Habermas' "constitutional patriotism" (Habermas 1996). With only a few exceptions, "professional" theory in the universities adapted itself to this; which may account for the limited social impact of German academia.

Scotland's situation was far from postmodern, and decidedly unpropitious. Germany had in 1945 the advantage of an influx of skilled manpower from the east. It could re-equip its manufacturing with up-to-date equipment. It settled for, and indeed devoted itself to, a hard currency which mattered more than the nation-state, and indeed served best when away from it: the *Deutschmark* won its greatest victories on the holiday beaches of Spain or Italy. Its social structure remained conservative; indeed became more so with the excision of the Communist East, and with the religious conservatism of Christian Democracy, which cleverly retained old institutions – village life, religious establishment, the *Hausfrau* mystique – as propellants of industrial growth.

In Scotland, the industrial deluge – particularly unavoidable in the 1960s – was more serious because not explicitly war-induced. There was no Zero Hour with the whole place cratered, but neither was there a foundation for gradual change. The marvel is that the resilience of local capitalists and artisans lasted so long after the disablement of their "world" of heavy industries. Following the downward plunge of the 1950s, it had to adapt to so many new régimes: incoming American light engineering in the 1940s and 1950s, the motor industry in the 1960s, North Sea oil in the 1970s, and the electronic industries of "Silicon Glen" in the 1980s. By the 1990s, however, this resilience was beginning to wear out. Financial services followed manufacturing industry in coming under takeover pressure by 2000; only at the low-tech or call-centre end of cybercommerce did Scotland do well.

Scotland wasn't a model European region so much as a hybrid composed of marginal Western European/North American (industrial ownership, financial services) practice and ex-collective Eastern European practice (housing, local government). The dominance of superfirms (Finlays, Tennants, Coats and Clark, North British Loco-motive, Colvilles, Lithgows, Scottish Brewers, Distillers) and their economics, and an historically early entry into international finance, made them behave as global actors, something evident in the personal returns to their industrial/financial leaders, which influenced the country's equally long-lived "rest and recreation economy" – deer forests and grouse moors, fishing and golf, yachting, spas, and so on. These returns are reflected in certain aspects of Scots servitor capital-ism: the developments recorded above have become the "Skibo Castle syndrome" – a malaise named after the luxury resort where the pop star Madonna married her film director husband Guy Ritchie.

4. Postmodernism Unbound

This stimulating but overdriven complexity, however, developed at the cost of the sociologist Max Weber's "ascetic capitalism", or the Calvinist or Social Catholic values which underwrote the German middle class. The weakness of the smaller employers ought to make Scotland's politics resemble East Europe, where the governmental superstructure has become the area of contest. In Poland or Slovakia the shallowness of party hinterlands expressed itself in policy and electoral instability. Yet, in Scotland, the Labour Party remained seemingly unbudgeable in power, oiling its authority with the use of patronage. The Conservatives, having no middle-class agenda, lost out to the Nationalists, yet the Nationalists, only able to collect votes on Labour's left, were split by the exertions involved in this process.

Scotland's political problem seemed a reflex of a deeper economic opacity: something resident in the metatheory its political

class thought it had in common with the west. It has been very difficult to find, in contemporary "neo-classical" economic theory, any
approximation to the "economic nation" whose sources of wealth
Adam Smith explored so graphically in 1776 in *The Wealth of
Nations*. Triumphalist neo-liberal discourse, in the gaps between
showering Nobel prizes on its devotees for micro-research, has – if the
contents of *Economica* or *The Economic Journal* are anything to go
by – little energy left to engage with the economics of mass-tourism,
organised crime, or even the influence of financial centres. This is despite the fact that the first two now overshadow the operations of
classical economics' building blocks, the entrepreneur and the firm.

One postmodern claim is thus endorsed by the malfunction of the
work ethic. This makes more than slightly suspect the "radical" response of developing opportunities for multi-modal or "hybrid" action. Attempts to bring the moral agnosticism of postmodernism to
heel can be observed in the recent separate critiques by Jeremy Rifkin
in *The Age of Access* (2000), Colin Crouch in *Coping with Post-
Democracy* (2001), and Scotland's own Pat Kane in his "play-ethic"
website www.theplay-ethic.com. Rifkin and Crouch concentrate on
the appropriation of the "national" public space by market-oriented
enterprise culture, and on the migration of the voluntaristic "third
sector" of the democratic/participatory ideal to the culture-nation or
region. Kane goes back to Enlightenment discourse to resume the idea
of *Spieltrieb* (the enthusiasm/compulsion of the game) advanced by
Adam Ferguson and Friedrich Schiller, as a means of providing cultural depth to the "third sector" – those activities centred on friendship, enthusiasm and trust which expand "civil society" and provide
ways of rearticulating community to cope with the stresses and nego-
tiations of market economics.

There are several problems about the Rifkind/Kane play ethic.
What happens if the political determinant of the rules of the game is
so remote as to be inaccessible? What if the cash-flow on which the
game depends has rules which are continually altered by privileged
performers? What if the "play" in question takes on, in default of any
explicit political targets, the rigid lineaments usually associated with
work or religion? And what if its liturgical elements don't work, even
as placebos?

Take sport: it's a huge quotient of household expenditure and attracts roughly a third of media coverage, yet in Scotland this particular *Spieltrieb* can only go so far in a situation that defines itself by competitiveness. The Tartan Army introduced a playful note of self-mockery into the World Cup, an intriguing reworking of patriotism in which the example of Mel Gibson anachronistically coated in woad in *Braveheart* (dir. Mel Gibson, 1995) was made over into an innocuous "Jimmy Hat"[1] regression to infantilism. This was valuable at the time – World Cups are *nicer* because of the Tartan Army – but where would *Spieltrieb* go when Scotland in 2002 didn't even manage to qualify, and when the country's two most successful clubs were anxious to compete in a bigger pond?

Perhaps not entirely coincidentally, scientists announced that they had detected a "laziness" gene which predisposed people to loll around in front of the television, watching football. The *Daily Record* duly made a connection between this and television's Scottish slob, Rab C. Nesbitt, only a few weeks after Francis Fukuyama, growing more pessimistic by the month, had forecast in *Our Posthuman Future* a new and ominously permanent class-division based on genetic endowment (Fukuyama 2002).

5. The Plutonic Economy

In the Scotland of semi-achieved nationality the cultural space of the play-ethic is contested territory. The country has done spectacularly well in some areas – computer-games, comics – and nurtured a world-beater in J.K. Rowling's *Harry Potter* novels. But who cleaned up on Harry the Boy Wizard? Round up the usual metropolitan villains! This entrepreneurial deficit is aggravated because of the absence of a middle class (along with all its accompanying organisations) and the dominance of a few large and highly-political concerns – the banks and insurance houses, "post-firm" public-utility concerns, and a highly-diversified media. These run businesses which depend on gov-

---

[1] A "Jimmy Hat" is a tartan cap combined with a crude orange wig. It could be seen being worn by supporters who had painted their faces blue and white in imitation of Mel Gibson's version of William Wallace.

ernments far removed from Scotland, something that poses problems of formal political theory. Where does sovereignty reside in an organisation like the bus company Stagecoach or the energy firm Scottish Power? And where does sovereignty in Scotland reside, when devolution to the Scottish parliament is paralleled by commitments to many Public-Private-Partnerships? The state sector (local government, the health service, education) is conscious both of being fought over, and of providing the bulk of the Scottish political class.

Postmodernity was supposed to dump the political historian or historian-politician on the dustheap. Instead he/she finds that this is exhilarating territory, not least because its practitioners have taken a process essentially political, and by treating it as something history-less, come horribly unstuck. It is in the nature of theory to assume continuity: the expectation that relationships will broadly follow patterns which are fairly predictable. History, inevitably, is messier, with lots of occasions where the patterns break down and the rule-book simply fails to explain what the major variables are up to. If the political morphology of the international firm is complex, no less so is the evolving social structure – from "stateless" to "state-lite"? – of Scotland, whose wayward development has permitted internal social gradients so steep as to set the concept of civil society at risk.

In 1996 the Scottish Council Foundation divided Scots society into thirds: "settled Scotland", "insecure Scotland" and "excluded Scotland" were sketchy but recognisable categories (McCormick and Leicester 1998). The first was made up of baby-boomers who were on solid salaries with pension-plans, and had invested in houses when they were cheap. The second, raised in the service-industry economy, might enjoy higher incomes but lacked job security and reliable pensions, and were beset by high mortgage payments. The third group had lost any foothold on affluence, were ill and/or old, depended on one sort of public subsidy or another, and at the most insecure level, had drifted into illegality as agents or victims. The problem is that a society penetrated to this degree by insecurity, and weak in any civic morality, can move into a much more questionable condition. To the techno-eupeptics of the play ethic, the "fourth sector" of crime provides a looming and ominous counterpoint.

In 1994 the Commons' Scottish Affairs Select Committee costed the drug problem in Glasgow alone at £633 million annually (Scottish Affairs Committee 1994). This sum was about 2% of Scottish GNP in that year. Since then the number of problem drug-users has gone up at least by a third, and involves perhaps 60,000 people. Since drugs spawn a complex shadow economy embracing not just the obvious crime and prostitution, but security firms, loan sharks, mini-cabs, tanning studios, gambling, money-laundering, restaurants and even art patronage, we are dealing here with an economic nexus far bigger than some respectable but ailing pensioner like shipbuilding.

What the Plutonic economy shows is the limit of civic republicanism. The decay of socialisation – family, church, education – is probably only to be expected in a secular and individuated society. If we add to this the problems of social exclusion, or a ghettoised immobility, and the destruction of the once-existing *Spieltrieb* of the heavy industries and their hypermacho skilled hierarchies, we get something much more disturbing. The internationalised nature of the Plutonic economy depends on plane- or container-borne drug imports from countries such as Afghanistan and Colombia. Domestically, it's under the violently-imposed hegemony of criminal bosses, something derived, perhaps, from the "ghetto justice" of "pacified" Belfast, diversifying into other operations.

This raises the question anent the play-ethic: granted its ethical/sociological acceptability, how compatible is it with the other imperatives crowding in on us – old-fashioned concerns like economic equality, freedom from being socially threatened, and so on? As these ventures into Scotland's Plutonic economy show, because our metatheories are in trouble, we don't register the problems generated as they decay.

6. Rebus is Right?

The premises of much postmodern theorising have been disproven by events. Globalisation didn't mean a rebirth of Smithian economic rationality and "sympathy" as forecast in *Trust*, Fukuyama's second book (Fukuyama 1995), or Robert Putnam's description of the foundations of successful economic regionalism in *Bowling Alone* (Putnam 2000). The multinational firm has turned out more likely to acquire its financial morality from the lower "Plutonic" end of the scale – notably from the behaviour of the élites it co-opts in third-world countries, than from the upper or academic end.

Nevertheless, by 2002, the strain on Scotland's body politic of trying to restore a type of state which ran so determinedly against the prevailing tendency looked as if it had led to stasis rather than the imaginative development that Nairn and others (the present writer included) had seen as embryonic within "civic nationalism". In the absence of a worked-out internationalist ethic and a theory of political organisation and delivery, an ethos of party egoism exerted itself, in which the priority became the defence of existing power-bases. The Labour Party had not reformed the inferior local-government system. Nor did the Liberal Democrats insist on this – their backing, too, was local rather than disseminated.

One post-Marxist political analysis which might be helpful here is that of the American leftist literary theorist Fredric Jameson. In *The Geopolitical Aesthetic* (1992), Jameson argues that the deliberately elliptical "spun" complexes of postmodernist, "conspiracy theory" – that old refuge of the paranoid – conserve a peculiar "modernist" value. In this (to revert to a theory stated at the beginning) the investigation of the dysfunctional and corrupt is more illuminating than attempts to establish general theories, because it exposes the paths and channels of power.

With this argument in mind, there seems to be the structure of an interpretation of Scottish misfortune in crime fiction, from Eddie Boyd's thrillers of the 1960s to the more recent work of Frederic Lindsay, Val MacDermid, William McIlvanney and Christopher Brookmyre – or, given a more documentary slant, Andrew O' Hagan's *The Missing*. Ian Rankin's Inspector Rebus novels have become a cult for good reasons, in the attention justifiably paid to them for their consistency of moral view and a cohesive, if less than optimistic, view of society. Rankin himself has likened Rebus's Edinburgh, a community conveyed largely by dialogue, to the nexus of relationships in Anthony Powell's twelve-volume *Dance to the Music of Time*, a sequence of novels which charts British society from the 1920s to the

1970s. Similarly, the extended temporality of Rankin's own sequence allows us to see how identity and relationships change. This may parallel shifts within Scottish society, particularly in that middle ground of "insecure Scotland" whose ambitions and fears have enveloped the Scottish Parliament.

The "procedural" crime novel evokes Georges Simenon. But while Superintendent Jules Maigret reflected the bourgeois solidity of Paris, albeit with a creepy echo of the years 1941-44, Rebus's environment is much more unstable, in spirit a regression to the gothic origins of the detective genre in "the novel of horror" of Edgar Allan Poe, or in Balzac's ultimately corrupt detective Vidocq in *La Comedie Humaine*. While Simenon's creation, Maigret, seems ageless, we know Rebus is past his career peak: the younger generation has got through the door, and she's smart. His marriage has ended and other relationships don't last; his child, now a young adult, is crippled. His diet is life-threatening, he drinks too much, he moons around in his own bubble-wrap of Saab and (somewhat anachronistic) pop. He is, like Vidocq, a guide to his society, and like Vidocq in mid-career, he compacts with the worse to try to stop the worst.

John Rebus takes every case as it comes. They don't just get harder, but become more representative of the disaggregated Scottish *polis* – in both senses of that term: Scottish Enterprise in *Let it Bleed*, North-Sea oil in *Black and Blue*, yuppie student life and cyberculture in *The Falls*, the new parliament in *Set in Darkness* (Rankin 1996, 1997, 2001, 2000). Edinburgh, with its art galleries and posh restaurants and law firms, is an official world which awkwardly combines a newly-fledged parliament with ambiguous loyalties. With classical economics gone global and enigmatic, a sophisticated multi-level state employing complex social theory and a well-educated élite is required, but a minimal "policeman" state is all that's paid for. Rebus is that policeman, and he's being overwhelmed.

To end on this note might be melodramatic. At the beginning of Christopher Brookmyre's *The Country of the Blind* his lawyer heroine is confronted by a prize clutch of dysfunctional Scots: the tenant who wants to sue the council for mental distress over a delayed repair to his gutter, and the underclass populist out to get "'the poofs next door'" (Brookmyre 1997: 18). When you read the "Voice of Scotland" section in the tabloid newspaper, the *Daily Record*, you realise this isn't far from the real thing (as presented by a popular press which is surely one of Europe's worst). In the case of Scotland, when one approaches the issues involved in transforming the simplest sorts of social theory into recipes for practical action, this primitivism – the work of the newspaper culture more than that of the actual readers of the *Daily Record* and *Sun* – means that the Scots don't even get started. In his next book *Boiling a Frog*, Brookmyre contrived to get the last priest strangled in the guts of the last tabloid editor: satirists and parodists at least know where the rotten teeth are. Beerbohm this wasn't, but at least it was a start.

Bibliography

Beerbohm, Max. 1922. *Dante Gabriel Rossetti and his Circle*. London: William Heinemann.

Brookmyre, Christopher. 1997. *The Country of the Blind*. London: Little, Brown.

—. 2000. *Boiling a Frog*. London: Little, Brown.

Craig, Cairns. 1999. *The Modern Scottish Novel: Narrative and the National Imagination*. Edinburgh: Polygon.

Crouch, Colin. 2001. *Coping with Post-Democracy*. London: Fabian Society.

Dicey, A.V. 1885. *The Law of the Constitution*. London: MacMillan

Fukuyama, Francis. 1992. *The End of History and the Last Man*. New York: Free Press.

—. 1995. *Trust: The Social Virtues and the Creation of Prosperity*. New York: Free Press.

—. 2002. *Our Posthuman Future: Consequences of the Biotechnology Revolution*. Farrar, Strauss and Giroux: New York.

Habermas, Jürgen. 1996. *Between Facts and Norms: Contributions to a Discourse Theory of Law and Democracy*. Cambridge, Mass.: MIT.

Harvie, Christopher. 1991. *"The Centre of Things": Political Fiction in Britain from Disraeli to the Present*. London: Unwin Hyman.

Jameson, Fredric. 1992. *The Geopolitical Aesthetic: Cinema and Space in the World System*. London: British Film Institute.

Kane, Pat. http://www.theplay-ethic.com.

Lang, Ian. 2002. *Blue Remembered Years*. London: Politico's.

Lippmann, Walter. 1955. *The Public Philosophy*. Boston: Little, Brown.

McCormick, James and Graham Leicester. 1998. *Three Nations: Social Exclusion in Scotland*. Edinburgh: The Scottish Council Foundation.

McCrone, David. 1992. *Understanding Scotland: The Sociology of a Stateless Nation*. London: Routledge.

—. 2001. *Understanding Scotland: The Sociology of a Nation*. London: Routledge.

Putnam: Robert D. 2000. *Bowling Alone: The Collapse and Revival of American Community*. New York: Simon and Schuster.

Rankin, Ian. 1996. *Let it Bleed*. London: Orion.

—. 1997. *Black and Blue*. London: Orion.

—. 2000. *Set in Darkness*. London: Orion.

—. 2001. *The Falls*. London: Orion.

Rifkin, Jeremy. 2000. *The Age of Access*. London: Penguin.

Scottish Affairs Committee. 1994. *Drug Abuse in Scotland Volumes 1 and 2*. HMSO: London.

Todd, Emmanuel. 1985. *The Explanation of Ideology: Family Structures and Social Systems*. Oxford: Blackwell.

Wallas, Graham. 1912. *Human Nature in Politics*. London: London School of Economics.

Phrasing Scotland and the Postmodern

A.J.P. Thomson

Influential discussions of Scottish nationhood by David McCrone and Cairns Craig
have drawn their legitimacy from appealing to the concept of postmodernity, raising
theoretical and political problems which have only been further obscured by devolution. Lyotard's work provides us with grounds to mistrust both "postmodern" and
"national" accounts of Scotland.
Keywords: David McCrone, Cairns Craig, Jean-Francois Lyotard, nationalism, postmodernism, differend.

In his *Nationalism and Modernism*, Anthony D. Smith suggests that
for many of those who have sought to link the idea of the nation to the
idea of postmodernity, there is not just "a deep ambivalence" but
"downright hostility" to the phenomenon of nationalism (Smith 1998:
219). If Smith is correct, this would place theorists of the Scottish nation in a somewhat surprising position, for a number of influential
accounts of Scotland's nationhood rely precisely on relating Scotland
to the postmodern. In this essay I examine the work of two such thinkers, David McCrone and Cairns Craig, in order to explore this
problem. Although both use the idea of the postmodern in very different ways, each is concerned to legitimate his own political and
theoretical positions by making such a link. However, by drawing on
the work of Jean-Francois Lyotard, whose analysis of the idea of the
postmodern should not be understood as the simple endorsement it is
often taken for, I will suggest a number of difficulties with their approach.

The sociologist David McCrone has most explicitly linked the
idea of Scotland with that of the postmodern in the first edition of his
Understanding Scotland. The connection is essential for McCrone
because it enables him to negotiate the problem of Scotland's exceptionalism. His bold introductory claim is that "Scotland stands at the
forefront of sociological concerns in the late twentieth century. Rather
than being an awkward ill-fitting case, [Scotland] is at the centre of
the discipline's post-modern dilemma" (McCrone 1992: 1). If sociology is understood to be concerned with the characteristics of nation-

states, as "a stateless nation" Scotland cannot be considered a coherent object of study. But from the viewpoint of postmodernity, following the questioning of "the classical paradigms of sociology associated with modernity" (McCrone 1992: 9), Scotland becomes not only a possible object of study, but an exemplary one:

> as the nation-state loses its *raison d'être* in a world economy, polity and culture, so Scotland seems to provide a glimpse into the future rather than the past. [...] Scotland stands at the centre of sociological concerns in this (post-) modern world. (McCrone 1992: 33)

The need to ground his work within a mutation of sociological paradigms testifies to the awkwardness of McCrone's attempt to carry out the sociology of "a landscape of the mind" (McCrone 1992: 16). Not only the apparent historical belatedness of a Scottish demand for self-government but also the problematic ontological status of the nation foreground the problem of the legitimation of any attempt to theorise "Scotland".

It is curious then, that McCrone chooses to build his understanding of Scotland on the controversial idea of the postmodern. The notorious plasticity of this term is in fact attested to by the contortions of McCrone's own discussion. Leaving aside the use of the term to describe a genre or style within literature or architecture, there are broadly two ways in which the postmodern has been understood: as a mode of thought, and as a historical epoch. McCrone's account hovers ambiguously between these two senses. Where modernity, for McCrone,

> had aligned the national economy, polity and culture in such a way that citizenship and an allegiance to the sovereign state provided a clear and unambiguous identity [...] post-modernity, on the other hand, pointed to the limited nature of state sovereignty in an inter-dependent world, and highlighted the often contradictory and competing identities on offer. (McCrone 1992: 9).

McCrone is using "post-modernity" as an abbreviation of what he refers to as "the post-modernity thesis" (within sociology); but while his grammar never makes entirely clear whether he takes the analysis offered by postmodern sociology to be correct, it is apparent that "the postmodern" is also intended to refer to "general processes at work in the contemporary world", to "political and cultural changes" (Mc-Crone 1992: 10). This oscillation between a historical and an episte-mological understanding of the term serves to make the reciprocal in-terdependence of Scotland and the postmodern in McCrone's work more complex than we might have first assumed. Not only does the link help the reader to understand Scotland by providing a suitable theoretical paradigm, it also legitimates McCrone's account within its proper disciplinary limits. Without the impact of a postmodern sociol-ogy, Scotland could not be properly constituted as an object of study. But this conjunction is not only theoretical, it is also historical. For it is only in the age of "postmodernity" that Scotland itself can develop the nationalist groundswell which was conspicuously lacking in the modern period: Scotland's exceptional status can only be reversed both in theory and in fact thanks to "the postmodern".

McCrone's suggestion as to how we might understand Scotland, however, has mutated following devolution and the subsequent elec-tion of a Scottish parliament. In the second edition of *Understanding Scotland*, the link between Scotland and the postmodern remains, but it has been downplayed. The reconstitution of Scotland as a partly-autonomous self-governing entity partially removes the need to legitimate its sociological study. Scotland's postmodern context be-comes part of a prior historical configuration, as a number of key syntactical adjustments make clear. While McCrone admits that "this new sociological agenda in the 1990s with its emphasis on post-modern diversity brought a new dimension to the study of Scotland" he is unwilling to advance the idea of a postmodern Scotland with as much force as before. In the 1992 text he cites Alberto Melucci ap-provingly: "Above all, and what is important for our purposes here, a new trans-societal order had emerged in which, argued Melucci, nation-states were extinguishing themselves" (McCrone 1992: 9). In 2001, this viewpoint is not so clearly underwritten by McCrone: "Critics like Melucci were arguing that a new trans-societal order was emerging in which traditional nation-states were losing their purpose" (McCrone 2001: 36). The postmodern sociology which both Scotland and McCrone needed in 1992 has become a historical curiosity by 2001. This is perhaps due in part to the increasing confusion sur-rounding the term postmodern, which leads McCrone to specify in his

"Introduction" that: "This is not a 'postmodern' book. 'Scotland' is not simply what you want it to mean" (McCrone 2001: 3). McCrone appears to sense that appealing to "the postmodern" might undermine what now seems to be the self-evident legitimacy of the national po-litical unit: but such a concern only reveals the extent to which de-volved Scotland still rests on premises which are not entirely self-evident. We might speculate about other motives however: if McCrone does not wish to rule out the possibility of Scotland as an independent state, announcing the death of the nation-state would certainly be counterproductive. Such a confusion of political and sociological criteria would only further heighten the apparent crisis of legitimation here, which would appear to have been exacerbated rather than solved by devolution.

A similar development also characterises the work of another critic to have related the idea of Scotland to that of the postmodern, if from a rather different perspective. In an article originally published in 1990, Cairns Craig locates Scotland in the context of "the postworld of our postmodernity" (Craig 1996: 218). This is reflected in the movement within Scotland from a "Marxian moment – the dissolution of myths in order to become part of the universal course of class his-tory – to the Nietzschean moment – the construction of new myths that will mobilise our actions" (Craig 1996: 220). Scottish thought has moved from the desire to find its true history behind the myths of tar-tan and kailyard to a more confident attempt to "reconstruct a mythic identity that is particular to Scotland and so redeem us" (Craig 1996: 220). Yet neither position is satisfactory for Craig, whose consistent and powerful argument in his essays of that same period of mythic reconstruction has been that to reshape our idea of Scotland into a sin-gle narrative equivalent to that of a unitary nation-state is misguided. Instead he offers us a somewhat elusive vision of a third way:

Neither the Marxian moment of demystified oneness with real history nor the Nietzschean moment of reconstituted and singular myth is sufficient. We have to see our cultural space precisely as the intersection of many narratives: an acceptance of simultaneity. (Craig 1996: 223)

For Craig, Scotland's perceived exceptionalism is generally expressed as a sense of a failure to be properly historical, to fit into the narratives of modernity. McCrone's sociological study of Scotland is grounded in a different story which suggests that these modern narratives have been exhausted and relieved by postmodernity. But in Craig's work there can be no simple choice between the modern and the postmodern, and it is clear that "the post-world" must be considered to be just one narrative amongst others. Rather than repeat the argumentative structure which redeems Scotland by both diagnosing and distancing its own strategies from earlier failed attempts, Craig seeks a way to revalorise the perceived flaw of Scotland's conceptual heterogeneity. So rather than replace a "modern Scotland" with a "postmodern Scotland", Craig is looking for a structure which can accommodate both ways of thinking about Scotland without subordinating one to the other. Yet he must also accept one of the fundamental tenets of the post-world he wishes to distance himself from, that "there may be discourses which see themselves as oppositional, but they are discourses like all the others, unvalidatable by anything outside their own internal structures" (Craig 1996: 213).

In an article written since devolution, Craig's position, like that of McCrone, appears to be somewhat different. The subject is ostensibly Walter Scott, but Craig's real target is Benedict Anderson's account of nations as "imagined communities". Anderson, Craig argues, "dissolves the nation as a space of debate about values, as the vehicle by which our collective agency sustains and enforces our values, and turns it into an atavistic refusal to enter the very world of politics" (Craig 2001: 27). Craig convincingly demonstrates the slippage between "imagined" and "imaginary" which serves to make the nation, for Anderson, always a form of ideology as false-consciousness, merely a function of the Marxian grand narrative of class struggle and the development of the economic base. Similarly, he shows that the idea of "political community" is always reduced by Anderson to a simple understanding of community in terms of projected (and imaginary) unity rather than a community structured by politics as dissension and conflict. As in the earlier article, Craig appeals to space to disconcert the relationship between time, nationhood and modernity. A nation is neither a history nor a myth, and certainly not a single narrative of any sort, but a cultural space in which an argument takes place. His authority is Alasdair MacIntyre's under-

standing of the nation as "an embodied argument": "to participate in a
nation is to participate in an ongoing debate, often about the very
founding principles of the nation, whose outcome is dissonance as
much as unisonance" (Craig 2001: 23). The nation, argues Craig, is
not "an imaginary medium", but "the medium of our imaginings"
(Craig 2001: 23). Whereas art and history can only conceive of a succession of presents existing in homogeneous temporal progression,
and present them as simultaneous, the nation in fact consists of the
simultaneous presence of "a series of alternative time frames" which
interact with one another. Craig wishes to hold on to a notion of the
nation as "a space of debate about values, [...] the vehicle by which
our collective agency sustains and enforces our values" (Craig 2001:
27). Where McCrone's Scotland is guaranteed by the narrative progression from modernity to postmodernity, for Craig Scotland
becomes the container of both modernity and postmodernity.

Up to this point the continuity within Craig's position is clear.
Although it is no longer premised on a postmodern context, this is another attempt to construct a discursive model of the nation in which
Scotland's singularity does not suffer in comparison against the traditional narratives of modernity and the nation-state. But in concluding
the article Craig's argument takes a surprising turn. The real value of
the idea of "imagined communities", he comments, is that it "puts
artists back in the position of being the 'unacknowledged legislators'
of the world, makes art again central to all those processes of politics
to which, in other views, it has seemed so marginal" (Craig 2001: 27-
28). Craig's conclusion is bullish:

Since every nation is an "invented nation," every artist is, potentially, the inventor of
the nation – and every critic the true interpreter of our only history, that of the creation
and recreation of our imaginary communities. (Craig 2001: 28)

Where in the earlier article Craig argued for neither what he called the
Marxian nor the Nietzschean options, here he appears to have relapsed
almost totally into the Nietzschean, or at least a pluralist version of
that position. What is important about the myth-histories being put
forward for Scotland, one presumes, is not the accuracy of their relation to any set of facts, but their co-existence as presenting alternative

frameworks of values, drawing on but also competing alongside all the other time-frames which constitute the nation:

the space of the nation, which has an apparently simultaneous existence, is actually a series of alternative time-frames, which [...] resist integration, retaining always the potential to disrupt the nation's contemporary order. (Craig 2001: 26)

Craig's strategy for legitimating this argument is more complex than in the earlier article, where a vague sense of a postmodern context, and of the impossibility of establishing a vantage point from which to judge the various forms of Scottish narrative identity, do the job. Here, the presence of competing value systems legitimates the diffuse and heterogeneous space of the nation as non-unified and dissonant; but the crucial difference is that the cultural imagining of the nation, and more importantly the cultural mediation of the critic, are what legiti- mate the idea of the national space in the first place. That such an understanding of the nation is, according to Craig, already present in advance in the work of Walter Scott should not surprise us either: following Lyotard we can recognise this as another form of the post- modern, that for Craig the postmodern exists within the modern rather than as its successor; "postmodernism is not modernism at an end but in its nascent state, and this state is recurrent" (Lyotard 1992: 22).

Whereas in *Out of History* Craig offers a vision of competing discourses, both in and out of history, in "Scott's Staging of the Na- tion" the same vision is presented, but set out on a single stage: that of the nation. The limits of the spatial mediation of competing discourses becomes coextensive with the idea of the nation; but because the idea of the nation, as Craig freely admits, has its own history, is an idea both of history and within history, it cannot be both within the discur- sive space and *be* that space. Or: for Craig, the space of the nation can be the contestation of the idea of the nation, or the values of the na- tion, but any such argument cannot present a non-national alternative; or at least not without betraying the true (historically constituted, but presented as natural) political value, that of the nation itself as the ideal political entity. From Craig's previous point of view the narra- tives of nationhood were single mythic choices among many others, but since devolution it appears that the idea of the nation has itself been elevated to a central and functionally transcendental role gov-

erning this discursive field.[1] Not only does this mean that the problem
of the legitimation of the national narrative is left hanging; also, as for
McCrone, it is devolution itself which has enabled Craig to obscure or
neglect the legitimation problem. The historical evidence of the newly
devolved semi-state makes the *de facto* suggestion that the Scottish
nation does exist, has existed and will exist *de jure*.

The central concerns of this discussion of McCrone and Craig's
work have been the relationship between the idea of "the postmodern"
– an epochal development for McCrone, and a mode of thought for
Craig – and that of "Scotland". In both cases, the writers draw on the
postmodern as a point of reference on which to ground their own accounts of the nation: as an object for sociological study in McCrone's
case, and as the space of dissensus and debate for Craig. Remarkably,
it seems that for both the idea of the postmodern functions to legitimate the idea of Scotland, at least in the absence of the legitimation of
the nation by the state. But in return, this mode of legitimation is only
justified by the prior existence of the continuing narrative of Scottish
nationhood which requires either a postmodern age, for McCrone, or a
postmodern view of the world, for Craig, to come to its maturity.

I turn now to Jean-Francois Lyotard's *The Postmodern Condition*
because it addresses precisely this interaction between narrative and
scientific discourses, the problem of legitimation and the postmodern.
In his now notorious "report on knowledge" Lyotard suggests that we
have entered a postmodern epoch in which the relation between narrative knowledge and scientific knowledge has become critical. Not
only does science's reliance on other, narrative, modes put its own
claims to legitimacy on the basis of its internal coherence and consistency into question, but the key narratives of modernity, those of
speculative thought and of universal human emancipation, also appear
uncertain. Against the dissolution of these "grand narratives" Lyotard
reports on the contemporary diffusion of competing language games
and argues that to seek consensus between them is to seek to unjustly
dominate these narrative modes with one metanarrative, drawing instead on the recent developments in scientific understanding as a
model of a paralogical discourse. Understood this way, Lyotard's ar-

---

[1] I have discussed a similar structure in relation to the concept of justice in
MacIntyre's work in Thomson 2001.

gument appears to subtend the positions of both McCrone and Craig. McCrone's sociological account aims for scientific legitimation but is forced to draw on two narratives which cannot be grounded objectively: the idea of a Scottish nation, and the claim to have entered a postmodern epoch. Craig, like Lyotard, seeks to maintain a spatial rather than temporal (historical) plurality of language games, but where Lyotard calls this "the postmodern condition", for Craig it is something more like a national condition. If this is an adequate account of Lyotard's book we appear to be presented with an arbitrary choice between narrative discursive modes (the sociological claim to scientificity, the nationalist philosophy of history, the postmodern mode of paralogical thought).

Lyotard's relationship to the idea of the postmodern put forward in this book has, however, caused both him and his readers some embarrassment. It has proved a point of debate between Lyotard and sympathetic readers such as Phillipe Lacoue-Labarthe; the first two book-length accounts of Lyotard's work in English dismiss the *Postmodern Condition* in favour of the somewhat later development of Lyotard's thought available in *The Differend*; more recently, in both of his books, James Williams has turned instead to Lyotard's earlier work *Libidinal Economy*, claiming that *The Postmodern Condition* has acquired "an illegitimate stature within Lyotard's work" (James 2000: 93).[2] Lyotard himself has taken steps to distance himself from *The Postmodern Condition*, and in particular from the idea of postmodernity as an epochal development following modernity, suggesting for example that his intentions might be better expressed as "rewriting modernity" (Lyotard 1991: 24). But despite referring to a "weariness with regard to 'theory', and the miserable slackening that goes along with it (new this, new that, post-this, post-that etc.)" (Lyotard 1988: xiii) in his introduction to *The Differend*, Lyotard also persists in locating *The Postmodern Condition* within the trajectory of his theoretical concerns (Lyotard 1988: xiv-xv). Moreover, Lyotard has continued to write about the postmodern, although he has not adopted a single account of the concept, in line with the suggestion of his work that there can be no final choice between different ways of

---

[2] See Lacoue-Labarthe 1984; Bennington 1988; Readings 1991; Williams 1998, 2000.

phrasing such a term. Indeed one recent survey of this work concludes that

after 1979, Lyotard's determinations of the postmodern are determined by a number of displacements among different positions that cannot be incorporated into one determination, but rather complement one another. The complexity and inconclusiveness of the postmodern must subtend any attempt at providing a satisfactory answer to the question: what is the postmodern in the work of Lyotard? (Brügger 2001: 92)

However, read from the perspective of *The Differend*, Lyotard's most comprehensive theoretical statement, this inconclusiveness can be understood as something other than a failure to construct a coherent position.

In the later book Lyotard recasts his earlier interest in language games and narrative in terms of a philosophy of heterogeneous phrases. But a phrase is not to be understood as a strictly linguistic entity; a phrase is a minimal event which could be brought into language: for example, silence, for Lyotard, is not the absence of phrases, but a phrase in itself. Lyotard's concern is with how phrase-events become linked together within different genres of discourse, and the conflicts between the competing genres which could establish a link to any particular phrase. The task of the philosopher is to recognise that these conflicts – differends – arise at the point where a phrase could be submitted to two or more different genres of discourse, but at which there are no criteria available on the basis of which to judge between the two genres, since that judgement would require there to be another genre, and another link to the phrase:

In the absence of a phrase regimen or genre of discourse that enjoys a universal authority to decide, does not the linkage (whichever one it is) necessarily wrong the regimens or genres whose possible phrases remain unactualized? (Lyotard 1988: xii)

The philosopher recognises and bears witness to differends; further, politics, for Lyotard, names "the threat of the differend, [...] the multiplicity of genres, the diversity of ends, and *par excellence* the question of linkage" (Lyotard 1988: 138).

Reconsidering the philosopher's task to be not that of formulating a legitimated logical or narrative structure but of testifying to differends between such structures opens up another way of making sense of *The Postmodern Condition*. Crucially, we do not need to accept the sociological and narrative account of the postmodern as subsequent to modernity to be Lyotard's own viewpoint, but one of the heterogeneous phrase-regimes set to work in his text. It is noticeable that in almost every place that "the postmodern" is used in this way it has the value of something reported: "I have decided to use the word *postmodern* [...]. The word is in current use on the American continent among sociologists and critics" (Lyotard 1988: xxiii). We might on the basis of this statement alone justifiably take every use of the word in Lyotard's text, even where it is not otherwise qualified, to have the quality of a citation. This sociological account, comparable to McCrone's understanding of the postmodern, is neither refuted nor endorsed by Lyotard: instead it is placed into conjunction with a number of other discursive modes, including the speculative and emancipatory narratives of modernity, the traditional narrative forms of mythic storytelling, and the postmodern science which "theorize[s] its own evolution as discontinuous, catastrophic, nonrectifiable and paradoxical" (Lyotard 1988: 60) and whose paralogical mode Lyotard seems to be advocating. Reading backwards through our argument so far, we might say that Lyotard is, in part, juxtaposing the kind of epochal sociology exemplified by McCrone with the more sophisticated position evidenced in Craig's awareness of the heterogeneity of narrative constructions of the nation. From the perspective of *The Postmodern Condition* neither could be said to conclusively dominate the other. McCrone would be unable to reduce Craig's account of the nation to the expression of a particular sociological phenomena; but neither could Craig dismiss McCrone's account of Scotland as society by incorporating it as one of the competing genres within his national space of dissensus. Each language game proceeds within different rules, is based on divergent forms of legitimation and has different outcomes. This does not mean that Lyotard withholds from us the means to choose between these different accounts. The desire for justice commands us to choose the language game which most acknowledges that heterogeneity of narratives: the "recognition of the heteromorphous nature of language games [...] implies a renunciation of terror" (Lyotard 1988: 66); on the account I've offered so far of

Lyotard's text, this would lead us to prefer Craig's earlier article to either his own later position, or either of McCrone's.

This conclusion, however, is criticised in Lyotard's subsequent work. Understanding why this should be the case throws a different light on the political implications of phrasing Scotland and the post-modern. In a later essay, Lyotard explains one of the key revisions of his ideas between *The Postmodern Condition* and *The Differend*:

> I think we now have to distinguish between different regimes of phrases and different genres of discourse. There is an uncriticised metaphysical element in general narratology that accords hegemony to one genre – the narrative – over all others, a sort of sovereignty of minor narratives which allows them to escape the crisis of delegitimation. It's true that they escape, but only because they never had any legitimating value. (Lyotard 1992: 31)

In *The Differend* this is made clear: "narrative is perhaps the genre of discourse within which the heterogeneity of phrase regimes, and even the heterogeneity of genres of discourse, have the easiest time passing unnoticed" (Lyotard 1988: 151). The emphasis on the heterogeneity of phrases replaces the weight attributed to narrative in *The Postmodern Condition*. Whereas in the former text narrative functions as a counterbalance to techno-scientific discourse, which was shown to depend on narrative forms of legitimation, in the later text narrative always has the object of reducing differends: "it 'swallows up' the event and the differends carried along by the event" (Lyotard 1988: 152). Philosophy, the genre of discourse which "has as its rule to discover its rule" (Lyotard 1988: 60) is not compatible with narrative which buries or passes over the problem of its own self-legitimation: as we have seen, both McCrone and Craig are tempted to do by the process of devolution.

The political stakes are high. Lyotard's conclusion to *The Post-modern Condition* is that he has sketched "the outline of a politics that would respect both the desire for justice and the desire for the un-known" (Lyotard 1984: 67). The work of both McCrone and Craig is also directed towards the future. For McCrone, "Scotland seems to provide a glimpse into the future rather than the past" (McCrone 1992: 33; 2001: 53), while Craig commends us to Scott's view that "the dramatization of the nation [...] was about the values which its imaginings tested and which they projected as the path of action for the future" (Craig 2001: 27). But the appeal to a postmodern world, or to a postmodern conception of discursive space, serves to elide the decision which has been taken in advance and presumed by both writers, as to the legitimacy of the nation itself, a decision which is both epistemological and political. Following devolution, the legitimation of their work on the narrative of nationhood ends up re-instituting a naturalised account of the nation which precisely blocks access to any other future than the national one: or as Derrida describes it in *Spectres of Marx*, "killing the future in the name of old frontiers" (Derrida 1994: 169). This circumscription of Scotland's political prospects is also a wrong done to politics itself, when politics is considered to be not the implementation of pre-determined political programmes but, as it is for Lyotard, the space of conflict and debate itself.

Bibliography

Bennington, Geoffrey. 1988. *Lyotard: Writing the Event*. Manchester: Manchester University Press.

Brügger, Neils. 2001. "What about the Postmodern? The Concept of the Postmodern in the Work of Lyotard" in Harvey, Robert and Lawrence R. Schehr (eds) *Yale French Studies 99, Jean-Francois Lyotard: Time and Judgement*: 77-92.

Craig, Cairns. 1996. *Out of History: Narrative Paradigms in Scottish and British Culture*. Edinburgh: Polygon.

—. 2001. "Scott's Staging of the Nation" in *Studies in Romanticism* 40 (Spring 2001): 13-28.

Derrida, Jacques. 1994. *Specters of Marx*. London: Routledge.

Lacoue-Labarthe, Phillipe. 1984. "Talks" in *Diacritics* vol. 14 no.3 (Fall 1984): 24-37.

Lyotard, Jean-Francois. 1984. *The Postmodern Condition: A Report on Knowledge* (tr. Geoffrey Bennington and Brian Massumi). Manchester: Manchester University Press.

—. 1988. *The Differend*. Minneapolis: University of Minnesota Press.

—. 1991. *The Inhuman*. Cambridge: Polity.

—. 1992. *The Postmodern Explained to Children*. London: Turnaround.

McCrone, David. 1992. *Understanding Scotland: The Sociology of a Stateless Nation*. London: Routledge.

—. 2001. *Understanding Scotland: The Sociology of a Nation*. London: Routledge.

Readings, Bill. 1991. *Introducing Lyotard: Art and Politics*. London: Routledge.

Smith, Anthony D. 1998. *Nationalism and Modernism*. London: Routledge.

Thomson, A.J.P. 2001. "MacIntyre and Levinas: History and Justice" in *Edinburgh Review* 107: 53-63.

Williams, James. 1998. *Lyotard: Towards a Postmodern Philosophy*. Cambridge: Polity.

—. 2000. *Lyotard and the Political*. London: Routledge.

Postmodernism, Nationalism and the Question of Tradition

Eleanor Bell

Recently, many debates in sociology and politics have focussed on the potential decline of the nation-state in an increasingly globalised world. To what extent might
such new configurations of power have an impact on Scottish literary studies? To
accommodate these developments, Scottish studies must become more conscious of
its own boundaries.
Keywords: postmodernism, nationalism, postnationalism, tradition, Michael Billig,
Benedict Anderson, David McCrone, Anthony Giddens.

In his work on contemporary politics, philosophy, and Irish studies, Richard Kearney is concerned with the changing nature of national identity, and, in particular, with the ways in which power is now being restructured at European levels. Kearney points out that as European identity continues to develop we should be increasingly conscious of the urge to replace nation-states with one super-nation-state (a United States of Europe), for this would only encourage the dominance of nationalist ideology rather than the reconfiguration of power at more regional levels which he sees as necessary. Additionally, Kearney is interested in postnationalism, which he associates with the re-ordering of identity at micro and macro levels beneath and beyond the tradi-tional concept of the nation-state. For Kearney, postmodern theory provides a useful means of understanding this transitional period:

It has been suggested [...] that postmodern theory can have radical implications for
politics. One frequently encounters the claim, for instance, that the postmodern
critiques of the centre – as logos, arché, origin, presence, identity, unity or sovereignty
– challenge the categories of established power. The most often cited examples here
relate to the critique of totalitarianism, colonialism and nationalism. The postmodern
theory of power puts the "modern" concept of the nation-state into question. It points
towards a decentralising and disseminating of sovereignty which, in the European
context at least, signals the possibility of new configurations of federal-regional government. (Kearney 1997: 61)

In this chapter, I would therefore like to consider some of the possible connections between postmodern theory and postnationalism, examining their applicability from a Scottish context. I will also discuss in what ways this focus on the postnational encourages a rethinking of the traditional concept of "Scotland".

While many critics have been commenting on the potential breakdown of the nation-state for some time, in Scottish literary studies these readings have still to be seriously taken into account.[1] Where, for example, in Irish literary studies there have been many heated debates surrounding this issue, in Scottish literary studies such critiques have yet to emerge. Although topics such as postmodernism and postnationalism remain highly contentious in Irish studies, there are nonetheless many engaging publications in these areas which explore the changing nature of national identity in the face of forces such as globalisation.[2] What I would like to argue, therefore, is that Scottish literary studies should be encouraged to move from its often insular focus on tradition-inspired approaches in order to take account of some of the wider influences now affecting the nature of belonging at wider European and macro levels.

In *Banal Nationalism*, published in 1995, Michael Billig is concerned with the changing nature of territory and the possible refigurings of the nation which are now at work. According to Billig, the gradual breakdown of nations and nation-states is leading to a new kind of sensibility; one predominantly linked with the personal, rather than conceived at a wider collective level:

It is as if the whole business of nationhood is being unravelled. At each turn, it seems that a whole group separates from a state to declare a new state in its own name and then minority groups within the new state claim national status. An infinite regress beckons, with states fragmenting into infinitely smaller units. These units, in their turn, cannot be culturally isolated entities. They are plugged into the vast networks of information, which respect no natural, political, or linguistic boundaries. Thus, the thesis of postmodernism proclaims a vision of the future world. In this world, no

---

[1] Perhaps one of the main theorists in this area is Zygmunt Bauman. See Bauman 1998 and 1999.

[2] See, for example, some of the tensions which exist between the following texts: Briggs, Hyland and Sammells (eds) 1998, Eagleton 1994, Graham 2001, and Kearney 2000.

longer is the national territory *the* place from which identities, attachments and patterns of life spring [...] In place of the bordered, national state, a multiplicity of *terrae* are emerging. And those who see their identities in terms of gender or sexual orientation, are [...] bound by no earthly *terra,* restricted by no mere sense of place. Thus, a new sensibility – a new psychology – emerges in global times. (Billig 1995: 134)

This new *terra* described by Billig reflects the power, for example, of niche marketing, the power of global capitalism to move from the national to the transnational in what Benedict Anderson describes as "the twinkling of an electronic eye".[3] This new focus on the personal, on consumer spending at the individual level, and on consumer control at the wider multinational level, therefore challenges the former dominance of the nation-state as *the* organising principle of human societies. Many critics of sociology and politics have suggested that nations are losing their dominant status to the forces of transnationalism and the impact of the global marketplace. For critics such as Billig, however, it is also vital to acknowledge the hegemony and ideological control which countries such as the USA continue to exert. For Billig, this is the most dangerous element of the general dissolution of the nation-state project. His notion of "banal nationalism" therefore refers to this paradoxical situation whereby the United States promotes itself as a global ideal, so that the "Americanisation of everyday life" is projected as the new norm throughout the western world. For Billig, banal nationalism refers to our unconscious identification with this supposed American global ideal.

Why then has there been an apparent hesitancy to address these postmodern and postnational concerns from a Scottish perspective? As Benedict Anderson points out, such forms of emergent identity based on the individual rather than the collective national level create a politics which is "radically unaccountable", and which is most probably a "menacing portent for the future" (Anderson 1998: 74). Perhaps, then, we can begin to understand this reluctance to challenge the nation. Interestingly, so far in Scottish literary studies there has only

---

[3] "The Tamil bus-driver in Melbourne is a mere dozen sky-hours away from his *land van herkomst* [...] The Filipina maid in Hong Kong phones her sister in Manila, and sends money in the twinkling of an electronic eye to her mother in Cebu. The successful Indian student in Vancouver can keep in daily e-mail touch with her former Delhi classmates" (Anderson 1998: 68).

been one book-length study of postmodernism, and this was primarily concerned with the writing of Alasdair Gray (Witschi 1991). A brief comparison with Irish literary studies, however, will reveal many books and articles in this area, ranging from postmodern readings of Joyce and Beckett, readings of feminism and postmodernism in literature, and readings of postmodernism as it intersects with postcolonialism and postnationalism.[4] So where, for example, Irish studies have books such as John S. Rickard's *Irishness and (Post)-modernism* (Rickard 1994), such publications have still to be written from a Scottish perspective.

While postmodernism has provided one of the dominant frameworks for reading contemporary literature in recent years, it is perhaps surprising that the discipline of Scottish studies has resisted this approach for so long. Arguably, Scottish literary studies have been more focussed on canon-building and the construction of the national tradition, and too immersed in tradition-inspired approaches to take account of such theoretical developments. The objective of this chapter is, therefore, to point out some of the potential pitfalls of this indifference, suggesting it is now imperative that Scottish studies take account of such ideas. It is also important to point out, however, that the inclusion of postmodern and postnational readings of the nation here are not intended to negate the importance of tradition and tradition-inspired readings. Rather, the objective is to suggest that these newer discourses may help enrich historical readings rather than undermine the discipline in an unscholarly fashion.

One of the few people so far to link postmodern and postnational theories with Scotland in a social and cultural context has been David McCrone. In *The Sociology of Nationalism*, published in 1998, McCrone addresses some of the growing debates surrounding the instability of national identity in the modern era. Referring to this sense of mutability he writes "today no-one is merely one thing", and goes on:

The "crisis" of self has entered the discourse, not simply as a theme of social psychology, but in response to radical change in the social structures which maintained a

---

[4] Rice 1997, Began 1996. On feminism, see, for example, the *Irish Journal of Feminist Studies*. On postcolonialism, see Briggs, Hyland and Sammells (eds) 1998.

fairly consistent sense of self – family, marriage, occupation. Self appears to have become more fragmented, composed of several competing identities, and the generic process of identification has become more problematic and contentious. Increasing rates of social change help to destabilise traditional social structures, opening up new anxieties as well as new possibilities. (McCrone 1998: 32)

Here McCrone describes the situation with which many contemporary sociologists are now concerned: namely, how to account for the perceived breakdown of tradition and how this impacts on our sense of identity at different levels, ranging from the personal to the national and beyond. In many respects McCrone also echoes Billig's earlier point that potentially a new psychology is emerging in postmodern times, one concerned with the need to re-map structures of belonging, and which highlights the self-conscious *process* of identity:

National identities become more problematic as conventional state-identities are corroded by forces of globalisation which shift the classical sociological focus away from the assumption that "societies" are well-bounded social, economic and cultural systems. What replaces conventional state-identities is not "cultural homogenisation" in which everyone shares in the same global postmodern identity because they consume the same material and cultural products. Rather, as Stuart Hall observes, "We are confronted by a range of different identities, each appealing to us, or rather to different parts of ourselves, from which it seems possible to choose". (McCrone 1998: 34)

McCrone is therefore concerned with how to account for what Kearney earlier described as the need to reorganise power at both micro and macro levels in order to take forces such as globalisation into account. It is also important to point out here that while McCrone discusses identity in terms of the postmodern condition, at no point does he suggest that Scottish identity is "itself" under threat. Rather, it is seen to be diversifying and changing, the widespread belief in it still being strong enough to keep it alive. As a sociologist who has clearly been committed to the development of devolution and the Scottish Parliament, McCrone would in no way wish to deny that "Scotland" as a cultural reality exists. Rather, he discusses Scotland in terms of the postmodern condition precisely in order to locate the nation and the changing nature of nationalism in the contemporary world. McCrone's reading of postmodernism therefore indicates some of the ways in which Scottish national identity now needs to be generally rethought. This is especially important in order to take into account what Zygmunt Bauman has described as the "fissiparous" nature of contemporary nationalism in which new nations emerge as old ones divide and split (McCrone 1998: 170). For McCrone, writing in 1992, in *Understanding Scotland: The Sociology of a Stateless Nation*, it is important to recognise that Scottish identity should no longer be depicted in essential or homogenous terms. Indeed, he states, the search for a unique Scottish identity "is rapidly becoming invalid":

What is on offer in the late twentieth century is what we might call "pick 'n mix" identity, in which we wear our identities lightly, and change them according to cir- cumstances. Those who would argue for the paramountcy or even the exclusivity of a single identity have a hard time of it in the late twentieth century. (McCrone 1992: 170)

So while Scottish identity should now be worn lightly it does none- theless exist.

Despite McCrone's belief in the actual reality of Scotland, he questions, in the final chapter of *The Sociology of Nationalism*, the extent to which nationalism and the general concept of the nation-state can now be considered to be in decline. In this section, McCrone examines a variety of perspectives and the work of several theorists in his general diagnosis of the contemporary situation. He begins by questioning the current validity of the nation-state:

Czechoslovakia has since disappeared; Ireland provides classic evidence of the differ- ence between the Irish nation (at least the whole nation, and substantial numbers abroad) and the Irish state (the twenty-six counties). This leaves only Finland as the solitary success story. In general, we appear to have a language of the nation-state, but not much of a reality. (McCrone 1992: 170)

Yet while the nation-state may in many respects be losing its former power and authority, McCrone is also keen to point out that there is also "an important conundrum to be tackled" (McCrone 1992: 171). Why should nationalism be growing when the nation-state is losing its foothold on power?

Nationalism shows no signs of dying. On the contrary, an elegy is premature as na- tionalism takes on new forms and meets new needs in the late twentieth century.

There is no shortage of putative gravediggers: industrialisation, post-industrialisation, modernity, postmodernity, globalisation, technology and so on. We have always been susceptible to the simple account. (McCrone 1992: 173)

From this statement we can begin to develop McCrone's reading of postmodernism. While he often generally refers to the postmodern sociological condition (as defined by Zygmunt Bauman amongst others), McCrone is ultimately hesitant of such broad forms of labelling. Whilst on the one hand he is conversant in such postmodern sociological readings, and finds these useful in his own discussions, he resists being labelled a postmodernist himself, preferring instead to return to his main pragmatic, political concerns. For McCrone, postmodernism may not contain what Kearney, from a more post-structural perspective, describes as "radical implications", yet nonetheless the culture of postmodernity needs to be mapped in his sociological accounts. Where both critics perhaps meet is in their impulse to trace the ways in which the much-discussed breakdown of tradition is now affecting the structures of the nation-state and our consequent sense of belonging.

How should we therefore account for this much-discussed breakdown of tradition in the context of Scottish studies? Does this deserve to be considered in detail? As suggested earlier, recent critics of Scottish literature have been more concerned with asserting tradition than in contemplating its potential demise.[5] Yet, for other theorists of the postmodern condition such as Anthony Giddens, the concept of a post-traditional society is becoming an ever-increasing reality. For Giddens, the notion of fixed local communities is now under threat, and this has implications for our future conceptions of tradition. Gid-

---

[5] See, for example, the work of Cairns Craig: "The tradition of the modern Scottish novel which this book seeks to explore is not an 'expression' of a national 'geist', nor a singular founding principle to which any work must conform to be 'Scottish': the tradition is a space of debate, a dialogue between the interacting possibilities of a medium shaped by the conditions of those living in Scotland – its languages and its economic and social circumstances – and within the institutions which give shape to its national imagining. [...] That there is a tradition of the Scottish novel is also, however, an index of the continuity of the nation and the national imagining to which it contributes" (Craig 1999: 33).

dens is therefore concerned with the ways in which such "cultural evacuation will affect our resultant sense of belonging":

> In the present day, the destruction of the local community, in the developed societies, has reached its apogee. Little traditions which either survived, or were actively created, during earlier phases of modern social development have increasingly succumbed to forces of cultural evacuation [...] The dissolution of the local community, such as it used to be, is not the same as the disappearance of local life or local practices. Place, however, becomes increasingly reshaped in terms of distant influences drawn upon in the local arena. Thus customs that continue to exist tend to develop altered meanings. (Giddens 1997: 101)

If, as Giddens points out, the impact of consumerism and the forces of global capitalism are now fundamentally weaving themselves into the fabric of the local, becoming part of our everyday communities (whether rural or urban), then this must eventually be reflected in our accounts of the national tradition. The effect of global capitalism on the local is therefore altering our sense of identity, and this for Giddens should not be underestimated in our readings of community.

Not surprisingly, some Scottish critics will be quick to dispute arguments which suggest that Scottish culture is being "evacuated". In both *Out of History* and *The Modern Scottish Novel*, Cairns Craig has challenged the notion that "each stage of development [...] wipes out what went before it and destroys the very possibility of continuity upon which tradition is founded" (Craig 1999: 18). In these texts Craig explores some of the ways in which Scottish writers and critics have continually sought to undermine previous eras of the Scottish tradition to negate their sense of the past in order to suit their own contemporary arguments. Yet, how would critics such as Craig account for the changes taking place as described by Giddens and others? While Craig suggests that the Scottish tradition represents "a space of debate", how then can the concept of post-traditional society be brought into this open dialogue? The debates surrounding post-tradition do not seek to evacuate our sense of the Scottish past, or even the Scottish future. Rather, they wish to interrogate the ways in which the concept of identity itself is now in the process of change. They also explore how common notions of national identity might now have to open up in order to accommodate a variety of other concerns. In this respect national identity necessarily becomes more global, and perhaps more local too.[6]

The discussion so far has introduced a variety of the debates currently surrounding postmodern theory, the alleged breakdown of the nation-state, and the weakening of tradition. Before going on to contextualise these in more detail, and consider their applicability to Scottish literary studies, it might first be useful to reflect on some of the wider concerns that the issue of globalisation brings to contemporary literary studies in general. The January 2001 edition of the *Transactions and Proceedings of the Modern Language Association of America* is solely devoted to "Globalizing Literary Studies" and its possible effects. In one of the articles, "Beyond Discipline?: Globalization and the Future of English", Paul Jay begins by stating that "the nation-state, to be sure, is alive and well as a political and military entity" (Jay 2001: 32). Jay then, however, goes on to explore the notion that "culture is now being defined in terms less of national interests than of a shared set of global ones" (Jay 2001: 32). In this article Jay begins to unravel some of the possible tensions of this contradiction between the strength of the nation and the apparent decline of national culture, and considers the readings of globalisation in the work of (amongst others) Roland Robertson, Anthony Giddens, David Harvey, Arjun Appadurai and Caren Kaplan. Jay opens out the potential origins of globalisation and also some of its future directions, and concludes that we need to recognise the inherent "multidirectionality" of the term: "globalisation" may in fact refer to many different concepts simultaneously – so we cannot hope for it to be contained (in

---

[6] See, for example, Mike Featherstone: "It has become a cliché that we live in one world. Here we think of a variety of images: the photographs of the planet Earth taken in space by the returning Apollo astronauts after setting foot on the Moon; the sense of impending global disaster through the greenhouse effect or some man-made catastrophe [...] Such images heighten the sense that we are interdependent; that the flows of information, knowledge, money, commodities, people and images have intensified to the extent that the sense of spatial distance which separated and insulated people from the need to take into account all the other people which make up what has become known as humanity has become eroded. In effect we are all in each other's backyard. Hence one paradoxical consequence of the process of globalization, the awareness of the finitude and boundedness of the planet and humanity, is not to produce homogeneity but to familiarise us with greater diversity, the extensive range of local cultures" (Featherstone 1993: 169).

much the same way as "the postmodern" also cannot). However, it is precisely also because globalisation cannot be pinned down in its many manifestations and consequences that Jay states:

> Whether we keep working under the increasingly ambiguous concept of English or develop new terms and paradigms to describe what we do, we need to find a way to accommodate the transnational and postnational perspectives of globalization studies in our programs and curricula without subordinating the heterogeneous literatures we deal with to outdated critical paradigms. (Jay 2001: 44)

Jay concludes his article by stating:

> The literature and culture of England will always have an important place in our curriculum, but I think we need to make a programmatic commitment to the study of English in a newer, global framework, one that recognises the transnational character of English in the past and the global context in which it will be produced in the future. If we do not make such a commitment, we may see the discipline of English become ever more marginal in the university of the future. (Jay 2001: 44-45)

Here we may also question the effect on Scottish literary studies: if the discipline remains hostile to forces such as globalisation, remains more interested in "outdated critical paradigms", will this not then in turn lead to the further marginalisation of Scottish literature within the more dominant discipline of English Literature?

So while on the one hand concepts such as globalisation and postmodernism may mean an infinite variety of different things to different critics, and may provoke endless debate as a consequence, it still remains necessary to account for some of these possible readings and their effects within the discipline of Scottish studies. While many critics of sociology have recently become tired of the circularity of postmodernist thought (the way in which postmodern theory often revolves around the concept of postmodernism rather than around more "real" cultural factors), many debates surrounding the condition of postmodernity nevertheless remain cogent. For example, in their recent book *Reflexive Modernization: Politics, Tradition and Aesthetics in the Modern Social Order*, Ulrich Beck, Anthony Giddens and Scott Lash all address issues surrounding postmodernity, yet are also clearly hesitant to overuse the term, or to label themselves as postmodernist in the process. While all of these critics have been deeply involved in mapping out the consequences of postmodernity, post-tradition and postnationalism, they are also clearly sceptical of the overuse of post-modern terminology and its circularity, often finding it an inadequate and limiting means of explaining social conditions.[7]

In his contribution to *Reflexive Modernization*, Anthony Giddens begins to map out some of the implications of living in a post-traditional society:

> The post-traditional society is an ending; but it is also a beginning, a genuinely new social universe of action and experience. What type of social order is it, or might it become? It is, as I have said, a global society, not in the sense of a world society but as one of "indefinite space". It is one where social bonds effectively have to be *made*, rather than inherited from the past – on the personal and more collective levels this is a fraught and difficult enterprise, but one that also holds out the promise of great rewards. It is decentred in terms of *authorities*, but recentred in terms of opportunities and dilemmas, because focussed on new forms of interdependence. (Beck, Giddens and Lash 1997: 107)

In this reading Giddens is also concerned that this new society of "indefinite space" should also break away from what he described as "the aporias of postmodernism" (Beck, Giddens and Lash 1997: 107). For Giddens the future direction of post-traditional society might be uncertain, yet he is also convinced that this should not lead to "irreparable fragmentation" (Beck, Giddens and Lash 1997: 107). Rather he advocates the move towards a society where there is a "renewal of political engagement" that might also seek to be democratic and ethical, one which, whilst anticipating what future collectivities might look like, does not seek to dismiss past traditions (Beck, Giddens and Lash 1997: 107).

It is now time for more discussion surrounding issues such as postnationalism, post-tradition, and the ways in which discourses of postmodernism might interconnect with these and affect the future of Scottish literary studies. This chapter therefore reflects an attempt to

---

[7] This can be noticed in their preface where they state, "For all of us, the protracted debate about modernity versus postmodernity has become wearisome and like so many such debates in the end has produced rather little. The idea of reflexive modernization, regardless of whether or nor one uses the term as such, breaks the stranglehold which these debates have tended to place upon conceptual innovation" (Beck, Giddens and Lash 1997: vi).

open out some of these connections, and does not intend to predict the future. If, as many critics suggest, the nation-state is now weakening alongside concepts such as tradition, then surely such cultural shifts need to be registered from a Scottish perspective. While this chapter does not aim to undermine the importance of the Scottish tradition, it does however call for more reflection upon what tradition might mean in a present and future context. As suggested earlier, if Scottish literary studies are to avoid further marginalisation then perhaps it is now time to welcome more self-conscious forms of dialogue.

Bibliography

Anderson, Benedict. 1998. *Spectres of Comparison: Nationalism, Southeast Asia and the World*. London: Verso.

Bauman, Zygmunt. 1998. *Globalisation: The Human Consequences*. Oxford: Polity Press.

—. 1999. *In Search of Politics*. Cambridge: Polity Press.

Beck, U., A. Giddens and S. Lash. 1997. *Reflexive Modernization: Politics, Tradition and Aesthetics in the Modern Social Order*. Cambridge: Polity Press.

Began, Richard. 1996. *Samuel Beckett and the End of Modernity*. Cambridge: Cambridge University Press.

Billig, Michael. 1995. *Banal Nationalism*. London: Sage Publications.

Briggs, Sarah, Paul Hyland and Neill Sammells (eds). 1998. *Reviewing Ireland: Essays and Interviews from* Irish Studies Review. Bath: Sulis Press.

Craig, Cairns. 1999. *The Modern Scottish Novel: Narrative and the National Imagination*. Edinburgh: Edinburgh University Press.

Eagleton, Terry. 1994. "A Postmodern Punch" in *Irish Studies Review* 6: 2-3.

Featherstone, Mike. 1993. "Global and Local Cultures" in Jon Bird *et al.* (eds) *Mapping the Futures: Local Cultures, Global Change*. London: Routledge. 169-88.

Graham, Colin. 2001. *Deconstructing Ireland*. Edinburgh: Edinburgh University Press.

Jay, Paul. 2001. "Beyond Discipline?: Globalization and the Future of English" in *PMLA* 116(1): 32-47.

Kearney, Richard. 1997. *Postnationalist Ireland: Politics, Culture, Philosophy*. London: Routledge.

—. 2000. "Towards a Postnationalist Archipelago" in *Edinburgh Review* 103: 21-34.

McCrone, David. 1992. *Understanding Scotland: The Sociology of a Stateless Nation*. London and New York: Routledge.

—. 1998. *The Sociology of Nationalism: Tomorrow's Ancestors*. London and New York: Routledge.

Rice, Thomas Jackson. 1997. *Joyce, Chaos and Complexity*. Urbana: University of Illinois Press.

Rickard, J.S. 1994. *Irishness and (Post)modernism*. London and Toronto: Bucknell University Press.

Witschi, Beat. 1991. *Glasgow Urban Writing and Postmodernism: a Study of Alasdair Gray's Fiction*. Frankfurt am Main: Peter Lang.

"Almost afraid to know itself": *Macbeth* and Cinematic Scotland

Willy Maley and Sarah Neely

The national context of Shakespeare's so-called "Scottish play" has frequently been underplayed in stage versions. Cinematic adaptations show a similar inability to represent Scotland as a nation. It is either overlooked, or reduced to a series of kitsch signifiers. Even recent trends in Scottish cinema are unlikely to foster a Scottish *Macbeth* in a context of global cinematic production and distribution.
Keywords: Shakespeare, Richard Kearney, Derrick McClure, *Macbeth*, Scottish cinema, postnationalism.

In the conclusion to *That Shakespeherian Rag* (1986), Terry Hawkes wonders what effect the rise of Scottish nationalism might have on the academic subject of English and on Englishness more generally (Hawkes 1986: 121). At the end of *Shakespeare in the Present* (2002) he returns to the theme:

> Could it possibly be that the Scots, the Welsh, the Irish might […] come to regard an involvement with Shakespeare as somehow condoning or even embodying the 'Englishing' by which, in some eyes, they were for too long moulded? (Hawkes 2002: 143)

The question is a good one, but it fails to take into account the degree to which the Americanisation of Shakespeare – and of global culture more broadly – has meant that there is more to breaking the mould of British politics than arresting an incorporating Englishness. Moreover, why throw out the Bardic baby with the British bathwater? There is more to Shakespeare's work than the conservative anglocentrism or global capitalism that it has been enlisted to serve.

In the case of Scotland, "an involvement with Shakespeare" is a particularly vexed issue. *Macbeth*, to take a striking example, is known in acting circles as "The Scottish Play", but its "Scottishness" is a touchy subject. Most incarnations of the play on stage and screen reveal a complicated and often ambivalent relationship to its connections with Scotland. The so-called "Scottish Play" is, paradoxically, unlikely to be discussed in relation to national identity, and for three related reasons to do with genre, history, and geography. Firstly, in terms of genre, *Macbeth* as a tragedy transcends locality. Secondly, the historical promotion of Shakespeare as an icon of an imperialist and universalising Englishness means the non-English constituents of early modern Britain, Ireland excepted, get short shrift. While Ireland looms large in New Historicist and Cultural Materialist readings of Shakespeare, Scotland is posted missing. *The Tempest* is now virtually "the Irish play", attracting increasingly ingenious postcolonial readings, but *Macbeth*, which is much more obviously tied to a specific national context, remains Scottish in name only, spared the emphases on nationalism that *Henry V* attracts (Baker 1997, Brown 1985). Finally, geographically speaking, Scotland's marginalised role within the British state, and within Renaissance studies, means that most critics lack the information or inclination to situate the play.

In a period when prominent thinkers like Richard Kearney argue against "the old forms of nation-state government", and put forward a "postnationalist" perspective, it is easy to see why there might be some hesitancy in calling for a specifically Scottish *Macbeth*. On the other hand, the critique of nationalism has always gone hand-in-hand with the persistence and pervasiveness of national identity. This can create a mix of patriotism and paranoia, as commentators cautious about the nation-state find themselves caught up, as citizens or subjects, in a political entity they would like to see as outmoded. Take the 1990 report of the Scottish Constitutional Convention, which Kearney quotes in *Postnationalist Ireland*. Here is a document clearly aimed at securing a measure of statehood for the Scottish nation, but whose authors are acutely aware of the pitfalls of patriotism in its most exclusive and insular manifestations:

The Scottish Parliament will look not only to Westminster, but also to Brussels and Strasbourg […] This does not mean struggling to re-establish a nation state at the very time Europe is moving away from this narrow concept. (Kearney 1997: 89)

We would dispute whether a move away from nationalism is anything other than wishful thinking on the part of an educated minority. Kearney's critique is as much a reaction against the recent "Troubles" in Ireland as a response to any sustained anti-nationalist shift in Europe. Ironically, the limited powers given to the new Scottish Parliament, which served as a model for the Northern Ireland assembly, coincides with an increasing tendency on the part of the British Government to look to the United States rather than to Europe, perhaps with the hope once more of empire-building. A premature postnationalism can be as dangerous as a strident nationalism if it masks a continuing colonial predilection on the part of particular nation-states.

This brings us to *Macbeth*, a postnationalist play in two senses, as a drama that depicts, in one reading, an old barbaric Scotland yielding to a new civilised one (with a little help from England), and as a play that despite being "Scottish" manages to go global in adaptations and interpretations. In Kearney's text, there is no sustained comparison of Ireland and Scotland – his book predates the recent upsurge of interest in Irish-Scottish studies – but there is a subtext that suggests that Scotland's "Independence within Europe" strategy (to cite a slogan of the Scottish National Party) is the way forward. However, the influence of America, in film as in politics, means that the European dimension gets lost somewhere between Holyrood and Hollywood. Scotland, still subsumed within an English-dominated British state, is visible on the international stage only as something less than a nation.

As recent cinematic versions attest, changing notions of Scotland and its representation are continually worked out in contemporary versions of *Macbeth*. This chapter explores the ways in which different forms of cinematic adaptation – from independent to mainstream – tackle the play's thorny relationship with its Scottish setting.

Unlike *Henry V*, Shakespeare's most English play, where national identity is of the essence, in *Macbeth*, Scotland is a blot on the landscape. Emptied of its Scottish context by a whole critical tradition, *Macbeth* is deracinated and denationalised. In terms of where Scotland stands on screen, the decontextualisation of *Macbeth* is clearly more than just a symptom of anti-historicist trends in Shakespeare criticism. The infrequency with which "The Scottish Play" and "Scotland" are juxtaposed becomes even more curious if we consider the significance of the setting in other Shakespearean dramas. While *Henry V* remains caught up in patriotism and propaganda – witness

Olivier's wartime version (1944) – few film versions of *Macbeth* are located in Scotland or take patriotism as their theme. This is a trend partly explained by the play's promotion as tragedy. Although Anne Barton insists that "*Macbeth* [...] is surely as much a history play as *Richard II*", its status as a tragedy and its alleged depiction of evil dictate its reception (Barton 1977: 70). *Macbeth*, as a tragedy, can rise above its station, becoming a transcendent "study of evil"; as a history, though, it needs to be fixed in time and place.

Nonetheless, the emptying out of the play's Scottishness, or the overloading of adaptations with stereotypes and tartan, has as much to do with a vexed cinematic history of representing Scotland as it does with the tradition of taking Shakespeare out of any historical context. For example, Orson Welles's version (1948), shot in three weeks, is indistinctly "medieval" rather than stringently Scottish, rendered in darkly lit, tightly framed compositions, and low-angle shots. The claustrophobic shooting style evokes a particular imagining of the "Medieval" which is attributable equally to flights of directorial vision and the constraints of a low budget. Akira Kurosawa's acclaimed in-terpretation, *Throne of Blood* (1957), heavily influenced by Noh theatre, shifts the violence of medieval Scotland to medieval Japan. Roman Polanski's *Macbeth* (1971), part-funded by Playboy Enter-prises, with Hugh Hefner as executive producer, is as notorious for its nudity as for its naked savagery. One reviewer cites Kenneth Tynan, Polanski's "script collaborator", saying of the Macbeths, "When we first see them they are young Mr. and Mrs. Scotland, the couple most likely to succeed" (Taylor 1971: 78). The review continues, however: "The exteriors have been shot, not in Scotland ('too touristy') but in Wales" (Taylor 1971: 78).

Can Scotland seriously be considered too touristy for a "medie-val" *Macbeth*? In seeking to avoid the accusation of kitsch, are adaptors neglecting Scotland? Directors taking on *Macbeth* must de-cide what to do with the debris and detritus of "Scottishness". The real problem lies in the available archive of images. According to Duncan Petrie, "it should come as no surprise to learn that the construction of a Scottish past is equally dependent on the construction of mythic projections rooted in fantasy, romance, and the power of imagination"

(Petrie 2000: 53). Ironically, one *Macbeth* filmed in Scotland, George Schaefer's 1960 version, was reviewed as a

new British version […] safe, tame, respectable […] perversely set against blue skies and sunny Highland landscapes which evoke the Scotland of the travelogues rather than the stormy, dark atmosphere of Shakespeare's play. (LGS 1961: 76)

Scotland, too touristy, too travelogue, is its own worst enemy as a location. From *Brigadoon* to *Braveheart*, Scotland the brand is marketed through heroism, landscape, and myth. A sense of being trapped in time, of history as heritage, and geography as tourism, persists. What gets lost between the local and the global is therefore precisely the national.

The stereotype of a scenic Scotland is, perversely, deemed insufficiently Scottish for Shakespeare's play. Since *Trainspotting* (dir. Danny Boyle, 1996), old stereotypes around the myth of tartanry associated with films such as *Whisky Galore!* (dir. Alexander Mackendrick, 1949) or *Brigadoon* (dir. Vincente Minelli, 1954) have been supplanted, and a darker Scotland has emerged blinking into the light. Shakespeare's Scottish play is as bold and bloody a portrait of violent masculinity as one could imagine, and it is easy to envisage a reworking of the story that would combine the most radical elements of recent cinematic depictions of Scotland: *Braveheart* meets *Trainspotting*. Such connections have been made in the BBC production, *Macbeth on the Estate* (dir. Penny Woolcock, 1997), set around a drug-ridden Birmingham housing scheme.

But is this new Scotland, illustrated by the recent trend in cinema, in fact a representation of Scottish nationality? These new films termed "Tartan Noir", and typified by *Trainspotting* and *Shallow Grave* (dir. Danny Boyle, 1994), are revered for displacing the Scotch "myth and mist" tradition with cosmopolitan flair. Yet, although one might read these new cinematic representations as getting closer to more "authentic" representations of "Scottishness", they might also be linked to an overall trend in contemporary filmmaking. Martin McLoone, for example, sees such films as representative of a new postmodern sensibility that undermines identification with place in favour of a rootless cosmopolitanism (McLoone 2001).

Such rootlessness is exemplified by less conventional versions of *Macbeth* which insist on representing Scotland in shorthand. In these films "Scottishness" appears through a variety of kitsch signifiers, and serves as a location upon which an American identity is played out. Actor Billy Morrisette's directorial debut, *Scotland PA* (2001), shifts its ground to 1950s America, where Duncan is the burger king of a budding fast-food empire, soon to be overthrown by his overworked, under-appreciated employee, McBeth. *Macbeth in Manhattan* (dir. Greg Lombardo, 1999), charts the progress of a theatre company putting on the play and, like *Looking for Richard* (dir. Al Pacino, 1996), uses this scenario as a springboard for reflections on the relationship between the States and Shakespeare. Several scenes in *Macbeth in Manhattan* are prefaced by medium shots of a kilted man from the waist down, traipsing through a downtown backdrop, a signifier which recalls various recent cinematic appropriations of kilts and tartanry, from ethnic chic to anti-fashion statement. Such appropriation is emblematic of the mythical projections of Scottish culture prevalent in contemporary filmmaking. Other films rely on the shorthand referencing of Scotland a great deal more. *Macbeth: the Comedy* (dir. Allison L. LiCalsi, 2001), which recasts Macbeth as a woman, offers a lesbian reading. Its references to Scotland are handled lightly. For instance, its female Macbeth, seated at her desk, is surrounded by a multitude of Scottish signifiers: the Lion Rampant Flag, thistles, whisky, and a "Thank God I'm Scottish" plaque. What these independent American cinematic readings have in common is their broad brush depiction – coolly detached or comically familiar – of the play's Scottish context.

The now-you-see-it, now-you-don't approach to "Scottishness" suggests a lack of specificity in line with Arthur Lindley's analysis of "ahistorical" or "dehistoricised" films, especially his view of the unfussy attitude to the circulation of medieval tropes in Welles's film (see Lindley 2001). But instead of staking a "claim to historicity", these more recent representations ally themselves to a version of "Scottishness" that lies seemingly outside history. This fresh turn in adaptations of *Macbeth* deploys a shorthand which values not the authenticity of reproduction of a cultural past, but the productivity and endless repetition of various cultural signs. These signs are important not in terms of what they stand for, but in a postmodern fashion for their recognition pleasure. In *Macbeth in Manhattan*, that swinging, streetwise kilt, seductively disembodied, in constant threat of disappearing from the frame, insists on ambiguity. In *Macbeth: the Comedy*, the tartanry is not worn without irony. The absence of haggis from the banquet is accounted for by the fact that the Macbeths are "strict vegetarians".

If an authentically Scottish cinematic *Macbeth* did exist, what would it look like? While it makes sense to look to other Scottish films for cues and clues, it is important to note that the very idea of a "Scottish film", or the determining of a "Scottish Cinema", has been fraught with difficulties. In addition to the questioning of the notion of a national cinema in a Scottish context, a general interrogation of the idea of national cinema has occurred across the board. Nevertheless, debates surrounding the development of indigenous cinema argue for its necessity in a transglobal industry that hinges on the acceptance of its product on a world stage. The importance of indigenous cinema in this commercial environment is to support and develop independent cinema against the dominance of the big players. However, as several critics have recognised, the possibility of a truly indigenous cinema remains remote (McLoone 2000, McArthur 1993). At various stages in the production and distribution of cinema, mainstream practices exert their pull. Even if a film is made independently, the global control and regulation of distribution requires at least some degree of compliance.

This influence is clearly an issue in one of the few recent adaptations of *Macbeth* shot in Scotland, Jeremy Freeston's 1997 version, shot in Blackness Castle and Dunfermline Abbey (but also Warwick Castle in England), and produced in association with a Scottish company, Grampian Television. Opening with a title sequence featuring penny-whistle music, an iron Celtic mask illuminated by torches flickering either side of the frame, and an abundance of dry ice, Freeston's take on *Macbeth* aligns itself through its promotional imagery and rhetoric with other films dealing with various aspects of "Scottishness" in the 1990s, specifically, the internationally acclaimed *Braveheart* (dir. Mel Gibson, 1995), and *Rob Roy* (dir. Michael Caton-Jones, 1994), but also lower budget productions, such as *Chasing the*

Deer (dir. Graham Holloway, 1994) and *The Bruce* (dir. Bob Carruthers, 1996). Freeston's portrayal of the opening battle sequence
immediately follows the title credits. Through a series of tightly
framed close-ups highlighting the grit and gore of general battle, the
scene stylistically mirrors its most successful precursor, *Braveheart*.
This can be illustrated by juxtaposing publicity stills from both films
portraying Wallace and Macbeth. Not only does Jason Connery's appearance have more in common with Mel Gibson than any cinematic
Macbeths of the past, the filmmakers frame and shoot the character in
a similar fashion.

What, then, are the prospects for *Macbeth* at the movies in a
post-devolutionary context, where a new confident Scotland is rede-
fining itself in cinema, culture, and politics, and at a time when
Shakespeare criticism is increasingly aware of the Scottish dimension
of the play? Writing in 1936, Edwin Muir said that "Scotland can only
create a national literature by writing in English [...] while we cling to
[Scots] we shall never be able to express the central reality of Scotland" (Muir 1936: 111-12). Since then, two things have changed.
Firstly, the variety and vibrancy of the Scots language have increased.
Secondly, fewer people are interested in "the central reality of Scotland". A Scottish context exists for Shakespeare's Scottish play now
more than ever, but precisely at a moment in history when an
obsession with specific national contexts is coming under intense
scrutiny, and is invariably eyed with suspicion.

Muir's claim that it was futile to "cling to" Scots appears ironic
when set alongside the appearance, in 1992, of two new Scots translations of *Macbeth*. Reviewing both renditions, Derrick McClure
wonders how translators can fit Shakespeare's view of Scotland into
contemporary Scots (McClure 1996, Lorimer 1992, Purves 1992).
According to McClure, "there is a *prima facie* inappropriateness in
using [Scots] to translate the supreme celebrant of the identity of the
rival culture" (McClure 1996: 3). McClure goes on to say that "Macbeth is now often perceived as the last champion of Scotland's Celtic
identity, and by extension of her historic independence: a simplistic
notion but a very appealing one" (McClure 1996: 4). Despite its alleged anti-Scottishness, translating *Macbeth* into Scots is a patriotic
act on two counts: because of the political commitment implicit in

translating from English to Scots (reversing the dominant dubbing practice in films); and because Shakespeare's tragic hero is heroic from a modern Scottish perspective in a way that he may not have been from a medieval or Renaissance standpoint.

In many ways, recent adaptations of *Macbeth* might seem to support Richard Kearney's prediction that eventually "future identities may, conceivably, be less nation-statist and more local and cosmopolitan" (Kearney 1997: 15). They seem symptomatic of a general blurring and borrowing of transglobal filmmaking practices. The question is why this is not the case in other recent adaptations of Shakespeare, such as Branagh's *Henry V?* It seems more likely that the tendency to transport *Macbeth* furth of Scotland reveals a particular problem with the representation of "Scottishness" on screen. Perhaps filmmakers, uncomfortable with existing representations of Scotland, choose to identify themselves with European filmmaking traditions. The medium of film also makes it difficult to represent the subtleties of "Scottishness". Mainstream cinema's reliance on recognisable tropes for its storytelling practices ensures that the stereotypes of tartanry continue to be exploited by filmmakers: Scotland's past is remembered through souvenirs, not sovereigns.

The dilemma is one affecting various facets of Scottish culture, not just cinema, and has to do with perceptions of Scotland's history and its perpetuation as a country of the mind, an imagined community. Adaptors of *Macbeth* must negotiate (albeit often unwittingly) with how to represent this imaginary Scotland. Colin McArthur, responding to a threat to remove *Macbeth* from the Scottish section of the school curriculum, argues that the play's historical ties to Scotland are worth maintaining, adding that although often such associations were merely indicative of contemporary ideologies, the play "since its inception, has followed closely the contours of what the world has perceived and imagined about Scotland and the Scots" (McArthur 1996). McArthur concludes with these dramatic words: "Given its history and evolution, it is hard to think of a more Scottish play" (McArthur 1996). *Macbeth* has made a lasting contribution to the Scottish imaginary even if successive adaptations and a long critical history have served to obscure the play's Scottishness.

Bibliography

Baker, David J. 1991. "Where is Ireland in *The Tempest*?" in Burnett, Mark Thornton and Ramona Wray (eds) *Shakespeare and Ireland: History, Politics, Culture*. London: Macmillan. 68-88.

Barton, Anne. 1977. "'He That Plays The King': Ford's *Perkin Warbeck* and the Stuart History Play" in Axton, Marie and Raymond Williams (eds) *English Drama: Forms and Development*. Cambridge: Cambridge University Press. 69-93.

Brown, Paul. 1985. "'This Thing of Darkness I Acknowledge Mine': *The Tempest* and the Discourse Of Colonialism" in Dollimore, Jonathan and Alan Sinfield (eds) *Political Shakespeare: Essays in Cultural Materialism*. Manchester: Manchester University Press. 48-71.

Hawkes, Terence. 1986. *That Shakespeherian Rag: Essays on a Critical Process*. London: Methuen.

—. 2002. *Shakespeare in the Present*. London: Routledge.

Kearney, Richard. 1997. *Postnationalist Ireland: Politics, Culture, Philosophy*. London and New York: Routledge.

LGS. 1961. "*Macbeth*, Great Britain, 1960" in *Monthly Film Bulletin* 28(329): 76.

Lindley, Arthur. 2001. "Scotland Saved from History: Welles's *Macbeth* and the Ahistoricism of Medieval Film" in *Literature/Film Quarterly* 20(2): 96-100.

Lorimer, R.L.C. 1992. *Shakespeare's Macbeth Translated into Scots*. Edinburgh: Canongate.

McArthur, Colin. 1993. "In Praise of a Poor Cinema" in *Sight and Sound* August: 30-32.

—. 1996. "Out, out damned Scot? (revision of Scottish higher education curriculum in English Literature)" in *New Statesman* October 18: 43.

McClure, J. Derrick. 1996. "When *Macbeth* Becomes Scots" in *Ilha do Desterro* 36: 29-51.

McLoone, Martin. 2000. *Irish Film: The Emergence of a Contemporary Cinema*. London: British Film Institute.

—. 2001. "Internal Decolonisation? British Cinema in the Celtic Fringe" in Robert Murphy (ed.) *The British Cinema Book*. London: British Film Institute.

Muir, Edwin. 1936. *Scott and Scotland*. London: Routledge.

Petrie, Duncan. 2000. *Screening Scotland*. London: British Film Institute.

Purves, David C. 1992. *The Tragedie o Macbeth*. Edinburgh: Rob Roy Press.

Taylor, John Russell. 1971. "Polanski's *Macbeth*" in *Sight and Sound* 40(2): 77-78.

Dislocating the Nation: Political Devolution and Cultural Identity on Stage and Screen

Ellen-Raïssa Jackson

Postcolonial theory may be used to explore the direction of Scottish and Irish cultural production in film and theatre. The political assessment of the relative merits of films such as *Braveheart* and *Michael Collins* reveals how cultural identity is shaped and challenged by contemporary re-imaginings of history. However, the effects of political devolution vary greatly: the lively cultural critique current in Scottish drama is not matched by a similar movement in Scottish cinema.
Keywords: postcolonial, Scottish Parliament, Irish film industry, Scottish film industry, *Braveheart*, *Trainspotting*, *Michael Collins*.

The 1980s and 1990s saw the rapid growth and acceptance of postcolonial theory in the academy, but this has been accompanied by continued debate, both among postcolonial practitioners and those committed to different theoretical standpoints, about the nature and scope of the term "postcolonial". After some initial resistance, Irish writing has generally been accepted into the body of postcolonial writing, largely through the work of theorists such as David Lloyd and Luke Gibbons, as well as through polemical projects such as the *Field Day* anthologies of Irish writing. However, whilst many non-Irish thinkers are happy to consider Ireland as "postcolonial" the response from within Ireland itself has been mixed. In particular, writers and academics from Northern Ireland have suggested that the postcolonial label assumes a homogenised Ireland that makes no distinction between the Republic and the North. In addition, critics like Edna Longley argue that postcolonial readings are often reductively nationalist and fail to respect or acknowledge Protestant and Unionist values and experiences. Similarly, Scotland has tended to suffer from an inability on the part of postcolonial critics to disaggregate Britain: for example, *The Empire Writes Back* (1985) refers to Scotland in passing as "in complicity" with the Imperial project and therefore worthy of little consideration (Ashcroft, Griffiths and Tiffin 1989: 23).

Although Scotland has received little attention from postcolonial critics, a few readings of Scottish history and Scottish writing in a

colonial context have been offered, most notably by Craig Beveridge
and Ronald Turnbull, Robert Crawford, and Willy Maley. In the main
however, postcolonial readings have been resisted or overlooked in
Scotland. At best, the core-periphery theories that underpin early postcolonial readings have been used to explain the troubled and troublesome relationship between Scottish and English cultural production.
In recent years, postcolonial theory has begun to question the dominance of the core-periphery model, which tends to focus colonial experience exclusively on the relationship with the colonising centre.
Critics such as Elleke Boheme and Bart Moore-Gilbert have called for
greater consideration of transverse forms of anti-colonial collaboration
and further study of the relations between different colonised nations
and regions. The challenge that postcolonialism presents to existing
critical frameworks is matched by the reluctance of critics to read
Scottish and Irish writing against and alongside one another. Whereas
a strong urge to bring together cultural analyses of Scotland and Ireland has been shown in projects such as the Irish-Scottish Academic
Initiative, the debate surrounding the New British History, and
through suggestions in the work of Robert Crawford, Marilyn Reiz-
baum and Seamus Deane, an equally forceful rejection of this approach has surfaced in the work of Fintan O'Toole, Colin McArthur
and others. The reasons for this divergence of opinion are not only
explicable in terms of the politics of the Republic, Northern Ireland
and Scotland, but are caught up in questions of canons, cultures and
critical perspectives. To some extent, such divisions are neither novel
nor surprising, and strong parallels exist in the complementary debates
in Scotland and Ireland about the direction a national literature should
take on the threshold of the twenty-first century.

However, more recently, all things Irish and Scottish have experienced a second revival – a boom in popularity that has exposed a
body of talented writers to international critique and acclaim. Similarly to the first revival, the new Irish fiction that wowed Britain and
America in the late 1980s was followed by a upturn in interest in
Scottish writers in the early 1990s. Without dismissing the value that
the confluence of such interest may hold, it is worth bearing in mind
that the labelling and marketing of Irish and Scottish culture can ho-
mogenise and stifle any creative effort that identifies itself with the

nation. In the conclusion to his book on the Irish novel, Gerry Smyth suggests that "it may be that 'The New Irish Fiction' is little more than an invention by a loose affiliation of London publishers, creating a critical category (and a market) where before there was only a set of vague impressions" (Smyth 1997: 175). Similarly, the boom in the market for Scottish fiction has tended to depend upon individual books creating an *impression* of what could be called "Kelmanism". Cultural products that do not fit the mould are, at best, criticised for their failure to do so and, at worst, completely ignored.

There are many reasons why both Scottish and Irish culture might be experiencing a boom in popularity, particularly in Britain and America. Yet, however valuable such interest may be, it has re-percussions in the form of a heightened antagonism between Scotland and Ireland, who compete for a similar share in the cultural market. This is particularly true in the case of the film industry, where tax in-centives and government co-operation (following the radical policies of Michael D. Higgins, the former minister for arts, culture and the Gaeltacht) have built up Ireland's potential as a location and base for filming at Scotland's expense. In particular, the filming of much of *Braveheart* in Ireland precisely because of the tax incentives and the burgeoning skills infrastructure stirred Irish-Scottish rivalries. The strong strategic line taken by the Irish Government following Hig-gins's lead ensured that external investment would provide the com-mercial and creative development of an indigenous film industry. This approach was much admired and envied, particularly in Scotland. The relocation of *Braveheart* provoked huge debate in the Scottish and Irish press, not only in terms of political and economic rivalry, but also about the extent to which the state could and should intervene in the representation of the nation. There was strong interest in the con-trast between the influence of the government and that of popular culture and the media, which continually generate, revise and reassert cultural identity in the public arena. At the same time as articulating a mutual jealousy, the debate opened up the possibility for a more open, participative relationship between the cultural and political identities of both communities.

The establishment of a Scottish Parliament in Edinburgh in 1999 was greeted in Scotland as a new opportunity for both Scottish culture and democracy. The Parliament allows Scotland to represent itself internationally, as a multi-faceted modern nation. It is not only a forum for competing political voices, but provides an international medium through which to display the many dimensions of Scottish experience, activity and preoccupations. In August 1999, the Scottish Executive published "Celebrating Scotland: a National Cultural Strategy", which prompted many Scottish commentators to consider in practice an idea that they had been debating since before the failed devolution referendum in 1979. The cultural strategy was of particular importance because it was the first time that the new Labour government had clearly stated its desire to expand and support film-making in Scotland. According to Duncan Petrie:

the devolution of political power from Westminster to Edinburgh carried major implications given the increasingly vital role played by public agencies in stimulating and supporting film-making in Scotland. The new Scottish Executive has already given clear indications of its interest in the field [...] instigating a new cultural strategy review under the new junior minister for culture, Rhona Brankin. (Petrie 2000: 222)

Sadly, the culture portfolio was then passed around the commutative Scottish Cabinet: Rhona Brankin was shuffled following Sam Galbraith's resignation, and Allan Wilson became a deputy without a boss (he also had a persistent habit of referring to himself as the "minister for sport" before he departed for pastures greener). Wilson was replaced by Mike Watson, whose interest in the arts element of his remit was overshadowed by the controversy stirred up by his member's bill to ban hunting with dogs. The identity of Scotland in political terms seemed destined to be caught between a discourse of sport and a discourse of culture.

However, all was not lost, as was demonstrated by later reports to the Education, Culture and Sport Committee of the Parliament on the Scottish film industry, the proposed national theatre, and the traditional arts. The film industry report was prepared by Mike Russell, the SNP spokesperson on all things cultural, an independent television producer and strong supporter of Gaelic. Russell's report outlined several key concerns about the industry, particularly in relation to training, fiscal incentives for indigenous and incoming production, and the creation of a film-friendly environment. Russell concluded that the

central issue was "the desire to increase the volume of film production
in Scotland, both from indigenous producers and from incoming productions with the aim of increasing its economic, social and cultural
impact" (Russell 2001).

In the committee debate on the report, the Conservative MSP
Brian Monteith spoke about the possibility of establishing a Scottish
film studio at Pacific Quay in Glasgow, and questioned whether such
a project would produce sufficient cultural and financial returns. In a
more recent debate on the progress of the national cultural strategy,
Mike Russell asked the Scottish Executive to deliver on its promise to
create a properly funded national theatre, and criticised the Executive's strategy for failing to gain the support of the Scottish
community. In the same debate, Brian Monteith also suggested that
the strategy had failed to capture the enthusiasm of the Scottish people. Mike Russell and Brian Monteith rarely saw eye-to-eye on any
subject (particularly anything relating to state funding or intervention),
and their agreement on this issue raised the question of exactly what
impacts or returns they were looking for and, more broadly, what
Scotland hoped to gain from the establishment of an active national
film industry and a dedicated national theatre. In Mike Russell's case,
it was fairly clear: his political aim was independence and the purpose
of a state-supported, strong indigenous industry was to demonstrate
Scotland's ability to compete against Britain in the cultural arena. Indeed, in one brief committee debate, Mike Russell managed to relate
the desire for a film industry with that for independence three times.
Furthermore, the SNP was keen to use images from Mel Gibson's
Braveheart during the 1997 general election campaign and again in
1999 in the run-up to the Scottish Parliament elections. The SNP frequently refers to the *Braveheart* effect, by which it means an increased
interest in Scotland and an accompanying increase in sympathy for
Scottish nationalism and the independence agenda. I note in passing,
that I have never heard an SNP member refer to the *Trainspotting*
effect in similar terms. Cultural critics, however, are perhaps more
interested in such a possibility. For example, Duncan Petrie talks
about *Trainspotting* as forging "a new sophisticated urban aesthetic"
(Petrie 2000: 196) which has paved the way for a flurry of energetic,
self-consciously British productions.

One key point in Russell's report on the film industry was the impact of the tax concession in Ireland and both the desirability of following the Irish model and the dangers inherent in ignoring it (which he referred to as the *Braveheart* example). Mike Russell linked such issues to the ability of the Scottish Parliament to raise taxes and the flexibility that would be the result of greater independence from Westminster. In contrast, Brian Monteith described the fiscal difficulties that Scotland faced as a British problem that required a British solution, clearly framing the issue within a unionist agenda.

What that discussion shows is that there are several tensions inherent in what appears to be a shared desire to relocate a national film industry and to support Scottish theatre. Firstly, the cultural value of such an enterprise is confused by the extent to which it depends on economic and social factors such as training and backing. Secondly, the political identity of such a project is also up for debate, since it can be seen to be used to fit both nationalist and unionist agendas. The commercial nature of the film industry, in contrast to say, that of the novel or theatre, makes the extent to which representation and related activity can be controlled extremely unclear.

The potential embodied in a flourishing and creative indigenous film industry presents a dilemma to the political bodies that might choose to encourage or emphasise it. Whereas political nationalism seeks to affirm a claim to nationhood underpinned by a coherent history, it must also assert a modern identity that lies outside history, to act as a given that can go beyond the historical moment. Furthermore, the contemporary importance of the nation must be attractive to the national public and provide an economic basis that is sustainable and successful. The welcome expansion of the Irish and Scottish economies in the early 1990s brought with it a boom in the marketing of both countries, and what the market wanted was a return to the romantic, sweeping landscape of *The Quiet Man* (dir. John Ford, 1952) and *Brigadoon* (dir. Vincente Minnelli, 1954). The traumatic search for a modern identity is a familiar postcolonial problem, but one that is complicated in a cinematic context by the commercial attraction of a ready-made brand. Although the resurgence in Irish film production in the late 1980s began with films that embraced an Ireland that was rooted in the pastoral and the past, such as Jim Sheridan's *My Left*

Foot (1989), and *The Field* (1990), this was followed by attempts to mediate urban, rural and emigrant identity in films such as *Into the West* (dir. Mike Newell, 1992) and *The Crying Game* (dir. Neil Jordan, 1992). As Martin McLoone has commented: "contemporary cinema suggests that Irish culture is still obsessed with coming to terms with its rural past, but has still not found an accommodation imaginatively with its urban present" (McLoone 2000: 6-7).

Nevertheless, filmmakers love Scotland and Ireland for their rural landscape, the space that it allows them to project their particular fantasies and, imaginatively, its ability to allow them to visualise the past. However progressive, innovative and dynamic the governments might wish their film industries to be, money, habit and genre all dictate a certain approach. In many respects, film, apparently a progressive and evolving medium, lags behind other cultural forms' rejection of received and rehearsed ideas of national identities. Whereas the Scottish theatre of the 1970s and 1980s sought to interrogate mythical and historical identity-narratives through plays such as John McGrath and 7:84's *The Cheviot, the Stag and the Black, Black Oil* (1973) to Liz Lochhead's *Mary Queen of Scots Got Her Head Chopped Off* (1987), filmic representations of Scotland have tended to dwell on a lost past and a static present. The reaction of Scottish theatre to the loss of national agency that was confirmed by the failed devolution referendum of 1979 was a critical engagement with collective responsibility. Rather than idolising a Scottish past in which a pure and elevated national identity was shared by all Scots in an uncomplicated fashion, Scottish theatre of the 1970s and 1980s tended to value people's solidarity in the past and their common frustrations in the present. However, as Randall Stevenson, Bill Findlay and others have commented, in many ways, Scottish theatre has suffered because of its fragmented and local focus. Although the smaller touring companies such as Borderline, Wildcat and Communicado have had significant success in developing community-based theatre that engages multiple Scottish identities in a broader contemporary cultural context, they have consistently struggled to secure funding, with the majority of the SAC budget going to the national companies – Scottish Opera, Scottish Ballet and the orchestras. Recent arguments have been fuelled by

the Executive's total inaction on implementing its much vaunted proposals for a national theatre.

In contrast, the Scottish film industry has struggled to get off the
ground, various proposals for a purpose-built national film studio have
come and gone, and the promotion of Scotland as location, rather than
nation, has seen it host a series of films that replay the familiar elegy
for a simple nation corrupted by contemporary culture. Even those
few films that could be said to take a critical approach to history, such
as *Ill Fares The Land* (dir. Bill Bryden, 1982), have lacked the necessary awareness to overcome the yearning of the "backward look".
From Hollywood vehicles, such as *Loch Ness* (dir. John Henderson,
1995), to UK drama such as *Mrs Brown* (dir. John Madden, 1997) to
home grown productions such as *The Bruce* (dir. Bob Carruthers,
1996), recent Scottish films frequently play to the idea that the cultural
value of Scotland is a past which bears all the hallmarks of noble savagery. Thus, the production notes of Michael Caton-Jones's film, *Rob
Roy* (1995) can boast that "the Scottish Highlands are virtually un-
changed [...] The making of Rob Roy was a daily adventure of scaling
the Highlands, outwitting the weather and recreating a lost and vener-
able culture".

The releases of *Shallow Grave* (dir. Danny Boyle, 1995) and
Trainspotting (dir. Danny Boyle, 1996) were broadly welcomed as an
antidote to the repeated identification of Scotland with the Highlands,
and the films have been hailed as providing "a new emphasis on the
city as the heart of contemporary Scottish experience" (Petrie 2000:
217). Ironically, one of *Trainspotting*'s most quoted moments is the
only scene shot not in the city, but at Corrour Station, by Loch Ossian:

> "It's nae good blamin it oan the English fir colonising us.
> "Ah don't hate the English. They're just wankers. We are colonised by
> wankers. We can't even pick a decent, vibrant, healthy culture to be colonised by. No.
> We're ruled by effete arseholes. What does that make us? The lowest of the fuckin
> low, the scum of the earth. The most wretched, servile, miserable, pathetic trash that
> was ever shat intae creation.
> "Ah don't hate the English. They just git oan wi the shite thuv goat. Ah hate the
> Scots."

Renton's expression of self-loathing brings together the masculinist
discourse of colonialism (the shame is that Scotland's conquerors are

"effete", thus further undermining the masculinity of Scots) as well as ambivalence about apportioning blame. Imperialism has consistently presented itself as inherently "progressive", a civilizing force brought to bear upon backward and incompetent natives. Renton's rant is double-edged: while it rejects the representation of the coloniser as the generous provider of a civilised culture, it retains the image of the colonised as weak and worthless.

Why is this passage so popular with academics, film critics, journalists and other trainspotters? In a rather confused review, Harlan Kennedy praises the scene for its subtlety and avoidance of "signposting":

The *non-sequitur* isolation of this scene makes sure we understand that while Anglo-Scottish tensions might underlie *Trainspotting*'s story, they lie *so* far under that like a seismic fault they aren't felt until they produce the occasional, seemingly irrational cataclysm. (Kennedy 1996: 29)

Andrew O'Hagan sees Renton's speech as a bold step beyond verbal innovation towards the "virtually unsayable": "There aren't many Scottish writers – previous to this generation – who could write such a thing, no films have given voice to this before" (O' Hagan 1996: 8).

For Kennedy, the strength of this moment lies in its positioning – the single, brief scene in the countryside. Yet this is an invention of Boyle's film; in the novel, Renton's iconoclastic words are to be found in "The Glass" section, set in a pub on Rose Street, which is about as central as you can get in Edinburgh. What is more, this is no great declamatory speech, but an interior monologue, an anxious and silent deliberation on Renton's relationship with his psychopathic "pal", Begbie. Commenting on this transposition, Angus Calder observes that

the reason [for the relocation] seems to be that the film's audiences south of Scotland will associate the country with Beautiful Highland Scenery. Removed from the complex pattern of interactions in Edinburgh [...] Americans and Germans will be challenged to set their romantic conceptions of Scotland against the frustrating reality of modern urban life. (Calder 1997: 218-19)

So, for Calder this scene is designed for the benefit of an outside audience (presumably Scots themselves have no need to be challenged by "the frustrating reality of modern urban life" since they are already living it), with Scotland functioning as an exotic "other": an object of desire – the beautiful Highland scenery; distaste – the speech itself; and finally similarity – modern urban life. All four critics seem to take Renton's speech at face value, in a way that they wouldn't consider interpreting the scene that takes place in "the dirtiest toilet in Scotland", for example, or Renton's self-justifications for the resumption of his heroin habit. What all of these critics appear unable to say is that this scene is a rupture in terms of both the film and the book because it claims a direct relationship between individual consciousness and the political status of the nation; something which is overwhelmingly denied by the introspective and self-obsessed junkie narrative. The reaction to this would suggest that any attempt to articulate the social consequences of the ambiguous colonial status of Scotland in cultural production will be subject to a similar form of self-censorship – to be condemned, either for being heavy-handedly prosaic or, conversely, for a lack of moral standpoint.

The release of *Braveheart* in particular sparked a furious debate between Scottish and Irish intellectuals about the comparative history of the two countries, their relationships to England, and the merits of their respective film industries. Irish critics condemned both the history and aesthetics of the film. Fintan O'Toole, for example, described *Braveheart* as "historical hogwash" (O'Toole cited in Hopper 1997: 10), and further challenged its integrity by drawing attention to the large amount of filming which took place in Ireland due to tax inducements and the availability of large numbers of extras taken from the ranks of the Irish army. Likewise, Keith Hopper compares the polarised popular and critical reception of *Michael Collins* to "Mel Gibson's 'Scottish' epic" – placing "Scottish" in scare quotes to further undermine any claim to national significance (Hopper 1997: 10). Having first set up the comparison, Hopper then seeks to undo it by claiming Gibson's film as a "cinematic commodity" in contrast to the artistic and "political integrity" of Jordan's work. He demands that critics:

make a commonsense distinction between an international costume drama, which backgrounds history as decorative object; and a national historical drama which foregrounds history as ontological subject. (Hopper 1997: 11)

The desire to separate cultural products along the all too familiar lines of low/high, popular/intellectual is accompanied by an equally familiar appeal to "commonsense". Even the terms which Hopper uses to distinguish the two films reflect his prejudices in this area. *Braveheart* is concerned with trivial appearances ("history as decorative object"), whilst *Michael Collins* gets to grips with complex, intellectual issues ("history as ontological subject"). The comments of both Hopper and O'Toole seem to privilege Ireland as a more genuine model of national or nationalist resistance. Furthermore, Hopper's distinction would suggest that a mass audience is incapable of understanding the issues raised by historical drama, implying that *Michael Collins* was less successful commercially because it demanded a more critical and discerning audience. Finally, the projected intelligence of the audience is used to further justify the distinction between the two films on the grounds that *Michael Collins* is "art", "a national event", where *Braveheart* is a Hollywood vehicle. This argument draws attention to an analytical discourse that rejects mobilising forms of identity or even figures of nationhood which are used and developed by working-class audiences.

Colin McArthur's position on *Braveheart* would seem to confirm O'Toole's opinion. Roundly condemning the film for historical inaccuracy, moral simplicity and cultural insincerity, McArthur's review tracks specific faults to the discourses of tartanry and "dark-Ageism":

darkness; religiosity and/or mysticism; grinding poverty and filth; physical deformity; and above all, unspeakable cruelty. These are the dominant tropes of *Braveheart*, although its simple-mindedness also owes something to Errol Flynn's star vehicle, *The Adventures of Robin Hood*. (McArthur 1995: 45)

Like Hopper, McArthur wishes to diminish the cultural significance of *Braveheart* by relegating it to the category of costume drama, where plot and message are secondary to action and style.

What these criticisms fail to take on board is the extent to which both *Michael Collins* and *Braveheart* are created and received in the context of both film genre and national mythology. In a response to McArthur's review in *Sight and Sound*, Sheldon Hall attacks "his insensitivity to the conventions of genre" and draws attention to the "narrative tradition" which informs both the style and content of the film:

> Linking Mel Gibson's excellent film to the "regressive discourses" of Tartanry and Dark Ageism, he neglected to relate it to the equally pertinent – and less odious – discourses of historical romances and mythic epic [...] no attempt was made to situate *Braveheart* within a narrative tradition which also encompasses El Cid, Spartacus, Ivanhoe, Jesse James and William Tell. (Hall 1995: 72)

Despite the value judgments of Hopper and McArthur, the debate identifies both *Braveheart* and *Michael Collins* as "national events" in the context of a global cultural market.

Could it really be that the financial, economic and social impacts that Scottish politicians were hoping for are, in essence, a form of re-newed national democracy? The possibilities inherent in an indige-nous film industry require a public engagement in cultural creation that has almost been lost to the political arena. Furthermore, the sup-port for a national cinema provides a practical tool with which to resist what Michael Higgins called "the colonisation of the imagination", which is brought about by the dominance of the Hollywood studios. Nevertheless, the impact of devolution on the Scottish film industry has so far been negligible. Even the excellent reception of several films such as Lynne Ramsay's *Ratcatcher* (1999) and Peter Mullan's *Orphans* (1999) have failed to stimulate the continued, national fund-ing structure necessary if the industry is to become strong enough to interrogate, engage with and give voice to the identities of Scotland. Ramsay's latest film, *Morvern Callar* (2002), an adaptation of Alan Warner's novel of the same name, has been strongly criticised for its failure to engage with its particular Scottish context, while Mullan's more powerful *The Magdalene Sisters* (2002) focuses on Ireland, where it has stirred vociferous debate, in contrast to its silent reception in Scotland. The political will to support a multi-faceted film industry is dissipated in the compromise of devolution. It is too early to say that the long-hoped for cultural revolution that would flow from devolution and self-determination has failed to materialise, but the impasse in the development of the national film industry is surely a bad sign.

Bibliography

Ashcroft, Bill, Gareth Griffiths and Helen Tiffin (eds). 1989. *The Empire Writes Back: Theory and Practice in Post-Colonial Literatures*. London: Routledge.

Calder, Angus. 1997. "By the Water of Leith I Sat Down and Wept: Reflections on Scottish Identity" in Harry Ritchie (ed.) *Acid Plaid: New Scottish Writing*. London: Bloomsbury. 218-38.

Hall, Sheldon. 1995. "Response to McArthur" in *Sight and Sound* October.

Hopper, Keith. 1997. "Cat-Calls from the Cheap Seats: The Third Meaning of Neil Jordan's *Michael Collins*" in *The Irish Review* 21: 1-28.

Kennedy, Harlan. 1996. "Kiltspotting: Highland Reels" in *Film Comment* 32(4): 28-29.

McArthur, Colin. 1995. "*Braveheart* – Review" in *Sight and Sound* September.

McLoone, Martin. 2000. *Irish Film: The Emergence of Contemporary Cinema*. London: British Film Institute.

O'Hagan, Andrew. 1996. "*Trainspotting* and Heartless Midlothian" in *Sight and Sound* February: 8.

Petrie, Duncan. 2000. *Screening Scotland*. London: British Film Institute.

Russell, Michael. 2001. *Issues in the Scottish Film Industry*. Scottish Executive.

Smyth, Gerry. 1997. *The Novel and the Nation: Studies in New Irish Fiction*. London: Pluto.

Nervous Men, Mobile Nation: Masculinity and Psychopathology in Irvine Welsh's *Filth* and *Glue*

Berthold Schoene

From the onset of modernity masculinity has been ineluctably bound up with con-structions of the nation and nationalism. From a postmodern perspective, however, where identity is perceived to be in crisis, this seemingly symbiotic relationship has been challenged. An examination of Irvine Welsh's *Filth* and *Glue* therefore high-lights some of the complexities of the contemporary gendered nation.
Keywords: modernity, masculinity, identity crisis, postmodernity, devolution, patriar-chy, trauma, autism, Irvine Welsh.

The nation and the self, as we traditionally conceive of them, repre-sent not naturally given entities but interdependent discursive con-structs that have been instrumental in modernity's project of mapping the world and employing human agency within it. According to Anne McClintock's suggestion that "nationalism becomes [...] constitutive of people's identities through social contests that are frequently vio-lent and always gendered" (McClintock 1997: 89), the correlation of micro-personal and macro-political identities must not be dismissed as merely contingent but should be taken seriously as definitive and spe-cific. By arguing that "the needs of the nation [are] typically identified with the frustrations and aspirations of men" (McClintock 1997: 89), McClintock insists that nationalism constitutes a significant part of the traditional masculine imaginary and that it is a direct corollary of men's deep psychological anxieties and desires. Moreover, if nation-alism is "always gendered", as McClintock proposes, then masculinity (unlike femininity) is always territorialist. Both the nation and the masculine self have traditionally been visualised as solid, im-penetrable wholes fortified by clear-cut, non-negotiable boundaries and informed by an uncompromising politics of self-sameness.

These imageries of man and nation persist in the present, but have not emerged entirely unscathed from the epistemological turmoil of the twentieth century. In anticipation of a new era inhabited by a previously inconceivable species of selves congregating in unprece-dented communal constellations, Virginia Woolf memorably remarked that "in or about December, 1910, human character changed" (Woolf 1966: 320), thus pinpointing the beginning of modernity's demise as brought about by increasing *post*modern diversification. The self of modernity, inalienably unique and autonomous, was rapidly superseded by the socio-historically determined subject of postmodernity, in itself not so much a clearly identifiable entity as an oscillating process of continuous dismantlement and reconstruction. This radical destabilisation of the self also gave rise to a twentieth-century crisis in national identity, exacerbated by the crumbling of imperial sovereignty and the troubled (re)constitution of old and new states that ensued. This crisis is by no means over, but continues to wreak havoc as nationhood remains caught up "in crisis" or, to phrase it more optimistically, finds itself "in transition" from modernity to a truly *post*modern age inhabited by emancipated post-selves cultivating flexible post-identities and living together peacefully in non-territorialist post-nations.

The transition from modernity to postmodernity is a quandary because, while some enthusiastically welcome and actively help to envision the new era, it is feared by others as a threat of ultimate cultural ruin and self-annihilation.[1] This conflict between a critical and creative avant-garde on the one hand, and the self-appointed custodians of tradition on the other, lies at the heart of twentieth-century culture. Whereas writers, artists and intellectuals have been inclined to cultivate an aesthetics of self-dispersal, reactionary national politics have been marked by hyperbolic resurrections of the pure and indivisible self, most manifest no doubt in the rise and endurance of totalitarian regimes. In *Male Matters*, Calvin Thomas interrogates this stark dichotomous irreconcilability at the core of modern culture:

Is modernity as self-hyperbole a repression of modernity as self-abolition? That is, are those philosophical, political, and aesthetic responses to and projects of modernity

---

[1] As Thomas Byers states, rather than being "only a matter of the subject's dislocation or transition from an old place to a new one […] the current crisis [i.e. postmodernity] threatens to transform or even overthrow the whole *concept* of identity" (Byers 1995: 7). Hegemonic masculinity in particular is left without strategies for viable self-identification. By promoting the demise of "man", postmodernity poses a threat to "the continued existence of the reified subject of bourgeois humanism [that is] the traditional subject, particularly the masculine subject" (Byers 1995: 6-7).

that gather themselves into self-hyperbole a repression of the experience of modernity as self-shattering? Is this hyperbolic gathering of modernity into a totalizing project staked not only on the repression of self-abolition but on the active abolition of the other? And is the acceptance or even celebration of the self-shattering experience of modernity the necessarily unorganizing rallying cry for the impossible communities of the postmodern? (Thomas 1996: 24-25)

Not only does the centuries-old struggle between the self and its margin of disempowered others continue, it has never been so fierce. As Thomas's questions indicate, sameness and alterity have rolled into an inextricable, potentially lethal embrace. The rise of postmodernity has resulted in an ever more pronounced championing of difference and marginality over homogeneity and hegemony, which means that ever greater violence, both discursive and actual, is now required to reassure the traditional self of the ongoing indisputability of its power.

At the beginning of the twenty-first century, it seems at first as if our culture were now ready to join with the postmodern. However, what Thomas Byers has described as modernity's *pomophobic*[2] anxieties – the "persistent fears on the part of a formerly dominant order that has begun to recognize that it is becoming residual" (Byers 1995: 6) – continue to exert their reactionary influence. The *post*-ing of nation and self is obstructed by the contradictions that agitate the post/modern paradigm shift. For example, contemporary masculinity finds itself torn between the old and the new: with most of their gender-specific self-fashioning still determined by manly propriety, men have now for decades also had to contend with feminist expectations for them to develop character traits diametrically opposed to patriarchal masculinity. Whereas residual patriarchy continues to insist on gender purity, and patriarchal masculinity must categorically abject the feminine, most contemporary feminisms celebrate the blurring of gender boundaries and actively endorse the cultivation of "female masculinity" and "male femininity". Accordingly, the "crisis" of masculinity derives from men's exposure to two antagonistic sets of imperatives – one patriarchal, the other feminist or post-patriarchal – resulting in a behavioural and self-constitutive predicament that is experienced as utterly irresolvable.

---

[2] Pronounced to rhyme with "homophobia", "pomophobia" is a neologism which refers to fear of the *postmo*dern, of that which is "po-mo".

Similarly, contemporary nationalism finds itself "in crisis" too, a crisis which assumes a somewhat peculiar shape in the case of previously subnational communities like Scotland. Until its recent devolution Scotland's rhetoric of nation was voiced mainly as minoritarian dissent and separatist desire. Scottishness represented an anti-unionist counterdiscourse, affiliated to the general postmodernist project of destabilisation and decentring, and thus chiming in with Thomas's "unorganizing rallying cry for the impossible communities of the postmodern". However, Scotland's situation has changed and, as a new nation with old traditions, it now faces a political and representational crossroads. It might opt for a swift transition from subnation to "post-nation", the latter designating "a society that has discarded the notion of a homogeneous nation-state with singular forms of belonging" (Hall 1996: 67). Alternatively, it might succumb to the nationalist imageries of blockbuster movies like *Rob Roy* (dir. Michael Caton-Jones, 1995) or *Braveheart* (dir. Mel Gibson, 1995) and allow itself to be lured back into its past as a traditional nation-state. Suspended between the utopian and the nostalgic, Scotland's crisis of nationhood mirrors the predicament of the contemporary masculine self, keen to become part of new communal configurations, yet held back by pomophobic anxieties over its exact status and position: if nationhood and/or masculinity were to yield wholeheartedly to postmodern diversification, how – if at all – might they come to reassemble? The nation and the masculine self have therefore become highly volatile entities, prone to violence and hypersensitive to violation.

1. Autism and the Acculturation of Hysteria

As Michel Foucault suggests in his preface to *Madness and Civilisation*, "mad" and "sane" are conspiratorial terms that remain open to discursive redefinition and, with histories of madness abounding, it may now be more urgent than ever to examine the mentality of the sane. Foucault writes:

We have yet to write the history of that other form of madness, by which men, in an act of sovereign reason, confine their neighbours, and communicate and recognize each other though the merciless language of non-madness; to define the moment of this conspiracy before it was permanently established in the realm of truth. (Foucault 1967: xi)

Behind "that other form of madness" stands, of course, the traditional masculine self. While this self deems itself infallibly rooted in the one and only (hu)man-making faculty of reason, it displays, both behaviourally and psychologically, a wide variety of "symptoms" typical of the psychopathological disorder of autism.[3] Autism refers to a spectrum of deep-seated and often irreparable disabilities affecting an individual's socialisation, communication and imagination. Uta Frith names "being alone mentally", "obsessive insistence on sameness", "repetitiveness" and "rigidity" as typical markers of autism (Frith 1989: 11), while Francesca Happé lists "social withdrawal or incompetence, obsessive delight in routine, and the pursuit of special interests to the exclusion of all else" (Happé 1994: 11). Other researchers highlight the lack of introspection (Bettelheim 1967) or the shocking "mindblindness" (Baron-Cohen 2000) characteristic of autistic impairment. In *The Empty Fortress*, Bruno Bettelheim conceptualises autism's projection of an imaginary hard outer-shell, thereby capturing the tendency among autistics to turn their bodies into fortress-like hiding places within which they seek to protect a sense of self often so vague that it is not only unviable but ultimately non-existent. Simon Baron-Cohen's concept of mindblindness, on the other hand, refers to the autistic person's emotional blankness, lack of empathy, and total inability to place himself in somebody else's position, or view himself through somebody else's eyes.

Even if one is reluctant to resort to crude stereotyping, one cannot deny that many of these classical symptoms of autism are reminiscent of character traits traditionally associated with the masculine gender. Protesting at once his fundamentally non-essentialist take on masculinity and conceding that all "gendered subjectivities do have a degree of 'conventionality'", Jack Norton writes:

---

[3] Autism remains subject to changing definitions by rivalling schools of medical scientists (Frith 1989, Happé 1994), psychotherapists (Tustin 1992) and cultural philosophers (Durig 1996). However, albeit variously described as an organic defect, a post-traumatic stress disorder, or simply a "different" mode of perception, it is commonly accepted that autism afflicts more males than females. The proportion most commonly given is 4:1.

Writings by men on male sexuality, and feminist literature, have identified a number
of common themes in contemporary male sexuality, including: desire for control,
resistance to vulnerability, need for independence as a means of distancing, repression
of insecurity, emotional inexpressiveness, denial of emotion as a source of knowledge, denial of needs, and compulsion to affirm one's (perceived) masculinity.
(Norton 1991: 155)

Whereas femininity has traditionally been linked with hysteria ("the
irrational, the will-less, the incomprehensible, the erratic, the convul-
sive, the sexual, the female, 'the Other'" (Micale 1995: 218-19)),
masculinity is the autistic gender. Both hysteria and autism represent
extreme responses to trauma. However, while hysteria signifies a
"feminine" falling apart of the self, autism represents a "masculine"
contraction of the self pulling itself together. Like traditional masculinity and femininity, autism and hysteria are locked into an antagonistic relationship, not only as metaphors of cultural critique but, more
importantly, also historically. First diagnosed by Ernst Bleuler in 1913
and further specified by Leo Kanner and Hans Asperger in the early
1940s, the emergence of autism as a specific mental disorder has been
co-eval with the cultural turmoil caused by World Wars I and II and
their impact on the history of masculinity. Simultaneously, the first
half of the century witnessed the increasing redundancy of hysteria so
that, as Mark Micale writes, "after twenty centuries of medical history, this extraordinary disease is for all intents and purposes disappearing from sight today" (Micale 1995: 29). Whereas Micale claims
that "nobody knows why" this happened, Juliet Mitchell explains hysteria's diminishing diagnostic credibility by referring to the display of
hysterical symptoms in World War I soldiers affected by shell shock.
"The need for men not to be feminine", Mitchell argues, "spelt the
demise of the hysteria diagnosis" (Mitchell 2000: 128). In other
words, no sooner had hysteria's gender-specificity as an exclusively
"female malady" revealed itself as a man-made fiction than its classi-
ficatory particularity became untenable (see also Showalter 1987: 167-
94). Within a patriarchal framework, male hysteria was ideologically
inconceivable. Hence, to safeguard modern manhood's imagery of
physical and mental incorruptibility, hysteria – both as a discourse and
as a disease – was prescribed a swift and total vanishing cure.

But in fact, so Mitchell argues, "hysteria has not disappeared, and never can" (Mitchell 2000: 133). Hysteria so perfectly blends in with postmodernity's general celebration of "difference" that it "has disappeared from sight in the clinic [while] in the real world, it is everywhere around us" (Mitchell 2000: 39). Hysteria, so Mitchell argues, has moved "from its relegation to the domain of 'the other' into the heart of society's 'self'" (Mitchell 2000: 134) and become "normalized [...] as the way in which we predominantly live" (Mitchell 2000: 133). This acculturation of hysteria is experienced as traumatic by the traditional masculine self, which has begun to stand out as a strait-jacketed anachronistic oddity, and whose self-contained posture strikes us now as a pathological affliction rather than the wholesome standard of human subjectivity. The same behavioural practices and modes of self-representation that, within patriarchy, would endow men with power and superiority disqualify them within a cultural framework informed by feminist and post-patriarchal thought. In this light, Penelope Vinden and Janet Astington's comment on the disparate degrees of disability caused by childhood autism within different cultural contexts appears to pertain equally to the fate of autistic masculinity:

Children with autism may be especially out of place in our culture, which is so mentally-oriented. While their restricted capacity for language [...] would severely limit their interactions in any society, their inability to relate intersubjectively might have different outcomes depending on the culture in which they grew up. For example, their desire for sameness, for predictability, might not work against them, as it does in our highly disparate society, but in fact might help them to adjust to living in a culture where there is less diversity. (Vinden and Astington 2000: 515-16)

At the same rate as we become immersed in, and learn to appreciate, postmodernity's pluralist diversity, we become increasingly impatient with traditional masculinity's fear of cultural destabilisation. To a growing majority of people, patriarchal manhood's insistence on its own normativity and hegemonic status seems indicative of a pathological disposition. By using Irvine Welsh's representation of Scottish masculinity and national belonging as a case study, I will explore how masculinity has responded, or is likely in future to respond, to its postmodern condition. Will it yield to a radical reconstruction within the hysterical climate of the postmodern, or will it invest what remains of its traditional power in an autistic backlash which ironically – due to its hyperbolic vehemence and phobic irrationality – eventually looks virtually indistinguishable from hysteria? How adaptable is masculinity? Will it perish on its own and in crisis, or will it eventually enter into a coalition with other new selves-in-transition?

2. *Filth* (1998): Masculinity as a Nervous Condition

Detective Sergeant Bruce Robertson, the protagonist of *Filth*, embodies a grotesquely caricatured example of contemporary Scottish masculinity. Commencing with Bruce's murder of Efan Wurie, a black journalist and allegedly his estranged wife's new lover, and concluding with Bruce's own suicide, the novel – thus bound up in "the murderous logic of traditional male subjectivity" (Silverman 1992: 389) – records the desperate failure of its hero's final effort at masculine self-assertion. As Calvin Thomas explains in *Male Matters*, "Death is the subject position of 'absolute master'" (Thomas 1996: 27); to identify with Death, to try and usurp that position of supreme subjectivity, is to claim infallibility, inviolability and indissolubility. Prompted by acute pomophobic anxiety, however, Bruce's killing of his alleged rival testifies not to his superiority but to his existential weakness and insecurity. The murder victim is not silenced by Death; rather, as in a picture-book return of the repressed, the pomophobic anxieties he represents become ever more pronounced and obtrusive: Efan Wurie becomes Bruce's "Effen Worry" (Welsh 1998: 228). *Filth* opens with an example of Bruce's warped perception of himself and others:

The trouble with people like him [i.e. Efan] is that they think they can brush off people like me. Like I was nothing. They don't understand the type of world we're living in now; all those manacled souls clamouring for attention and recognition. He was a very arrogant young man, so full of himself. (Welsh 1998: 1)

Bruce – *not* Efan, the son of the ambassador for Ghana – is the "very arrogant young man, so full of himself", who is alienated and rendered redundant by the post/modern paradigm shift. That, as a Scotsman, Bruce fails so disastrously to relate to Efan's postcolonial position indicates his generally unselfconscious and irreconstructible disposition. Most of the novel is narrated from Bruce's perspective as an interior monologue, beating in ever more claustrophobic circles about the gaping black hole of what remains of his precarious identity. Bruce's narrative is a battle for the self, divided between self-awareness and repression: on the one hand the text resolutely occludes introspection while on the other it spawns its own mutinous counterdiscourse. From the visceral depths of his being emerges the irrepressible voice of "the Self" (Welsh 1998: 70), Bruce's speaking tapeworm, which recurrently ruptures the flow of the main narrative, and even eclipses it at times, thereby exposing the specious authenticity and coherence of Bruce's first-person narration. Bruce is diagnosed as suffering from "what seems to be a persistent nervous condition" (Welsh 1998: 243). A nasty rash has developed on his scrotum and is rapidly spreading all over his abdomen: Bruce is being consumed by a psychosomatic return of the repressed. Significantly, the centre of this hysterical insurrection of the body is the testes which, in contradiction to their biological centrality, are traditionally associated with the feminine, that is, with men's vulnerability and the fleshy softness of their anatomy (see Flannigan-Saint-Aubin 1994). Bruce's wishful projection of a phallic identity finds itself undermined by the most elementary constituents of the human, whose categorical repression forms the very basis of his masculinity. Now the itch of the repressed has become insufferable and threatens his self with abject liquid(is)ation as "shite [is] coming oot every orifice" (Welsh 1998: 79). The abject becomes visible as an attribute of the self, whose body is disclosed as a permeable surface of (feminine) openings rather than an impenetrable fortress of (masculine) integrity.

Although *Filth* demands to be read as a novel about the hysterical disintegration of the masculine self, it is also, at least potentially, a curative text, promising to make Bruce's divided self whole again by untying the knot of his traumatic masculine individuation. What Bruce can only recognise as a disease represents an attempt by his subconscious to induce a process of psychic reassembling. All of Bruce's symptoms of increasing physical discomfort are signals of acute mental distress. "My guts feel sick and heavy", Bruce complains, "It's like there's something in me, I can almost feel it growing, getting stronger" (Welsh 1998: 50). As the novel proceeds, it turns into an excruciatingly reticent talking cure, which only circuitously unveils a response to the question of Bruce's doctor: "You don't have anything on your mind, anything you have not told me about?" (Welsh 1998: 243). Bruce becomes seriously impaired by the babble of voices in his head (Welsh 1998: 234-38) and, in the final quarter of the book, he suffers a mental breakdown, which is perhaps most evident in the sudden synonymous interchangeability of first-person singular and plural pronouns: "we, I, we (we're all here now)" (Welsh 1998: 331). And yet, the schizophrenic unravelling of his accustomed subjectivity could still be regarded as an ultimately very positive development, as a process which might enable Bruce to retrieve the emotional complexity of his "inner" self, that is, as a curative cracking-open instead of an irremediable cracking-up.

My interpretation of *Filth* takes its cue from the correspondences Welsh establishes between the physical health and mental stability of the individual and the wider political organisation of systemic power. My reading of Bruce's nervous decline is led by Peter Logan's assertion in *Nerves and Narratives* that:

> within each nervous body lies the story of the social conditions that created it and, having created it, compel it to act out its nervous fit. This narrative is also a history of its own production, a somatic *Bildungsroman* that tells the story of how it came into being, of how this particular body came to have a story to tell. (Logan 1997: 29)

While a multiplicity of different factors, familial as well as sociocultural, have contributed to the making of Bruce, many of these could only exert such a (de)formative influence on him because he suffered severe trauma in his boyhood. Not only does he witness his brother's death, he is also held solely responsible for it. Bruce furthermore discovers that he is not his parents' legitimate firstborn but his mother's premarital child of rape, sired by "The Beast", a notorious and – judging by the novel's description – almost mythical sex-offender. Most unsettling, however, is that it appears to be specifically Bruce's badly traumatised psyche which renders him such a good impersonator of traditional masculinity. It seems as if the damaged male psyche in particular fits the ideals, and complies with the imperatives, of patriarchal masculinity most perfectly. While Bruce's emotional and social impairments may very well originally have been caused by childhood trauma, life as "a law enforcement professional" (Welsh 1998: 134) has done nothing to alleviate or correct his condition but only compounded it. As the Worm puts it, "you came not to feel. Your life, your circumstances and your job *demanded* that price" (Welsh 1998: 262; my emphasis).

Bruce's cultivation of macho impassivity displays conspicuous similarities to the psychiatric diagnosis of "hard-shell" encapsulation, a particular form of autism, described by the psychotherapist Frances Tustin as "an intensification and entrenched exaggeration of an in-built set of reactions which are specific to trauma. It is of the nature of a post-traumatic stress disorder. It is also a survival mechanism" (Tustin 1992: 11). Although according to his estranged wife, Bruce is "a very sensitive man underneath [...] his hard front" (Welsh 1998: 42), he continues to find it impossibly difficult to relate to, let alone empathise with, others. If Bruce's emotional impairment is indeed due to trauma, then there would of course be no shortage of moments of terror, loss, betrayal and extreme emotional cruelty in his childhood that might have caused it. However, it seems worth noting (if one chooses to give credence to Freud's theory of the Oedipus complex) that trauma plays a crucial part in every "normal" boy's transition from childhood to manhood. According to Freud, to achieve masculine status the boy must detach himself from his mother and counter-identify with the father, meaning that the inception of the masculine not only always coincides with, but in fact demands, an experience of loss and separation, which inevitably burdens the young boy with feelings of acute vulnerability, exposure and aloneness. To win recognition as a man, Oedipal boys must radically cut themselves off from the feminine, which is accomplished through repression and ineluctably results in neurotic self-division. They must split the world, as well as themselves, into a heroic manly "me" on the one hand and a despicable effeminate "not-me" on the other because, as Lawrence Kramer explains, "for Oedipal sons, the social subject-position inscribed as masculine is paired with a psychical position inscribed as feminine" and "what counts as normal masculine subjectivity involves a continual effort to defer the arrival, which is to say the return, of the castratory moment" (Kramer 1997: 26, 28).

Hence, whereas Bruce's childhood trauma may be exceptional in degree, it is not so in kind; within patriarchy, all heterosexual men's emotions towards the feminine are ambivalent, mixed up with longing and loathing, desire and fear. Only once in *Filth* does Bruce experience a momentary reunion with the feminine and that is when, after rushing to the aid of a dying man in the street, he briefly finds himself holding the man's grief-stricken wife in his arms:

At first it feels awkward and invasive, but our bodies settle into a natural convergence, we fit each other like a hand in a glove [...] The woman is in my arms, her head in my chest. I want to hold her forever, to never let her go.
They take the dead man in the ambulance and we break our embrace and I feel the cold shallowness of isolation as she's led away. (Welsh 1998: 114)

If anything at all is capable of breaking up Bruce's autistic aloneness, it is such an intimate reintroduction of the feminine into his life. Symptomatically, however, such a redemptive merger can only come about *in extremis*, and accidentally, when for an instant Bruce is oblivious to the internalised frown of the father. For every Oedipal boy, the father's love is conditional and revocable; unlike, the mother's it is something that has to be earned. In Bruce's case, however, the situation is compounded by the fact that, no matter how outstanding his conduct, the love of both his biological and adoptive fathers is forever courted in vain (the former is despised by Bruce, whereas the latter despises Bruce). Hence, to achieve a sense of wholeness and empowerment, without incurring shameful emasculation, a suitable substitute for the maternal body has to be found, a substitute that would also have unconditional patriarchal approval. In Bruce's case, this surrogate super parent is the police force, which provides him at once with (maternal) security and (paternal) sanction, with both a sense of cosy at-home-ness and a hard protective armour.

3. "Please Police Me": Masculinity and its Institutions

In *The Way Men Think*, Liam Hudson and Bernadine Jacot refer to "the ways in which his institutions can serve the adult male as his 'exoskeleton'; a secure structure within which the irrational elements of his thought are contained" (Hudson and Jacot 1991: 82). While Hudson and Jacot's imagery points at a complex cause-and-effect relationship between the individual male's emotional needs on the one hand and the construction of a specific systemic superstructure on the other, it also resounds with one of Bruce's own comments on his work as a policeman: "The job. It holds you", he declares, "It's all around you; a constant, enclosing absorbing gel" (Welsh 1998: 3). Bruce's identification with two traditionally male-dominated institutions – The Force (the police) and The Craft (the Masonic brotherhood) – is total and, as his magical terms of invocation signal, his membership affords him an almost metaphysical sense of wizardly self-empowerment. Welsh draws pertinent connections between the personal and the public, the psychosomatic and the socio-political, as well as between the masculine and the national. Bruce's intestinal parasite, for instance, also stands for Margaret Thatcher's "enemy within". Concentrating on the psychodynamics of abjection, which inform the construction and maintenance of both patriarchal masculinity and traditional nationalism, Welsh's narrative frequently resorts to allegorical signification. Bruce's intolerance of rave culture reflects on his own internal struggle for emotional impassivity and self-containment: "These things [i.e. raves] are springing up everywhere", Bruce registers with exasperation, "It's a threat to the great British way of life and it has to be stopped before it gets a toehold. Cunts think they can live just by looking after each other and dancing to fuckin music" (Welsh 1998: 84). And, indeed, how could Bruce possibly manage to keep up masculine appearances if he allowed his feelings free rein?

The more anxious Bruce becomes, the more vehement and exclusive are his abjective responses to the world around him, until the "rubbish" encompasses the whole of "the great fucking British public" and not just ethnic minorities, gays, lesbians, feminists, old people, the disabled, working-class people, the homeless, as well as "communists" and "papists" (Welsh 1998: 11). As a result, in an ironic reversal of effects, Bruce fails dramatically to empower himself, set himself free, or alleviate his increasing panic; rather, all his efforts at self-protection lead him to fence himself in, drawing ever tighter circles around his beleaguered ego and thereby aggravating his autistic encapsulation. Moreover, he comes very close to recognising himself as

"filth" (a derogatory slang word for police) while, in one of his col-
league's eyes, he takes shape as "the type of sad case who preys on
vulnerable, weak and stupid women in order to boost his own shat-
tered ego" (Welsh 1998: 338). Eventually his self-inflicted exclusion
from society is complete, with all that remains of his manhood nothing
but "a mess" (Welsh 1998: 338). What Bruce's increasingly precarious strategies of self-assertion expose are the many contradictions that
inhabit and haunt the masculine gender, especially when employed in
patriarchal service. On the one hand, membership in the police force
instils in Bruce a sense of power and autonomy. On the other hand,
Bruce is aware he is only an instrument of power, a means to an end,
and as such he is expected to yield whatever personal ambitions he
may have to the mysterious ways of the law. Somehow, the Force's
alluring promise of autonomous selfhood coalesces with its less en-
ticing imperative of subjection, which is why Bruce sees no contradiction in criticising his colleagues at the same time for coming together as a "motley crew" (Welsh 1998: 226) of individuals and for
deferentially welcoming anonymity as "uniformed spastic[s]" (Welsh
1998: 246). Now and then, presumably in order to remind us of
Bruce's all-consuming desire to police others, Welsh inserts what
looks like the expression of a semi-conscious thought into Bruce's
conversations with women or clients: "Please. Police. Me" (Welsh
1998: 298). But this phrase also gives voice to Bruce's own desire for
being policed, as he invites domination by a powerful superego to
whose rigid structures he appears more than willing to succumb.
    As David Savran illustrates in *Taking It Like a Man*, this seem-
ingly self-defeating sado-masochism is germane to traditional masculinity and derives from a complex psychological disavowal without
which not only modern subjectivity, but modernity itself as a sociocultural formation, would have remained unthinkable. Savran
identifies humanist "man" as a self-disciplinary masochistic subject
who places as much emphasis on self-control as on the control of others. Practising oppression, abjection and repression in equal measure,
man's discursive (and actual) imprisonment of alterity is accompanied
by self-division and psychical self-incarceration. Savran delivers a
perfect character sketch of Bruce the policeman when he concludes
that to prosper within patriarchy the traditional masculine self must

disavow the knowledge that his independence requires submission to an economic system in which he remains a cog, and a despotic superego that has internalised the Law, the Father, and the Word [...] Constantly impugning his desires, this new bourgeois must tirelessly police himself and his desires while calling this submission "freedom". He must work vigorously to confound pleasure and pain [...] He must always be ready to discipline himself for his shortcomings and irresponsibilities, and, if he is to win esteem (from either the superego or others), never allow the introjected rod to fall from his grip. (Savran 1998: 25)

The similarities between Welsh's portrayal of Bruce as an individual and Savran's blueprint of the modern self are conspicuous; so are the correspondences between the psychodynamics of masculine subjectivity and the organisation of the traditional nation-state. A reading of *Filth* in terms of Scottish masculinity and nationalism is invited by the protagonist's patronymic name, Bruce Robertson, which appears to identify him as a fictitious descendant of Robert the Bruce. Significantly though, unlike his daunting heroic ancestor, Bruce is a policeman, not a soldier, employed not to fight an external enemy but to ensure the uniformity and concurrence of the unruly elements within the nation's own borders. Published only a year after Scotland's devolution in 1997, Welsh's depiction of Scottish nationalism in *Filth* is devastatingly pessimistic, not least because of its dubious choice of protagonist. If Bruce is the new Scotsman, then the new Scotland is not a postcolonial nation rejoicing in its newly won independence but, on the contrary, a compulsively autocratic power sharing imperial masculinity's "voracious appetite for expanding its domain of ownership and its territory of control in a bid to suppress all other competitors and to achieve omnipotence" (Hatty 2000: 11). Rather than being inspired by feminist and multicultural thought, its political stance is racist and sexist, as Bruce confirms in conversation with one of his colleagues, "Scotland's a white man's country. Always has been, always will be" (Welsh 1998: 46).

Despite its extreme idiosyncrasies Bruce's life story reads like an allegory of traditional masculinity's quandary within the postmodern, as well as a poignant allegorical rendition of the political state of Britain since 1979 (the year of Scotland's first referendum as well as the beginning of Margaret Thatcher's career as Prime Minister). Judging from Bruce's reference to Arthur Scargill and the mid-1980s Miners' Strike, I suggest we read Bruce's struggle against the unruliness of his

body as a parallel to the brutal oppression of counterdiscursive discontent within the nation by Thatcherite conservatism. "I know it's up
there, inside of me", Bruce remarks on the presence of his tapeworm,
"twisting and growing, biding its time, like an Arthur Scargill in the
healthy body politic of eighties Britain, the enemy within" (Welsh
1998: 171). Later in the novel, Welsh contrives a striking parallel
between Margaret Thatcher's treatment of Arthur Scargill and Scotland's attitude to homosexuals and the English. Bruce's campaign
against his allegedly gay rival for promotion, Peter Inglis, not only
resuscitates nationalistically motivated associations of Englishness
and effeminacy but is also reminiscent of Thatcher's rhetoric against
"the enemy within": "The worm called Inglis is being flushed out the
system; outed and routed, before further infestation can take hold"
(Welsh 1998: 250-51). Bruce's psychosomatic distress becomes emblematic of political strife within the British national body at large; in
both instances, autocratic self-assertion finds itself under siege from
voices of dissent whose heralding of new, more dialogic and compas-
sionate constellations of power can no longer be ignored.

Stefan Herbrechter writes that in *Filth* "Welsh zooms in on the
extreme masculinist position in order to further dissect and advance its
psychotic self-dissolution" (Herbrechter 2000: 112) by showing how
"the protagonist is eaten up from inside by an unspeakable Other"
(Herbrechter 2000: 121). But is this really the case? And if so, would
the disintegration of Bruce's "hard-shell" ego, and the emergence of
his own internal alterity, not deserve to be described in somewhat
more positive terms? The most frustrating aspect of *Filth* is that Bruce
can never allow himself to fall apart, or to be consumed by internal
alterity; on the contrary, at the end of the novel he feels compelled to
pull himself together in a final suicidal act of manly self-
(de)termination. If only Bruce were able to give in to hysterical self-
dissolution, it might release him from a life lived in autistic isolation
and enable him to enter into genuine communication with others. As it
stands, the ending of *Filth* identifies Bruce as both a victim and a per-
petrator of what Leo Bersani calls "the sacrosanct value of selfhood, a
value that accounts for human beings' extraordinary willingness to kill
in order to protect the seriousness of their statements" (Bersani 1987:
222). Bruce's suicide is a desperately pomophobic reflex. Unable to

experience his increasing self-embodiment as anything but acute emasculation, Bruce resorts to violence – masculinity's ancient panacea – which, "in the service of the modern self", so Suzanne Hatty explains,

preserves individuality and forestalls the possibility of fusion with the dangerous not-self. Violence, as a modern strategy, guarantees both individual and social control, while maintaining and perpetuating hierarchy and inequality. (Hatty 2000: 10)

In a bitterly ironic reversal of Bruce's intentions, however, his particular choice of suicidal violence – death by hanging – transforms what could so easily have been mistaken for an act of phallic self-assertion into a scenario of the most shameful detumescence. Exposing in its final vision Bruce's flaccid, dangling and incontinent body, Welsh's novel thwarts patriarchal man's attempt at a heroic self-identification with Death, "the symbolically uncastratable" (Kramer 1997: 203). As the Worm slips out of the unclenching grasp of Bruce's bruised body, his suicide turns him into a spectacle of pathetic self-abjection.

4. *Glue* (2001): a Festival Atmosphere

In *Glue*, which focuses on the friendship and life stories of four Scottish working-class men, Welsh initially appears to merely reiterate the monologic mode of narration that characterises *Filth*. However, this changes dramatically in the final part of the novel when traditional realism gives way to a tumultuous kaleidoscope of spontaneously interweaving and unravelling narrative moments. This radical shift in form marks a drastic change in the way in which the men relate to each other. Welsh endows Billy, Carl and Terry with the ability to see through and unlearn the self-destructive dynamics of traditional masculinity and eventually, in an act of friendship, break the armoured shell of emotional invulnerability.

The first three parts of the novel – set in the 1970s, 1980s and 1990s – follow the same repetitive pattern of strictly autistic narration and give the impression that each of the friends lives in his own individual reality capsule. Together with a considerable portion of pomophobic sentiment, this manifests itself perhaps most pertinently in Billy's brief comment on his own mental strategies of coping:

> I don't like it when the shite of modern life flies through your nut. It's brutal and it drains your energy. The real fights are fought in yir heid, that always has to be right. And you can train yourself in your heid as well as your body; train yourself tae sift oot or bury aw the shite you get bombarded wi daily.
> Focus.
> Concentrate.
> Dinnae let them in. Ever. (Welsh 2001: 160)

The boys' alternating blocks of narration remain rigidly self-contained and their relation to each other is one of mere juxtaposition. The boys are given monosyllabic walk-on parts in each other's lives and they routinely refer to each other as "mates", but such declarations of closeness are belied by their discretely confined minds. They never open up to one another as friends, and their culture is one of self-defensive silence and emotional inarticulacy. They bully each other for the sake of bravado and as a result cry "tears that nae cunt'll see. Ever" (Welsh 2001: 107), revealing a girlfriend's observation that "youse are so beautiful tae yir pals, ah love the wey thit yis aw look eftir each other" (Welsh 2001: 215) to be little more than a delirious, ecstasy-induced hallucination. The boys cannot bear talking to each other, which becomes only too evident when we watch Gally – "the maist sensitive ay the lot" who, according to Carl, is "like a clitoris blown up tae five foot five and moulded intae a human figure" (Welsh 2001: 215) – struggling to disclose to the others how he feels. The boys are desperate to change the subject, frightened because "Gally's never talked like this before" (Welsh 2001: 276) and relieved when "at last the cunt starts laughing" (Welsh 2001: 278). Each of them claims to be worried about Gally, but when it comes to acting on their feelings, they seem paralysed by a homophobic fear of male-to-male intimacy or, as Terry so inimitably puts it, "that shite wi other guys" (Welsh 2001: 214).

The mere fact that Gally wants to talk, and does talk, is enough to call his masculinity into question. A "real" man like Billy, for example, has little time for the ghoulfest of the confessional culture; when [fear and doubt] threatened, he bit hard on it as if it was a pill and swallowed the energy that was released from it. Better that than giving some other cunt the power to dismantle your head. (Welsh 2001: 427-28)

In contrast, Gally's verbal incontinence testifies to a gross lack of manly self-composure, and his heightened self-consciousness is interpreted as advanced emasculation. Terry suspects that whilst in prison Gally "wis probably gittin shagged by some big fuckin soapdodger" (Welsh 2001: 278-80), adding that "ah ken he's hud a bad time. Ah lap the cunt up [...] Eh's ma best mate [...] Thir's just some fuckin funny shite gaun oan wi that cunt sometimes" (Welsh 2001: 280). Welsh portrays Gally as a victim of masculinity's culture of silence. In slavish compliance with Carl's father's law of male homosocial propriety – one of the rules of which is that "ye never grass anybody" (Welsh 2001: 118) – the other boys let Gally go to prison for a crime they know he did not commit. Released after some miserable years inside, Gally feels "part of the grey matter in his brain setting into breeze-block concrete" (Welsh 2001: 456), quite as if his previously intact emotionality were now about to congeal into the exact shape and texture of the masculine culture of autism that has ruined his life. The rest of his story is a downward spiral as he drifts into drug addiction, contracts HIV, and eventually jumps off a bridge during a boys' night out. No doubt Gally's suicide traumatises the other boys profoundly. However, while Carl's and Terry's immediate reactions are patently hysterical (uncontrolled shrieking and violent shaking), Billy, who holds his friend's broken body piéta-like in his arms, momentarily resembles an icon of maternal tenderness.

In his review of *Glue*, James Campbell describes it as "carefully crafted", adding that "the main interest is generated by the overlapping lives of the principal characters" (Campbell 2001: 8). No doubt the structural organisation of the novel is important as it follows a narrative trajectory from "the concrete of the block of flats" (Campbell 2001: 3) on the outskirts of the city to the city centre itself, and from the realist fixity of individual life stories to a rambling tale of spontaneous communal encounter. However, the main focus is clearly on how the boys' lives come to overlap. After years of mutual detachment, "the bricks of maleness" (Welsh 2001: 437) shatter in the fourth part of the novel. As a result, the narrative becomes more dynamic and

its pace accelerates, celebrating momentariness, delighting in fragmentation, and yielding to the apparent pleasures of collective self-
dispersal. The atmosphere is carnivalesque (the title of this fourth part
is "A Festival Atmosphere"), an ideal breeding ground for an exuber-
ant and self-liberating cross-, counter- and re-identification. All
throughout this part we witness previously subordinate identities
crowding in on the former centre. Thus, it seems to be no coincidence,
for example, that one among the first batch of subchapters is set in "A
Fringe Club", or that we find Billy's younger brother Rab suddenly
promoted from his supernumerary status to a major leading role.

The greatest novelty in the fourth part of *Glue*, however, is the
introduction of a group of young women characters, who have their
own stories to tell and whose lives are, at least initially, perfectly unrelated to that of the men. (In contrast, in the first three parts of the
novel all female roles are occupied by sisters, mothers, girlfriends or
"shags".) James Campbell rashly dismisses Welsh's introduction of
this new female point of view by suggesting that "in their appetites
and instincts, the girls are simply XX-chromosome versions of the
lads" (Campbell 2001: 8). In fact, the appearance of Lisa and Charlene
as emancipated females, who categorically reject woman's inferior
place, has complex and far-reaching repercussions, not only on how
the men relate to the women, but also on how the men relate to each
other. Changes in the perception and impersonation of femininity inevitably trigger corresponding changes in masculinity. As Catherine
Waldby explains, "phallic fantasy can only be maintained when it has
penetrable bodies to feed on, and if women systematically refuse to
bear the weight of these kinds of projection then it falters" (Waldby
1995: 273). It is of crucial significance that, with the support of her
best friend, Charlene stands up to the father that sexually abused her.
But what seems more significant is that Welsh portrays his women
characters as capable of forming strong homosocial bonds, without the
mediation of men, and that their practices of resistance and self-
assertion are presented to us as a true alternative to the men's. While
the women's approach to conflict-solving is both assertive and con-
frontational, unlike the men's it never employs violence or involves
the exploitation of others. Consequently, it is also superior to the
men's in that it keeps the women out of trouble. In a heated discussion

between two of the boys' mothers and fathers at an earlier point in the novel, Carl's mother concedes that "Terry's had a hard life". But then she continues to point out that "soas Yvonne [his sister], n she's turned oot awright. Soas wee Sheena Galloway, n she's never been in the jail or oot ay her heid oan drugs like thet Galloway laddie!" (Welsh 2001: 157). So the question remains, in the words of Billy's mother, "what is it wi you stupid, daft bloody men" (Welsh 2001: 157).

Campbell's reading of the women as exact mirror images of the men denies the former their difference, a difference which shows them to be far less (self-)destructive, and much more emotionally mature, than the men. Interestingly, one definitive symptom of autism is its insistence on sameness and its concomitant inability to recognise and acknowledge difference. Both are features that are not only noticeable in Campbell's misreading, but also in one of Terry's radically egalitarian exclamations which, albeit only at a first cursory glance, seems almost pro-feminist in its sentiment: "How they expect fanny tae be different fae cock in this day n age is beyond me" (Welsh 2001: 206). Whatever the apparent similarities between Welsh's men and women, it is important to remember that even though Lisa and her friends' "cocks oot fir the Lassies" (Welsh 2001: 305) attitude may appear "sexually aggressive" – for example, we witness Lisa push a finger up Terry's bum (Welsh 2001: 388) and Kathryn's insatiability cause Johnny to "swallow" repeatedly (Welsh 2001: 389) – it is never violent. What happens in the latter part of *Glue* is that femaleness casts aside demure feminine passivity and catalyses a turbulent reshuffling of the "sexual and bodily choreographies of masculinity and femininity" (Waldby 1995: 267). What ensues is a dramatic deconstruction of traditional gender polarity, and the tentative beginnings of a radical communal reassembling, strikingly similar in fact to what Lawrence Kramer in *After the Lovedeath* theorises as "the practice of gender synergy" (Kramer 1997: 16), a never-ending process of playfully crossing, blurring, blending and repositioning of traditional gender roles.

Protesting that "authority, truth, and pleasure inhere in the *ad hoc* ensemble of positions rather than in a fixed and prepotent masculine position" (Kramer 1997: 12), Kramer proposes the introduction of "an unsystematic system" of gender that would dissolve the coercive fixtures of traditional gender assignment, and translate gender into a dynamic process of constant re-identification. Importantly, however, Kramer concedes that "gender synergy cannot establish itself culturally unless men come to embrace it, and not grudgingly or resignedly but with enthusiasm" (Kramer 1997: 16). This would involve a mobilisation of precisely that "faculty of recognising value in outsiders" which Campbell finds so blatantly lacking in Welsh's men who, as far as he can see, fail to "ever get the hang of communal life" and to whom, invariably, "others remain the Other" (Campbell 2001: 8). But Campbell appears mistaken when he writes that *Glue* "charts the rites of passage from boyhood to ladhood (no Welsh character has progressed beyond the latter)" (Campbell 2001: 8), for Terry, Carl and Billy do grow up into "three middle-aged men" (Welsh 2001: 464). At the end of Part Four, as we see them take responsibility for their part in Gally's suicide, they relate to each other genuinely for the first time. "We kept away from each other because we reminded each other of our failure as mates", reflects Carl as he realises that "for all our big talk, our friend had died alone" (Welsh 2001: 414). As demonstrated by the men's eventual admission to "The Golden Era" – that is, the novel's coda set in the future of 2002 – Welsh is highly optimistic concerning his protagonists' ability to recover and make a change. Nevertheless, his description refrains from indulging in a hyperbolic utopianism and instead, by concluding the fourth part of the novel with a carefully reserved understatement, stays solidly within the realm of the realistic: "They [Terry, Carl and Billy] never said that much to each other, but they gave the impression of being close" (Welsh 2001: 464).

Introduced by their female contemporaries to the practice of gender synergy, Welsh's men manage to free themselves from the autistic shackles put upon them by traditional masculinity's definitive norms, imperatives and ideals of claustrophobic self-containment. This is a freedom that had formerly only been accessible to them through the use of drugs when, so Rab confesses, they still needed "a good pill to decondition us; loosen us up, get rid of the uptight shit" (Welsh 2001: 381). Whereas initially the novel's title may have alluded to glue-sniffing, in the novel's final vision it signifies a collective plunge into the contingent stuff of communal adhesion that postmodernity is made of – its fluidity, flexibility, and ceaseless mobility. Living up to the expectation expressed by David Buchbinder in *Masculinities and Identities* that "in the future men will have learned that difference does not also mean superiority or inferiority" (Buchbinder 1994: 87), the new masculine self, as envisaged by Welsh, unfolds as a versatile, multifaceted and mobile interlocutor, healthily immersed in communal intercourse and far removed from the filth of its unfortunate predecessor's death. As certain aspects of Paul Gilroy's recent work indicate, this new synergetic concept of subjectivity has also found its way into contemporary debates on nationhood where it materialises as a self "that is no longer plausibly understood as a unitary entity but appears instead as one fragile moment [caught up in the flux of] dialogic circuits" (Gilroy 2000: 109). As a result, although perhaps still imagined in terms of gender, the nation ceases to be one-sidedly or divisively gendered. Like masculinity, the traditional nation-state mobilises, not in order to repeat yet again its territorialist statement of rigid integrity, but to embrace a future of nomadic circulation within a tapestry of international identities-in-flux.

Bibliography

Baron-Cohen, Simon, Helen Tager-Flusberg and Donald Cohen (eds). 2000. *Understanding Other Minds: Perspectives from Developmental Cognitive Neuroscience*. Oxford: Oxford University Press.

Bersani, Leo. 1987. "Is the Rectum a Grave?" in *October* 43: 197-222.

Bettelheim, Bruno. 1967. *The Empty Fortress: Infantile Autism and the Birth of the Self*. New York: Free Press.

Buchbinder, David. 1994. *Masculinities and Identities*. Melbourne: Melbourne University Press.

Byers, Thomas. 1995. "Terminating the Postmodern: Masculinity and Pomophobia" in *Modern Fiction Studies* 41(1): 5-33.

Campbell, James. 2001. "Scratch'n'Sniff" in *The Guardian* (28 April 2001): 8.

Durig, Alexander. 1996. *Autism and the Crisis of Meaning*. Albany: SUNY Press.

Flannigan-Saint-Aubin, Arthur. 1994. "The Male Body and Literary Metaphors for Masculinity" in Brod, Harry and Michael Kaufman (eds) *Theorizing Masculinities*. Thousand Oaks: Sage. 239-58.

Foucault, Michel. 1967. *Madness and Civilisation: A History of Insanity in the Age of Reason*. London: Routledge.

Frith, Uta. 1989. *Autism: Explaining the Enigma*. Oxford: Blackwell.

Gilroy, Paul. 2000. *Between Camps: Nations, Cultures and the Allure of Race*. London: Penguin.

Hall, Catherine. 1996. "Histories, Empires and the Post-Colonial Moment" in Chambers, Iain and Linda Curtis (eds) *The Post-Colonial Question: Common Skies, Divided Horizons*. London and New York: Routledge. 65-77.

Happé, Francesca. 1994. *Autism: An Introduction to Psychological Theory*. Hove, East Sussex: Psychology Press.

Hatty, Suzanne. 2000. *Masculinities, Violence, and Culture*. Thousand Oaks: Sage.

Herbrechter, Stefan. 2000. "From *Trainspotting* to *Filth*: Masculinity and Cultural Politics in Irvine Welsh's Writings" in West, Russell and Frank Lay (eds) *Subverting Masculinity: Hegemonic and Alternative Versions of Masculinity in Contemporary Culture*. Amsterdam: Rodopi. 109-27.

Hudson, Liam and Bernadine Jacot. 1991. *The Way Men Think: Intellect, Intimacy and the Erotic Imagination*. New Haven: Yale University Press.

Kramer, Lawrence. 1997. *After the Lovedeath: Sexual Violence and the Making of Culture*. Berkeley: University of California Press.

Logan, Peter. 1997. *Nerves and Narratives: A Cultural History of Hysteria in Nineteenth-Century British Prose*. Berkeley: University of California Press.

McClintock, Anne. 1997. "'No Longer in a Future Heaven': Gender, Race and Nationalism" in McClintock, Anne, Aamir Mufti and Ellen Shohat (eds) *Dangerous Liaisons: Gender, Nation, and Postcolonial Perspectives*. Minneapolis: University of Minnesota Press. 89-112.

Micale, Mark. 1995. *Approaching Hysteria: Disease and Its Interpretations*. Princeton: Princeton University Press.

Mitchell, Juliet. 2000. *Mad Men and Medusas: Reclaiming Hysteria and the Effect of Sibling Relationships on the Human Condition*. London: Allen Lane.

Norton, Jock. 1991. "My Love, She Speaks Like Silence: Men, Sex and Subjectivity" in *Melbourne Journal of Politics* 20: 148-88.

Savran, David. 1998. *Taking It Like a Man: White Masculinity, Masochism, and Contemporary American Culture*. Princeton: Princeton University Press.

Showalter, Elaine. 1997. *Hystories: Hysterical Epidemics and Modern Culture*. London: Picador.

Silverman, Kaja. 1992. *Male Subjectivity at the Margins*. New York and London: Routledge.

Thomas, Calvin. 1996. *Male Matters: Masculinity, Anxiety, and the Male Body on the Line*. Urbana and Chicago: University of Illinois Press.

Tustin, Frances. 1992. *Autistic States in Children*. London: Tavistock and Routledge.

Vinden, Penelope and Janet Astignton. 2000. "Culture and Understanding Other Minds" in Baron-Cohen, Simon, Helen Tager-Flusberg and Donald Cohen (eds) *Understanding Other Minds: Perspectives from Developmental Cognitive Neuroscience*. Oxford: Oxford University Press. 503-19.

Waldby, Catherine. 1995. "Destruction: Boundary Erotics and Refigurations of the Heterosexual Male Body" in Grosz, Elizabeth and Elspeth Probyn (eds) *Sexy Bodies: The Strange Carnalities of Feminism*. London: Routledge. 266-77.

Welsh, Irvine. 1998. *Filth*. London: Jonathan Cape.

—. 2001. *Glue*. London: Jonathan Cape.

Woolf, Virginia. 1966. *Collected Essays: Volume 1*. London: Hogarth.

Queer Readings, Gay Texts: From *Redgauntlet* to *The Prime of Miss Jean Brodie*

Christopher Whyte

Scottish literary criticism typically ignores potential "queer readings" of canonical texts. Subjects such as crossdressing in Walter Scott's *Redgauntlet* and the homo-eroticism of Muriel Spark's *The Prime of Miss Jean Brodie* have been ignored by orthodox interpreters. That these potential readings have been suppressed indicates the prohibitions and taboos involved in the formation of the Scottish canon.
Keywords: queer theory, crossdressing, homoeroticism, Walt Whitman, Walter Scott, Muriel Spark, Edwin Morgan.

On one of those compèred programmes of classical music broadcast on BBC Radio 3 which partake of the nature of a medley, I happened to hear the American composer John Adams' setting, for baritone and orchestra, of Walt Whitman's poem of the American Civil War, "The Wound Dresser".[1] I knew that Whitman had been homosexual, and that his work as a nurse among the wounded of Pittsburgh had a strongly erotic colouring, almost certainly expressed in physical relationships with some of those he cared for (Shively 1989). Adams' choice of words to set aroused my curiosity. It seemed fair to define Whitman's poem, in many of its aspects, as a gay text. Was the musical setting a gay text as well? I looked around for information about Adams' private life, not easy to come by in the case of a living composer. He had lived, worked and taught in San Francisco for many years. But it was not till I read, in the booklet accompanying a CD recording of his *Harmonielehre* for symphony orchestra,[2] that the third movement had been inspired by a dream, in which he saw his daughter Quackie flying through the air, whispering the secret of grace into the ear of the medieval mystic Johannes Eckhardt, that I

---

[1] First performed in February 1989, *The Wound Dresser* is a setting (with the exclusion of the first section and the opening paragraph of the second) of a poem of the same name, dated 1865 (Whitman 1977: 227-29). A recording made in August 1989 by Sanford Sylvan with the Orchestra of St Luke's, conducted by the composer, is available on Elektra Nonesuch CD 7559-79218-2.

[2] EMI CD 7243 5 55051 2 5, issued in 1994. The notes are by Mark Swed.

understood I had been jumping to unwarranted conclusions. Adams was drawn to Whitman's poem by the experience of witnessing his mother nurse his father through Alzheimer's disease. What was in origin a gay text had been drawn towards a parallel but distinct experience, in which there was no significant homoerotic component.

The incident was instructive in two ways, both relevant to the discussion which follows. Texts, be they musical, visual, or verbal, are of their very nature chameleons, apt to elude the labels we try to glue onto them. A text which could with justification be defined as gay in one context had lost this definition in another, or had at any rate acquired a different meaning which co-existed alongside the first, without erasing it. I was no doubt still at liberty, like any other listener, to forget about Adams' parents and daughter and to see in the musical setting an expansion of the homoerotic experience which had prompted the words in the first place. Nevertheless, I realised that the question about a gay text is emphatically not a question about the sexuality, known or imputed, of its author. One can claim that *Redgauntlet* offers material for homoerotic reading without necessarily having to posit that Walter Scott was himself homosexual, or experienced homoerotic drives in his own person. The two issues are distinct. What is more, gay texts are capable of functioning as "straight" texts, and vice versa, thus rendering the urge to divide cultural products into two mutually exclusive camps no less ridiculous than the urge to divide up individual human subjects in a similar way.

It is worth pausing for a while to reflect on the chameleon nature of texts. It is a quality which can be remarkably productive under the conditions of censorship obtaining until recently (and in many cases still in force) with respect to homoerotic content. Crouching forward in my seat in the gods, intent on Tatiana while she sang the letter scene from the First Act of *Eugene Onegin*, as if this change of physical posture could somehow have allowed me to get closer to the composer's mind, I asked myself what it was that had permitted the homosexual Tchaikovsky to find such convincing music for these words. In particular, why had he set Tatiana's avowal "Ja [...] vljubljenà" ("I have fallen in love") in such a way as to imply that no greater disaster could befall a human being? The heterosexuality of Pushkin was beyond question, for all that in a verse epistle to the exiled Filip Vigel he affectionately satirises this friend's passion for anal intercourse (Karlinsky 1986: 55),[3] and though the man who shot him in a duel is said to have been the lover and protégé of the notoriously gay Dutch ambassador to St Petersburg at the time, Baron van Heeckeren. Nonetheless, by patching together selected phrases from the libretto, it was possible to frame a rather different, if related narrative for this section of the opera. A young man who feels isolated and misunderstood in the rural setting where he has grown up ("ja zdjes' odnà,/ Niktò menjà ne ponimàjet") is profoundly shaken by the arrival of a stranger, an older man who breathes an air of urban sophistication. Prey to alternate impulses of trust and mistrust ("Kto ti, moj àngel li khranìtel/ Ili kovàrni iskusìtel"), and worried that his lack of experience may be deceiving him ("Obmàn neòpytnoj dushì"), he throws caution to the winds, and confesses his feelings in a letter. The following day he receives a humiliating lecture. The older man has decided to let him off lightly. While he cannot approve of the young man's conduct, he replies with equal frankness ("No vas khvalìt' ja ne khochù;/ Ja za njejò vam otplachù/ Priznànjem tàkzhe bez iskùsstva"). On no account should the young man again risk his good name in a similar fashion. He might not be so lucky the next time ("Uchìtes' vlàstvovat' sobòju;/ Ne vsjàki vas, kak ja, pojmjòt." (Pushkin 1991: Chapters III (Stanza XIX and Tatiana's Letter) and IV (Stanzas XII and XVI))).[4] In other words, it was feasible to imagine a similar sequence of events affecting a young man, whose homosexual feelings have remained at an inchoate stage because of his circumstances, who identifies (rightly) a visiting stranger as someone who shares these feelings, and is rebuffed with icy courtesy, in such a way as to cause him infinite and lasting pain. Could this be how Tchaikovsky had avoided the creative anorexia which plagued E.M. Forster after *A Passage to India*, provoked at least in part by his unwillingness to

---

[3] The poem in question was not published in full until the centenary of Pushkin's death. This Italian publication is an extended version of an essay which Karlinsky, better known as an outstanding Tsvetaeva scholar, first published in *Gay Sunshine* in 1976.

[4] My use of Pushkin's text may seem daring. But it is nothing compared to the change wrought by the opera libretto, which so crucially omits the voice of the narrator from its source poem. Where possible in the Russian, of course, words referring to Tatiana are marked as feminine in gender.

represent in a published text love and sexuality as he experienced them? In a setting like Tchaikovsky's, where same-sex love could not be represented on the operatic stage (and have things changed?) it was logical that the composer should identify with the heroine of the story. *Cherchez la femme.*

One further instance: the Scottish poet and playwright Edwin Morgan has confided to me that there is every likelihood that the historical Cyrano de Bergerac, hero of the play by Edmond Rostand which Morgan rendered into Scots to such acclaim, was homosexual. Shortly afterwards Morgan set to work on a play of his own, based on the Mesopotamian epic of Gilgamesh, perhaps the earliest written text available to us which speaks clearly of the overwhelming love of one man for another. When I later heard that he had broken the mould by translating into Scots for the Lyceum Theatre in Edinburgh, not a text couched in a popular idiom, but Racine's *Phèdre*, I could not help but speculate whether Morgan's sexuality had again conditioned his choice of subject. *Phèdre* has always struck me as ripe for reinterpretation in homosexual terms, especially where stringently repressive conditions obtain. As with Tchaikovsky, the homosexual subject would be projected onto the female protagonist. Phèdre becomes obsessed with a man much younger than herself, aware from the start that her passion goes against the norms of the family and of civil society. When she avows her love and attempts to enjoy its fruits, a dreadful monster, which surely is also a symbolic representation of her feelings, emerges from the sea and tears the young man in question to pieces. Were one to switch the gender of the main character, the play would offer a concise expression of one particular brand of homosexual self-hatred. Such a reading does not depend upon research into the sexual practices of its author for substantiation. To do so would be to misunderstand the issues at stake.

Texts, then, are liable to cross the bounds we set for them without even the flimsiest of warnings. John Adams could use Walt Whitman's words to give voice to a very different experience of his own, without feeling the need to erase their original import. (I am thinking here of the emphasis given in his setting to the penultimate word in Whitman's unnecessarily, and therefore all the more forcefully revealing, final line: "Many a soldier's kiss rests on these *bearded* lips" (my italics)). Living and working in San Francisco, the composer might well have felt that the impact of AIDS on the community around him made "The Wound Dresser" relevant in a painful way to contemporary gay experience. *Eugene Onegin* perhaps tendentiously, and Racine's *Phèdre* more explicitly, offer room for readings in terms of situations and an agenda which characterise the fate of gay people in a range of repressive environments. The term "gay text" must therefore remain an elusive one. It is a quality texts may take on for a while, at the hands of an adaptor or a critic, but which they may lose in other circumstances. One could even posit a ranking of co-existent readings, which would vary according to the specific circumstances of a text's reception.

This is where the concept of "queer reading" shows its usefulness.[5] If you do not have to be homosexual to be queer, then the idea of "queer reading" may be helpful in extending the range of responses to canonical and non-canonical texts, thereby alerting readers to possible interpretations which may have been unnoticed or suppressed, often moving against the apparent grain of the author's conscious intentions and against that of traditional critical approaches. "Queer reading" is apt to detect a "gay text" where there were no suspicions of such a possibility. But, and this is one of its most valuable contributions, it can also alert us to the willed and wilful silences within the literary academy.

There are further reasons why it should be especially welcome in a Scottish context. I am far from being the first to bemoan the apparent difficulty of integrating international literary theory with a prevalently nationalist critical tradition like the one in Scotland. The reasons for the difficulty are not far to seek. Since the 1920s, Scottish Literature has constituted itself as distinctive and independent through a predominantly oppositional discourse, whose principal concern was whether a given text could be shown to be Scottish and, in the case of a positive response, just how Scottish it could be proved to be. One could refer to this as the "Scottishness litmus test". Pertaining to the national tradition was what mattered. Literary theory, by contrast, refuses to prioritise the nationality of a text or texts. Theory's potential

---

[5] For an overview, see Jagose 1996 and Sedgwick 1997.

for renewal and subversion rests on its tendency to relate texts to one another on a radically innovative basis. This is why the marrying of Scottish criticism with literary theory has proved so problematic. It is inevitable that the theorist and the nationalist should find themselves at loggerheads. The theorist threatens to dissolve the very basis on which the nationalist has struggled to create a canon. Yet in a context like the Scottish one, where national identity has been, frankly, over-emphasised, other possibilities of approach to the same texts, such as queer theory, become unusually valuable.

"Queer reading" is also, quite simply, about pleasure: not what we were instructed to look for in a text, or the things we are supposed to find there, but the pleasure that it gave us, the impulse(s) that kept us reading. We are at last allowed to talk openly of our *jouissance* as readers, particularly when it was a kind of *jouissance* we might initially have hesitated to confess to. Queer reading draws our attention to issues which tend to be thrust to one side or glossed over in academic discussion, whether the context be a seminar room, a lecture theatre, or a published journal. Nothing could be further from the old fashioned approach which required that an informed or academic reader should struggle to suppress whatever features might distinguish him or her amongst the larger body of educated readers. Queer reading gives us permission not just to acknowledge our positionality, but to revel in it as a fount of pleasure.

What is more, it works against a once dominant, perhaps now dying but not entirely dead mode of hermeneutics, characteristic of the Protestant tradition, which implies that we read creative literature in order to improve ourselves. We do not turn to literature for pleasure, but so that we may become better individuals and better citizens. At its most blatant, this mode prescribed that the main figure in a fictional narrative should undergo a process of self-discovery and self-improvement. The reader's task was to identify with this process and to be, as a consequence, similarly instructed and uplifted. What violence has been done, for example, to the novels of Jane Austen in the name of this approach!

Could any gay man reading Scott's *Redgauntlet* fail to be swept up in the dynamic of Darsie Latimer's relationship with Alan Fairford? As much as, perhaps even more than Redgauntlet's determination to enlist his nephew for the Stuart cause, it is Alan's willingness to set his father's wishes, his professional career and even his personal safety aside in order to rescue his friend, that keeps the story moving. One could make a case for merely assigning the novel to one kind of romance pattern, as Northrop Frye does:

In this type of story one brother goes out on a quest or in search of adventure, the other remaining home, though able to tell from some sign how his brother is faring, and going into action when help is needed. This structural device is still useful in displaced stories where the look-alike twins are replaced by close friends, as in Scott's *Redgauntlet*. (Frye 1976: 111)

What matters, however, is that the bond existing between Alan and Darsie is strong enough to function convincingly as a substitute for their being children of one father. Rather than acting as an underpinning structural device, the strength of their relationship allows the text to come into being, for the letters they exchange as a consequence of their separation make up more than one third of its totality, and the opening third at that. Their separation and reunion constitute the basic movement of the novel, standing as they do at its beginning and its conclusion. The scene in which they are reunited tellingly suggests that, if the kind of pleasure mentioned above may be alien to its author's intentions, it is hardly alien to the substance of his text:

The situation of Darsie was indeed something awkward; for Cristal Nixon, out of caution perhaps to prevent escape, had muffled the extreme folds of the riding-skirt with which he was accoutred, around his ankles and under his feet, and there secured it with large corking-pins. We presume that gentlemen-cavaliers may sometimes cast their eyes to that part of the person of the fair equestrians whom they chance occasionally to escort; and if they will conceive their own feet, like Darsie's, muffled in such a labyrinth of folds and amplitude of robe, as modesty doubtless induces the fair creatures to assume upon such occasions, they will allow that, on a first attempt, they might find some awkwardness in dismounting. Darsie, at least, was in such a predicament, for, not receiving adroit assistance from the attendants of Mr Redgauntlet, he stumbled as he dismounted from the horse, and might have had a bad fall, had it not been broken by the gallant interposition of a gentleman, who probably was, on his part, a little surprised at the solid weight of the distressed fair one whom he had the honour to receive in his embrace. But what was his surprise to that of Darsie's, when the hurry of the moment, and of the accident, permitted him to see that it was his friend Alan Fairford in whose arms he found himself! (Scott 1997: 322)

There can be no doubt of the narrator's evident enjoyment of this scene. The coy reference to male horsemen's interest in the ankles of their female companions is just one sign of the sensual arousal the situation provokes in him, and is followed by an invitation to them to imagine what it would be like to have their own ankles similarly enveloped, in a word, to be dressed up as women. It is not sufficient for Scott merely to reunite Alan and Darsie, with the passionate joy which might have been "innocently" characteristic of dear male friends at the time of which he writes. In female garb, Darsie more or less falls off his (her) horse into Alan's arms. What more explicit, or provocative homecoming could Scott have devised? In a stimulating and compelling essay, symptomatic of the opening of a new, transgressive and fruitful strand in studies of the novelist, Chris Fearns notes how, at the conclusion of *Redgauntlet*,

the scandal of barely concealed homosocial desire between male rivals is ultimately defused by the convenient plot device of making the woman in the case the sister of one, onto whom the other's desire can safely be deflected. (Fearns 1996: 161)

The triangulation by means of which this is achieved is, of course, rather more than just a "convenient plot device", and we shall return to it at a later point in the discussion.

Cross-dressing is a favoured device of Scott's, which recurs with noteworthy frequency in his fiction. Such is his predilection for cross-dressing that it even crops up in the case of minor characters, without further exploitation in terms of the plot. I am thinking here of the blind fiddler Wandering Willie's wife, his "female companion", who first appears "in a man's hat, a blue coat, which seemed also to have been an article of male apparel, and a red petticoat" (Scott 1997: 94). His work as a whole is permeated to a remarkable extent by that of Shakespeare, and Shakespeare certainly acted as an inspiration and, to a certain degree, a validation, even an alibi, for Scott's use of the device. After all, Shakespeare's theatre was, to a degree we are still today reluctant to acknowledge, a transvestite spectacle. Given the prejudices of his time and country, transvestism alone permitted the drama to take place. It was an integral part of the experience of the audience and the actors. This may be why Shakespeare tends to favour cross-dressing of females as males, since it allowed his boy actors to (re)assume an identity which his audience knew to correspond to the anatomical realities on stage. Whether or not one should view this kind of cross-dressing as the "recovery" of a "genuine" gender identity is a moot point. What is certain is that, in Scott's verbal texts, no such anatomical realities exist beneath his character's clothes. Nor can they offer a pragmatic justification for his use of the device.

When Darsie first assumes female dress (under coercion), the narrator has the following comments to make:

> the fair reader must be informed, that in those rude times, the ladies, when they honoured the masculine dress by assuming any part of it, wore just such hats, coats, and waistcoats, as the male animals themselves made use of, and had no notion of the elegant compromise betwixt male and female attire, which has now acquired, par excellence, the name of a habit. Trolloping things our mothers must have looked, with long square-cut coats, lacking collars, and with waistcoats plentifully supplied with a length of pocket, which hung far downwards from the middle. But then they had some advantage from the splendid colours, lace, and gay embroidery, which masculine attire then exhibited; and, as happens in many similar instances, the finery of the materials made amends for the want of symmetry and grace of form in the garments themselves. But this is a digression. (Scott 1997: 289)

If any *jouissance* demands attention in this paragraph, it is the *jouissance* of the author himself, fondly envisioning a vanished transgender paradise, and uncertain who is more deserving of his envy: the women, who got to dress up like men and even had voluminous "pockets" (what on earth did they conceal in them?) or the men, who got to wear all sorts of fussy, feminine things like lace and "gay" embroidery, as well as colours no self-respecting lawyer of the Regency period could have risked being seen abroad in. Scott even deploys an obscure and ambivalent verb, "trolloping"[6] to denote what our grandmothers and great-aunts got up to. No, Walter, one is tempted to reply, this is definitely not a digression.[7]

Is it possible that Scott's undisguised delight in costume, in the minor details of the garments which his characters put on, more than

---

[6] It both implies "something hanging down, dangling", and a connection with loose or immoral women. See *OED* s.v. "trollop".

[7] Chris Fearns' description of an earlier passage in the novel is equally applicable to this "explanation that fails to explain, an explanation whose clichéd prolixity suggests if anything a reluctance to examine the issue too closely" (Fearns 1996: 160).

the expression of antiquarian enthusiasm, or of a pedantry which confronts impatient readers with superfluous material to struggle through before they are rewarded with the next stage in the story, can be explained by the fact that these characters, being made of words, have no anatomical reality by which they can be gendered, and must rely on their clothes to tell them (and us) whether they are male or female?

Homoerotic dynamics in *Redgauntlet* are not confined to the relationship between Alan and Darsie. There can be little doubt that the most erotically charged figure in the novel is that of the man after whom it is named. Darsie first comes upon him in a suitably Gothic setting. It is close to sunset, and it cannot be long before the notoriously dangerous tides of the Solway Firth begin to race. Darsie is watching a group of men fishing for salmon on horseback:

The feats of one horseman, in particular, called forth so repeatedly the clamorous applause of his companions, that the very banks rang again with their shouts. He was a tall man, well mounted on a strong black horse, which he caused to turn and wind like a bird in the air, carried a longer spear than the others, and wore a sort of fur cap or bonnet, with a short feather in it, which gave him on the whole rather a superior appearance to the other fishermen. He seemed to hold some sort of authority among them, and occasionally directed their motions both by voice and hand; at which times I thought his gestures were striking, and his voice uncommonly sonorous and commanding. (Scott 1997: 33)

Dallying unadvisedly, Darsie risks being carried away by the treacherous currents and drowned. In the very best tradition of a Gothic heroine,[8] he is swept up onto the horse of the older man for whom he experiences such hypnotic fascination:

as I stood irresolute, he extended his hand, and grasping mine, bid me place my foot on the toe of his boot, and thus raised me in a trice to the croupe of his horse. I was scarce securely seated, ere he shook the reins of his horse, who instantly sprung forward [...] The rider sat like a tower. (Scott 1997: 34)

It is probable that only a rather primitive Freudian would encourage us to linger on the implications of Redgauntlet's "longer spear than the others", or of his sitting "like a tower". What is certain is that, were

---

[8] See, in this respect, Kathryn Sutherland's introduction to the Oxford University Press edition of the novel (Scott 1998: xviii).

the rescued person in this case to be a woman, critics would not hesitate to discern a powerful erotic charge in the passages quoted. If we hesitate to acknowledge it in Darsie's case, is this simply because of a presupposition on our part that such a dynamic could not be present in a Scott novel?

Once the comparative safety of Redgauntlet's home has been reached, we are treated to a further, meticulous description of the older man, so extensive that it can be quoted only in part:

His shirt was without ruffles, and tied at the collar with a black riband, which showed his strong and muscular neck rising from it, like that of an ancient Hercules. His head was small, with a large forehead, and well-formed ears. He wore neither peruke nor hair-powder; and his chestnut locks, curling close to his head, like those of an antique statue, showed not the least touch of time, though the owner must have been at least fifty. His features were high and prominent in such a degree, that one knew not whether to term them harsh or handsome. In either case, the sparkling grey eye, aquiline nose, and well-formed mouth, combined to render the physiognomy noble and expressive. (Scott 1997: 39)

Another factor which may tend to blind us to the real import of such a description is an expectation, drawn from a heterosexual matrix in narrative tradition, that erotic attraction will emerge between characters of a roughly similar age (though the Gothic elements present here tend to undermine such a hypothesis). Were the only fragmentarily preserved annals of gay love over the last few centuries to be available to us in full, it is highly probable that the fascination exerted upon a younger man by one some twenty or thirty years older would play a major part in them.

Such is the intensity of interest centred around Redgauntlet that when the young woman who is, after all, the novel's female lead, puts in an appearance, she is dismissed in a matter of lines. Darsie writes that if Alan expects "a fine description [...] thou shalt be disappointed". Having categorised her as "very pretty [...] a sweet and gentle-speaking creature", Darsie has "said all concerning her that I can tell thee" (Scott 1997: 41). Such laconism arouses his friend's suspicions ("thou sayest so little of her, and so much of everyone else, that it excites some doubt in my mind" (Scott 1997: 47)), and perhaps it should arouse doubts in the reader's mind too. Is it pushing things to suggest that Darsie has no time to look at Greenmantle because he cannot take his eyes off his uncle, even for a minute?

If there is an erotic dynamic that goes beyond simple friendship in Darsie's relationship to Alan, it is possible that the same may be true of his abduction at the hands of Redgauntlet. Apparently it was customary, in certain ancient Greek communities, for a mature male to abduct a younger male and disappear with him for a limited period into a wild place, thus removing him from normal social intercourse. In captivity, Darsie behaves like a traditional romance heroine, who must resist the suitor being forced upon her by a tyrant and preserve her virginity for the right man, though in Darsie's case the virginity is ideological rather than anatomical. He will not espouse the cause his uncle wishes to marry him to, yet judges it prudent to keep silent about his true political sympathies until he is freed from his captor's clutches.

Darsie's falling from the horse in female dress into Alan's arms resembles a mock marriage. It was impossible for the two actually to marry one another in a novel of this sort (or in most social realities known to us before the later twentieth century). Instead, Scott resolved the homoerotic dynamic through triangulation,[9] somewhat to Darsie's detriment for, while Alan achieves emotional and sexual fulfilment, there is no suggestion that Darsie pairs off with anyone in the longer term. Officially, we are supposed to believe that both young men are equally interested in Greenmantle as a potential bride. Yet Scott remarks of Darsie that "the romance attending his short-lived attachments had been of his own creating", so that it "disappeared soon as ever he approached more closely" (Scott 1997: 311). In other words, he has never got nearer to any woman than appraisal from afar. The revelation of his and Greenmantle's kinship takes place while he is in drag. Any possible erotic tension is further defused by what he interprets as her unjustified familiarity. He is "vexed with her forwardness, and affronted at having once more cheated himself" (Scott 1997: 313).

---

[9] Those who are familiar with the work of Eve Kosofsky Sedgwick will see clearly how indebted my thinking at this point is to her treatment of the Girardian love triangle: see Girard 1976.

When Greenmantle is revealed as Darsie's sister, Alan is free to marry her. She is as close to Darsie as Alan can ever get.[10]

An identical pattern of triangulation is used towards the close of Muriel Spark's most celebrated novel, *The Prime of Miss Jean Brodie.* It may help to visualise the triangle as a diagram. In the case of *Redgauntlet*, a dotted line would link Alan and Darsie, signifying an erotic tension which cannot be named within the world of the novel, no matter how powerfully it is enacted. A zigzag line between Darsie and Greenmantle would indicate an erotic tension which cannot be given expression for reasons which are made explicit, namely that they are brother and sister. A straight line, linking Alan and Greenmantle, would indicate the only possible pairing, and the one through which the plot reaches a problematic resolution. In Spark's novel, Miss Brodie occupies Darsie's position and the art master, Mr Lloyd, Greenmantle's, while Sandy Stranger stands in the same position as Alan Fairford. Sandy never comes close to avowing her passion for Miss Brodie, though the narrator gives repeated hints as to the nature of her attachment (dotted line). Miss Brodie refuses to have an affair with Teddy Lloyd because he is married (zigzag line). For Sandy to sleep with Mr Lloyd is as close to sleeping with Miss Brodie as she herself, or her creator, will allow her to get (straight line).

The implications for the interpretation of this novel are significant. The "Protestant" hermeneutics outlined above (even at the hands of a proclaimed Catholic critic such as David Lodge)[11] have

---

[10] Readers wishing to explore queer approaches to Scott's fiction further are referred to Chris Fearns' excellent essay "That Obscure Object of Desire: Sir Walter Scott and the Borders of Gender" cited earlier (Fearns 1996). I came upon this essay, which analyses *Redgauntlet* in the context of a brilliant series of queer readings of Scott novels, after work on the present paper had been completed.

[11] Lodge seems to suggest the novel would be better titled *The Menopause of Miss Jean Brodie*: "Miss Brodie's 'Prime' may be a euphemism for, or a sublimation of, the experience of the menopause, which would be particularly traumatic for a spinster, and would explain many of the vagaries of her behaviour" (Lodge 1992: 168). More than once in the course of Lodge's study, Miss Brodie's prime is contrasted casually, but significantly, with "normal", "fertile" sexuality. Is the implication that, if she had simply got married and had children like ordinary women do, there would have been no problem? There would, of course, also have been no novel. And for Miss Brodie to be afflicted with the menopause at forty is perhaps a punishment even the most moralistic of critics should hesitate to wish upon her.

claimed that the novel is about good and bad teachers, about the dangers of fascism as embodied in Miss Brodie herself, or a critique of Calvinism, again as represented by the heroine. The reality is that Sandy betrays Miss Brodie, not for her politics, or for her unusual educational practices, but because she is heterosexual. Had Jean Brodie been able to respond to Sandy's feelings, she might have survived. If, that is, Sandy had been capable of dealing with her response to them.

In Scott's case, given his horrified reaction when a longstanding friend had to flee the country to escape charges of pederasty,[12] it is safe to assume that, if homoerotic dynamics are indeed present in *Redgauntlet*, the author was oblivious as to the implications. A scene such as Alan's embracing of a cross-dressed Darsie may only have been possible because of the degree of Scott's lack of awareness. The dynamics are so explicit because they never reached the stage of being disavowed. With Spark the circumstances are different. She both gives signs to the reader which are obvious enough for one to be puzzled that so few have managed to draw the appropriate conclusions, and kicks over her traces. Sandy's mental jibe that "the woman is an unconscious Lesbian" (Spark 1965: 120) is a good example of the latter tactic. The very mention of the word "Lesbian" serves to distract the reader's attention, as if it could reassure us that the issue has been dealt with satisfactorily, and that we need look no further for manifestations of woman-to-woman sexuality in the text. The tactic is all the more wily in that Sandy herself is the major lesbian character in the book.

The novel is scattered with ambivalent passages which, if we are willing to consider them clear-sightedly, give a vaguely malicious tinge to the relationship the novelist establishes with her readers. The hints need to be there, in the interests of the novel's overall coherence, although she herself does not necessarily believe us astute enough to put two and two together. One almost has the sense of the narrator

---

[12] "Richard Heber, a book-collector, had been a close friend of Scott and his family for over twenty years. He was caught with a young man; the newspaper *John Bull* published the story; Heber got a tip-off from a friend that he was about to be prosecuted, and fled the country to avoid execution, since homosexual acts were still a capital offence" (Morgan 1995: 211-12).

playing a game with herself from which the majority of her readers are excluded. The critical reception of the novel has proved her conjectures (if they were such) to be justified.

Take, for example, the judicious appraisal, not clearly attributed to either the narrator or Sandy, that "Miss Brodie looked admirable in her heather-blue tweed with the brown of a recent holiday in Egypt still warming her skin" (Spark 1965: 106), or the passage where "Sandy considered Miss Brodie not only to see if she was desirable, but also to find out if there was any element of surrender about her" (Spark 1965: 89). The alibi, in the latter case, is that Sandy, strictly speaking, is mulling over a heterosexual affair between her former teacher and Mr Lowther, rather than over something that might directly involve herself. Nevertheless, her concern is with what Mr Lowther might feel about Miss Brodie, rather than the other way round. She is, as it were, putting herself into Miss Brodie's lover's shoes (or should one say, his trousers?). The episode of the "wonderful policewoman" with whom Sandy "fell in love" (Spark 1965: 67) can of course be dismissed as an "inevitable" stage, the kind of infatuation every young woman must pass through before "moving on". (Sandy never succeeds in moving beyond Miss Brodie. This is the thematic justification for the circularities present in the novel's narrative structure.) The fact that the policewoman said "nesty" rather than "nasty" is sufficient to "put [Sandy] off the idea of sex for months" (Spark 1965: 68). Off sex with whom? The phonetic stumbling block is, however, not enough to stop Sandy and her heroine, who looks "very nice in her dark uniform and short-cropped curls blondely fringing her cap", from gazing "into each other's eyes, their mutual understanding too deep for words" (Spark 1965: 69).

The diffused ambivalence sets other, apparently disconnected, phrases in the text reverberating disconcertingly. I am thinking of Jenny's sense of "the hidden possibilities in all things" (Spark 1965: 81); of Sandy's "feeling of leading a double life, fraught with problems that even a millionaire did not have to face" (Spark 1965: 21); of her reflecting, in a conversation with Miss Brodie at a much later date, which concerns both Mr Lloyd and Mr Lowther, that "it was not the whole story" (Spark 1965: 60) (so what is "the whole story"?); and of the intimation that, in her crucial interview with the headmistress,

Sandy "was moved by various other considerations to betray Miss Brodie" (Spark 1965: 94). What "other" means remains uncertain. Sandy has a peculiar idea of heterosexual marriage, which she visualises briefly in the scene of a wife infuriated because her husband was not at home to repair a fuse (Spark 1965: 31). The Marcia Blane School for Girls is presided over by a "manly portrait" of the founder, regularly honoured by "a bunch of hard-wearing flowers such as chrysanthemums or dahlias" (Spark 1965: 6) (flowers as a "feminine" symbol are "defeminised"). An imaginary Alan Breck (from Robert Louis Stevenson's *Kidnapped*) assures Sandy that she is "a brave lass and not wanting in courage that any King's man might possess" (Spark 1965: 30).

Amidst so much that is half-lived and half-said, two passages stand out. In one, Sandy engages in an abstracted dialogue with Tennyson's Lady of Shalott:

> The Lady of Shalott placed a white hand on Sandy's shoulder and gazed at her for a space. "That one so young and beautiful should be so ill-fated in love!" she said in low sad tones.
>
> "What can be the meaning of these words?" cried Sandy in alarm, with her little eyes screwed on Miss Brodie and her lips shut tight.
>
> Miss Brodie said: "Sandy, are you in pain?" (Spark 1965: 22)

Is it too daring too propose that Sandy's question functions as a prod directed at the reader, a kind of signpost that this puzzling, tangential incident, like so many elements in the story, needs to be given close attention if we are to grasp the novel's actual import? Crossing the Meadows, Sandy considers her teacher's inconsistencies, for it is hard to reconcile her contempt for the Girl Guides with her admiration of Mussolini's fascists. Yet "the group-fright seized her again, and it was necessary to put the idea aside, *because she loved Miss Brodie*" (my italics) (Spark 1965: 32). There it is, squeezed in at the end of a sentence, at the end of a paragraph concerned with totally different issues. In a text such as this one, where everything is either casual and chaotic, or (as I would maintain) intentional and carefully planned, if surreptitious, it is hard to overstate the importance of such a simple statement. It explains Sandy's conduct, her choice of Teddy Lloyd as lover, her betrayal of Miss Brodie and the prison of self-suppression to which she condemns herself, symbolised by the bars of the convent grille she grips so desperately. She is the victim of her own refusal to acknowledge and live out her sexuality, to actualise human love as she is capable of knowing it. She turns that potential into something very different.

An assessment of *Redgauntlet* which overlooked its homoerotic dynamics could still teach us much about the novel. The same is not true of *The Prime of Miss Jean Brodie*, precisely because the book makes such an issue of obfuscation, of its own seeming in-explicability. Consideration, from a "queer" perspective, of what has been neglected in both books may usefully bring us to reflect, at the close of this essay, upon the prevailing silences within the Scottish academy. By the phrase "the Scottish academy" I mean the putative collective of those who write, teach and write about the literature, and more generally the culture, of Scotland. When I discussed the contents of this essay in an informal conversation with Martin Bowman, co-translator with Bill Findlay of the works of Montréal playwright Michel Tremblay, he was astonished that the novel's lesbian dynamics should be so prevalently ignored in Scotland. He had, he insisted, been teaching *The Prime of Miss Jean Brodie* as a lesbian novel in Canada for at least a decade. His reaction set me thinking about what can and cannot be said about certain texts within a Scottish context. I wondered if the lesbian dynamics in Spark's novel had been ignored because of the role attributed to it in the formation of a Scottish canon. It is among the most popular of Scottish texts from a teaching point of view. The secondary literature on Spark, despite its evident omissions, compares favourably with that of most other Scottish novelists from the same period. Nevertheless, in the course of over fifteen years teaching in two Scottish universities, I had never heard the issue mentioned in an academic context. It might not have existed.

This is a useful place to call a halt, because it should mark the beginning of another, very different essay. Silences and spaces, once identified, are valuable because they are pointers. What was not, or could not, be said is, so to speak, the negative image of the forces which dictate the silence. Any prohibition is rich in indications as to the nature of the interests which enforce it, their purposes and their positionality. To what extent can these interests be identified with those which have subtended the formation of a canon of modern Scottish literature? Though it is intended to render them invisible, the prohibition can, if handled carefully, bring the prohibitors and their agenda firmly into view. But that is the subject of another essay.[13]

---

[13] This essay derives ultimately from a paper offered to the postgraduate seminar series of the Glasgow and Strathclyde School of Scottish Studies in November 1998, and was read, in truncated form, at a plenary session of the "Resisting Alterities" conference at Macerata University, Italy, in December 1999.

Bibliography

Fearns, Chris. 1996. "That Obscure Object of Desire: Sir Walter Scott and the Borders of Gender" in *Canada* 22(2): 149-66.

Frye, Northrop. 1976. *The Secular Scripture: a Study of the Structure of Romance*. Cambridge, Mass. and London: Harvard University Press.

Girard, René. 1976. *Deceit, Desire and the Novel: Self and the Other in Literary Structure* (tr. Yvonne Freccero). Baltimore and London: John Hopkins University Press.

Jagose, Annamarie. 1996. *Queer Theory: an Introduction*. New York: New York University Press.

Karlinsky, Simon. 1986. "Omosessualità nella letteratura e nella storia russa dall'XI al XX secolo" in *Sodomo: rivista omosessuale di cultura* 3: 47-70.

Lodge, David. 1992. "The Uses and Abuses of Omniscience: Method and Meaning in Muriel Spark's *The Prime of Miss Jean Brodie*" in Hynes, Joseph (ed.) *Critical Essays on Muriel Spark*. New York and Toronto: G.K. Hall and Maxwell Macmillan. 151-73.

Morgan, Edwin. 1995. "A Scottish Trawl" in Whyte, Christopher (ed.) *Gendering the Nation: Essays in Modern Scottish Literature*. Edinburgh: Edinburgh University Press. 205-22.

Pushkin, A.S. 1991. *Evgenij Onegin*. London: Bristol Classical Press.

Scott, Walter. 1997. *Redgauntlet* (ed. G.A.M. Wood with David Hewitt). Edinburgh: Edinburgh University Press.

—. 1998. *Redgauntlet* (ed. Kathryn Sutherland). Oxford: Oxford University Press.

Sedgwick, Eve Kosofsky (ed.). 1997. *Novel Gazing: Queer Readings in Fiction*. Durham and London: Duke University Press.

Shively, Charley. 1989. *Drum Beats: Walt Whitman's Civil-War Boy Lovers*. San Francisco: Gay Sunshine Press.

Spark, Muriel. 1965. *The Prime of Miss Jean Brodie*. Harmondsworth: Penguin.

Whitman, Walt. 1977. *The Portable Whitman* (selected and notes by Mark Van Doren). Harmondsworth: Penguin.

The Muted Scotswoman and Oliphant's *Kirsteen*

Anne McManus Scriven

Until recently, writing by Scottish women has often gone unrecognised, and Scottish-ness has often been equated with maleness. Feminist analysis of the work of Margaret Oliphant, in particular of her novel *Kirsteen*, reveals some of the ways in which women function as a "muted group" within a dominant male discourse.
Keywords: Margaret Oliphant, canon, Elaine Showalter, gynocriticism, nationality, fraternity.

To point out the phallocentrism of the Scottish literary canon is nothing new. David McCrone notes that women in Scotland "have been relegated to walk-on parts" (McCrone 1992: 190); Douglas Dunn highlights "the extent to which Scottish literature was, and is, controlled by male psychologies" (Dunn 1994: 1); Christopher Whyte argues that the "tentative" Scottish literary canon is made up of texts "almost exclusively by male authors" (Whyte 1995: x). Yet, despite these and many other acknowledgements of the imbalance in the Scottish literary canon, writing by women in Scotland is still largely a forgotten discourse. The neglect of Margaret Oliphant's novel *Kirsteen* (1890) by critics is a prime example of the silence surrounding nineteenth-century Scottish women's writing. In the following chapter, I argue that Oliphant's distinctive construction of a Scottish heroine functions as a muted counter-culture to dominant national narratives which presuppose that the word "Scottish" signifies maleness.

A gendered view of nationality is continually reinforced by biased academic works claiming to be reflective of nineteenth-century Scottish literature. The focus on male writers such as Galt, Hogg, Scott and Stevenson excludes critique of contemporaneous female writers such as Brunton, Ferrier, Oliphant and the Findlaters. Some critics include a chapter on the writing of Scottish women in their edited anthologies – but the fact that this token quota is deemed "proper" or "enough" is itself a statement about the significance of Scottish women's writing. As Joanna Russ notes in her essay "Anomalousness":

Groups in which women actually number 50% tend to be seen as being *more* than 50% female. It is not impossible that some similar, unconscious mechanism controls the number of female writers which looks "proper" or "enough" to anthologists and editors. (I am reminded of the folk wisdom of female academics, one of whom whispered to me before a meeting at which we were the only women present, "Don't sit next to me or they'll say we're taking over.") (Russ 1997: 103)

Having edited or written a token "women's writing" chapter, many scholars then continue to focus on critiquing Scottish male writers, designing University courses foregrounding male writers, running annual conferences on these writers, and re-publishing work by them. As Douglas Gifford and Dorothy McMillan argue in their ground-breaking *A History of Scottish Women's Writing*:

Histories of Scottish literature have tended in recent years to include more women [...] It seems, however, that gradualism in writing the history of Scottish women's writing will not be enough to secure for women a more than vestigial presence in whatever larger stories are being told about either the national or the female canons. (Gifford and McMillan 1997: ix)

Why the correlation of "Scottish" and "female" is viewed as problematic is, I argue, elucidated by the theory of the "wild zone" pioneered by gynocritic Elaine Showalter in 1981. This model, although a "weel-kent" one in feminist literary criticism, is well worth a re-visit as it argues that women constitute "a *muted group*, the boundaries of whose culture and reality overlap, but are not wholly contained by, the *dominant (male) group*" (Showalter 1986: 281). Showalter's theory is today still an appropriate and useful argument for a reading of Scottish women's writing as literature that displays a different understanding and experience of nationhood than that con-structed by male writers. Precisely because it offers a different narra-tion of nation than the "male-stream" tradition, writing by Scottish women has not been deemed central to the construction of Scottish national identity. What it is to be female and Scottish remains very much within the untheorised realm symbolised by Showalter's "wild zone".

In the majority of her novels set in Scotland,[1] Margaret Oliphant explores the peculiar position women hold in relationship to their nation, and yet the double-voiced discourse of her "Scottish" heroines has never been properly examined. There have recently appeared two edited anthologies of criticism on Scottish women writers – Aileen Christianson and Alison Lumsden's *Contemporary Scottish Women Writers*, and Carol Anderson and Aileen Christianson's *Scottish Women's Fiction 1920s to 1960s*. Vital as these works are, they emphasise the lack of published criticism focussed solely on the nineteenth-century foremothers of twentieth-century Scottish women writers. During the writing of this chapter, the volume *Scottish Literature in English and Scots*, edited by Douglas Gifford *et al.*, also appeared on the scene. Although it contains chapters focussing on Ferrier's *Marriage* and Oliphant's *Kirsteen*, the same marginalisation of nineteenth-century women's writing is again in evidence. The editors state that their book is "not a history of Scottish literature", that their "brief survey must grossly simplify" (Gifford, Dunnigan and MacGillivray 2002: 313), but why need this be once more at the expense of nineteenth-century Scottish women's literature? Every anthology which highlights the dominance of male writing does little to negate the belief that Scottish writing is a male prerogative. As Adrienne Rich has argued:

Until we can understand the assumptions in which we are drenched we cannot know ourselves. And this drive to self-knowledge, for women, is more than a search for identity: it is part of our refusal of the self-destructiveness of male-dominated society. A radical critique of literature, feminist in its impulse, would take the work first of all as a clue to how we live, how we have been living, how we have been led to imagine ourselves, how our language has trapped as well as liberated us, how the very act of naming has been till now a male prerogative, and how we can begin to see and name – and therefore live – afresh. (Rich 1995: 35)

Even when interest *is* rekindled, what nineteenth-century Scottish women writers say about women and nation can often be overlooked.

---

[1] Oliphant's "Scottish" novels number some two dozen. Unlike her English contemporaries, Oliphant often gives her heroine's name as the title of her book (e.g. *Katie Stewart* (1853), *Effie Ogilvie* (1886), *Joyce* (1888), *Lady Car* (1889), and obviously *Kirsteen*), thus reinforcing her deliberate narrative focus on a woman's life.

In the case of Margaret Oliphant, none of her prominent critics give more than superficial attention to the Scottishness of Oliphant's fictional heroines.[2] Any critique that has been done on national identity and Oliphant's writing tends to hang on the best known of her supernatural stories, which have managed to retain a place in various anthologies and critical works.[3] But Oliphant's narratives of the relationship of nineteenth-century Scottish women to their nation are a field largely unploughed.

There are very simple reasons for this particular lack of criticism. Despite the fact that Oliphant penned and published over ninety novels in her lifetime, the only two novels still in print are *Miss Marjoribanks* (1998) and *Phoebe Junior* (2002). The vast majority are available for the determined researcher in the National Library of Scotland, or are occasionally found languishing in some dark corner of an obscure second-hand bookstore. It is little wonder then that critics of Oliphant's writing usually give the best part of their energy to discussion of her Carlingford novels – an inter-connecting series set in the English home-county town of Carlingford. While these novels criticise the position of women in England during Victoria's reign through the eye of the satirical Scot, they obviously do not focus on the experience of the nineteenth-century woman in Scotland.

Readers of Oliphant will also find problems in the range and availability of critical literature. For example, the unpublished PhD thesis by Margaret King Gray, "The Fiction of Margaret Oliphant" (1979), lays the foundations for research on Oliphant and her Scottish heroines. Yet, while Gray's thesis is important for its recognition of Oliphant's great influence on the shape of the Scottish literary canon, it is nonetheless unpublished and does not theorise the literary construction of the nineteenth-century female Scot. Furthermore, critics beyond Scotland have little or no appreciation of what Joy Hendry has

---

[2] To date there are only a handful of published critical works concentrating solely on Oliphant. A brief bibliography of significant criticism includes Colby and Colby 1996, Williams 1986, Calder 1992, Rubik 1994, Trela 1995, Jay 1995 and Kamper 2001.

[3] See Manlove 1994 and Fielding 1996. Fielding is the only critic, to date, that I am aware of who offers a very interesting theorisation of "ventriloquism" in Oliphant's stories of the supernatural.

termed "the double knot in the peeny" (Hendry 1987: 38) – i.e. the argument that Scottish women writers are marginalised and kept silent both by their gender and by their nationality.[4] Bearing out Hendry's argument are the disappointing colonial overtones which creep into Elizabeth Jay's otherwise excellent scholarly biography *Mrs Oliphant: A Fiction to Herself* (1995), where Oliphant's "Scottish" novels are referred to as "regional". The legacy of a dominant neighbour is also (ironically) found in Showalter's important gynocritical study *A Literature of Their Own* (1987) where Oliphant and other Scottish writers such as Mary Brunton and Jane Welsh Carlyle are positioned as "English" writers.

All of what I have just indicated, however, does not discredit the foremost critics of Oliphant or downplay any of their efforts to reinstate her as a writer worthy of re-assessment. Nevertheless, their work indicates the truth of Anne McClintock's argument that if "the invented nature of nationalism has recently found wide theoretical currency, explorations of the gendering of the national imaginary have been conspicuously paltry" (McClintock 1989: 89). Oliphant's narratives of her Scottish women have to date gone untheorised because it is only very lately that theorists of nationhood have woken to the fact that the dominant arguments of nationhood, are, like the recognised Scottish literary canon, reflective mostly of the male viewpoint. As Glenda Norquay has argued, "we need to reconsider the myths in which issues of national identity are formulated" (Norquay 1998: 198). It is all too ironic that when, seeking to expose the myth of national identity in his seminal study *Imagined Communities: Reflections on the Origin and Spread of Nationalism*, Benedict Anderson argues with words rooted in male experience:

Finally, it is imagined as a *community*, because, regardless of the actual inequality and exploitation that may prevail in each, the nation is always conceived as a deep, horizontal comradeship. Ultimately it is this fraternity that makes it possible, over the past two centuries, for so many millions of people, not so much to kill, as willingly to die for such limited imaginings. (Anderson 1983: 16)

---

[4] "Peeny" is a Scots form for "pinafore", a loose feminine work garment secured by a bow knot.

In the opening scene of Oliphant's novel *Kirsteen* (1890) we find an immediate enactment of nationhood as Anderson's idea of "comradeship" and "fraternity" when Robbie Douglas, Kirsteen's brother, is preparing to leave home accompanied by his childhood friend for service in India – a destination that they had been bred for "from their cradles". A farewell grand supper is given, a tradition "on the eve of the departure of one of the boys to make their fortune in the world" (Oliphant 1984: 15). Their health toasted in champagne and with tears and blessings from near and dear ones, the young lads take leave of their Highland village. But this is not the only image of nationhood presented to the reader at the opening of the novel. From the very first page the disparity between Kirsteen the Scot-as-woman, and her brother Robbie, the Scot-as-male, is made starkly obvious. While her brother sets his sights upon adventure and new experience, Kirsteen is left with nothing but the thankless task of looking after her hypochondriac mother and younger siblings – her only sustenance being the memory of a promise to her brother's friend Ronald that she would "wait" for him. In her father Drumcarro's complete disregard for his daughters, the muting of Scotland's women is underlined:

"Where is Kirsteen away to?" […] said her father.
"I'm here, father," said Mary in her mild voice.
"Oh, ay, you're there," said the inconsistent head of the house, "for you're just nobody, and never had two ideas in your head," he continued in a lower tone. "Now, Robbie, my man, take your glass, there is no saying when you will get another. It's just second nature to a Scotsman, but it's as well for you to be out of the way of it, for though it's the most wholesome drink, it's very seductive and you're much better without it at your age. It's like the strange woman that you're warned about in Scripture." (Oliphant 1984: 15)

The opening scenes of *Kirsteen* are a statement on what occurs when "nation" signifies "fraternity". As Carole Pateman argues in *The Sexual Contract* (1988), in a fraternity, men rule over women in the private domain, but agree a "contract" which provides for social equality between men in the public domain. Oliphant illustrates this fraternal understanding of nation as Robbie, the male Scot, is viewed by his father as responsible, visible, and active – as the proud carrier of tradition out into the wider world – while Kirsteen, the female Scot is, by contrast, relegated to privacy and invisibility – she is of little consequence and is expected to keep the home fires burning.

These opening scenes of Oliphant's novel therefore enact an understanding of nationhood much like that espoused by John Locke in his second *Treatise of Government* (1690). Locke presumes the primary qualification for citizenship and the right to participate in public affairs to be rationality – a quality he attributes only to men. Political power is viewed as including the rule of husbands over wives, as men are argued to be "abler and stronger" (Locke 2002: 321). Integral to their relegation to the private sphere is also an understanding that women should take on the work of formation and nurture of future citizens. As Yufal Davis argues:

Women, however, are not just the biological reproducers of the nation, but also its cultural reproducers, often being given the task of guardians of "culture" who are responsible for transmitting it to the children and constructing the "home" in a specific cultural style. (Yufal Davis 1997: 116)

While her brothers reach young adulthood and are sent off to make their name and fortune in the world, Kirsteen is expected to be content with a caring supportive role in her family, an identity which is little more than domestic servitude. Events develop so that Kirsteen's situation becomes intolerable for her. Having given her heart to the friend of her brother and having promised to wait for him until his years in India are over, she is then distraught when her father expects her to marry the aged laird of Drumdochart. Kirsteen's father, who is constructed as a monster figure, a former slave-trader and epitome of the brutal male – an obvious precursor to Douglas Brown's John Gourlay in *The House With The Green Shutters* (1901) – speaks to her in words reflective of the full weight of patriarchal Scotland. He regards her as little more than a female body signifying "a creature of no account. A lass that has to obey her father till she gets a man, and then to obey him" (Oliphant 1984: 86). When Kirsteen attempts to reason with her father that her aged suitor will understand her refusal, Drumcarro moves into new heights of temper and threatens to kill Kirsteen where she stands. Searching for a way of escape it is to Marg'ret, the faithful servant of the Douglas household, that Kirsteen turns.

Marg'ret, along with other spinsters of Oliphant's pen such as Margaret Maitland of *Lilliesleaf*, Catherine Douglas of *Merkland*, Margaret Murray of *It Was A Lover And His Lass* to name but a few, is given the task of speaking out against the dominance of the patriarchal Scot. Where Austen reduces the elderly single woman to the dependent and wittering character of Miss Bates in *Emma* (1816), or where Ferrier caricatures her in Lady MacLaughlin of *Marriage* (1818), Oliphant constructs Marg'ret (again an obvious precursor to Stevenson's Kirsty in *Weir of Hermiston*) as the only woman in the Douglas house capable of dealing with the brutish Drumcarro. Marg'ret, and the other fictional women of her ilk, are the straighttalking, upright, morally heroic women, whom Oliphant praises in her essay "Scottish National Character":

This class of celibates behaved themselves with great energy and emphasis in the world, and have worked their opinions and reminiscences into the history of their time with a force and clearness not to be surpassed [...] In these thoroughly excellent women – for such they were in spirit of their peculiarities – the national genius for contradiction attained its climax; not that they were argumentative or disputatious, like slower wits, but only possessed of a strong intolerance of other people's opinions, and in the clear rapidity of their own intellects entertained a sharp impatience and contempt of dullness, which they did not choose to veil under any haze of charity. (Oliphant 1860)

When Marg'ret tackles Drumcarro over his neglect of his daughters' future, she refuses to be silent in the face of a dominant male discourse which, following Lockean standards, wishes to relegate her to a position of voicelessness. Refusing to be identified solely as a woman in domestic service to the Douglas household, she challenges Drumcarro from the standpoint of one human being to another – a brave challenge to which even Drumcarro finds himself listening. As Penny Fielding argues of Oliphant's oral women:

Oliphant thus uses speech not so much to make women visible in history as to make them heard. Speech, then, represents not the acceptance of a process of socialisation which already exists and already privileges sight, but something like an alternative. (Fielding 1996: 210)

The inclusion of this strong articulate older woman also acts as a counter-argument to the possible challenge that Oliphant's construction of the female Scot is an essentialist one. In *Kirsteen,* alongside the heroine's story are the stories of other women who both collude with and question the symbolic order around them. It is significant that all these women oscillate between various states of being or understandings of themselves. This supports the argument that the untheorised "wild" zone of femaleness and Scottishness does not necessarily denote a homogeneity. When Kirsteen seeks help from Marg'ret this multiplicity of selves is underlined:

To keep Kirsteen back was, in the circumstances and with the strong convictions of the Scotch serving woman as to the force of a troth-plight and the binding character of a vow, impossible. But to let her go thus unfriended [...] was something more than could be borne. (Oliphant 1984: 108)

Marg'ret finally opts to help Kirsteen's flight by providing her with money towards a journey to London and "a new world of meaning" (Oliphant 1984: 107). In contrast to her brother's public exultant leaving where sadness mingled with jubilance, Kirsteen slips unseen out of her childhood home very early one morning, alone and unprotected, to walk first to Glasgow and then travel by coach to the unknown city of London, in full "consciousness of having no home or refuge to which she belonged" (Oliphant 1984: 126). In the face of such disregard for Scotland's daughters it is tempting to agree with Virginia Woolf's argument in her extended essay *Three Guineas* (1938), where she says:

"Our country" [...] throughout the greater part of its history has treated me as a slave; it has denied me education or any share in its possessions [...] in fact, as a woman, I have no country. As I woman I want no country. As a woman my country is the whole world. (Woolf 1992: 313)

But Woolf's conclusion is not Kirsteen's. The latter runs from a home which rejects her, but still retains some sense of belonging to her birth country. In conflict with herself as well as her country, Kirsteen struggles to identify what it means to be a female Scot, and in the London chapters we see Oliphant's real genius as a narrator of this problematic position. The little luggage that Kirsteen carries with her to London is supplemented by her heavy mental baggage which is loaded with questions of identity. Dismissed as unimportant from her birth by her father – a fallen figurehead of the existing Douglas clan – Kirsteen experiences nationhood in metaphorical images rather than in active participation. Homi Bhabha's argument that nations "only fully realise their horizons in the mind's eye" (Bhabha 1990: 1) can be seen in the nostalgic memory Kirsteen holds of her home (a memory which, however, in typical Oliphant style, is tinged with realism):

That she should be seized with a yearning now and then for the sound of the linn, for the silence of the hills, for the wholesome smell of the peats in the clear blue Highland air, was as natural as that she should hear that wail for Kirsteen in the midst of her dreams. These longings gradually built up in her mind an ideal picture of the beauty and perfection of nature as embodied in her own glen, such as is a stay and refreshment to many a heart in the midst of alien life – to many a heart which perhaps in presence of that glen not idealised would be unconscious of any beauty [...] Go back! Oh, no; she would not if she could go back, and she could not if she would. (Oliphant 1984: 177-78)

The story of Kirsteen narrates an awakening to the fact that nationality is a gendered discourse, an awakening that is abrupt and painful. As a fugitive from her place of birth Kirsteen initially tries to retain a pride in having "Douglas blood in her veins", but she is at the same time aware of the reality that her claim to this ancient lineage as a woman is but a fragile one. All of her brothers before her would, by law, inherit any of the existing Douglas land, and her family name, in which she takes so much pride, would have been relinquished had she married her sweetheart Ronald Drummond (or indeed the aged Glendochart). The fluid identity of the clans*woman* is underlined in the interchange between Kirsteen and the Duke of Argyll:

"No, my lord Duke, I cannot go home," she said, with a curtsey so respectful that his Grace could only take refuge in the recollection that she was not his clanswoman.
"If ye had been of my name I would not have taken a denial," he said.
"And she would have been of your name if she had married Glendochart," cried the Duchess exasperated. (Oliphant 1984: 176)

While in London, Kirsteen hears of the death of her lover, and with this news sees through the cloud of illusion that hovers around her idea of Scotland. With the passing of a young girl's dream comes a complete awakening to her own strengths. Kirsteen returns to Scotland to ask for the handkerchief she had once given Ronald as a keepsake, and which he had kept until his death. In this journey we see the new Kirsteen emerging "no longer afraid of any danger on the road, or of the world unknown" (Oliphant 1984: 233). Kirsteen journeys to Scotland heartbroken, but she is no longer the poor confused girl who had left it some years ago. She is now a grown woman, a mantua-maker of some high distinction, and financially independent. She retrieves the precious handkerchief and returns to London. The narrator comments "and thus life was over for Kirsteen; and life began" (Oliphant 1984: 241).

In the latter part of the novel the crossover with Oliphant's own life is seen. A widow after only seven years of marriage, working constantly to meet the needs of her dependant family, coping with the death of her ten-year-old daughter Maggie in 1864, and the later death of her nephew in 1879, worried over the poor health of her eldest son who died some few months after the publication of *Kirsteen*, and dealing with the death of her remaining son in 1894, Margaret Oliphant must surely have lived Kirsteen's experience:

The worst had happened to her that could happen. No postscriptal life or new love was possible to her. Her career was determined, with many objects and many affections, but of that first enchantment no more. (Oliphant 1984: 241)

The other obvious parallel to Oliphant's own life is the fact that Oliphant lived most of her adult life in England, visiting Scotland frequently but never making it her home. From the perspective of another culture, Kirsteen, like Oliphant herself, reconfigures her relationship with Scotland and decides on what terms she will re-engage with it, and what borders she will recognise.

Kirsteen must be read ultimately as a *Bildungsroman*. As Kirsteen evolves towards a coherent self,[5] she recognises that she has outgrown the narrative that patriarchal Scotland would have her live by. In the final chapter of the novel, Kirsteen returns, at her father's

---

[5] For a fuller discussion of the trajectory of the female *Bildungsroman*, see Abel, Hirsch and Langland 1983.

bidding, to visit her old home in full awareness now that her identity as a Scottish woman is an existence or experience beyond the dominant male sphere. But as Showalter argues, "the concept of a woman's text in the wild zone is a playful abstraction" (Showalter 1981: 263); the reality is that Kirsteen, like any woman of any nation, only has the discourse of the symbolic phallogocentric order to speak through. When Drumcarro sends for her, Kirsteen, thinking that her father is dying, "obeyed this letter with a speed beyond anything which was thought possible in the north" (Oliphant 1984: 338). The haste in which Kirsteen journeys to Scotland can be read as a desire to find belonging and an acceptance of her life. But this acceptance is given in a much diluted form. When Kirsteen, at her father's request, buys back the lost family lands of Rosscraig there is no warm embrace for her from a repentant father, but only the amazement of a sick old man who is incredulous that it is to his daughter that the family is indebted:

"Your hand upon it," he cried. The hot clutch made Kirsteen start and shiver. He dropped her hand with an excited laugh. "That's the first bargain," he said, "was ever made between father and child to the father's advantage – at least, in his house. And a lass, – and all my fine lads that I sent out for honour and for gain!" (Oliphant 1984: 339)

Kirsteen's purchase of Rosscraig, the old Douglas land, could be read as symbolic of the Scotswoman moving out from the private sphere to the public, but Kirsteen remains for her family "a rare and not very welcome visitor in the house she had redeemed" (Oliphant 1984: 341). Her brother returns from India, now a distinguished colonel, and is startled to find that he is indebted to his sister "a London mantua-maker", "sewing" as he puts it to himself, "for her bread". Like the rest of his family, he deplores "the miserable way of life she had chosen, and that she had no man" (Oliphant 1984: 341). For the remainder of her life Kirsteen is both a misfit and mystery to all around. Single, rich and successful, bountiful and still beautiful in her later years, Kirsteen settles in Edinburgh – a city both near and far enough from her childhood home. Living her life financially independent of her family but providing for their needs, Kirsteen continues to refuse any stereotypical pattern of the Scottish woman.

In the introduction to *Studies in Scottish Fiction: Nineteenth Century*, Horst Drescher asks "is there something which could be described as a typical nineteenth-century experience of Scottishness?" (Drescher 1985: 12). If we apply this question to Oliphant's *Kirsteen,* any response must surely reflect the marginalised and unmapped life of this nineteenth-century Scotswoman. Like Woolf's concept of the elusive semiotic female sentence,[6] to be female and Scottish is a construction yet to be properly identified or written. As Homi Bhabha has argued, "What emerges as an effect of such 'incomplete signification' is a turning of boundaries and limits into the in-between spaces through which the meanings of cultural and political authority are negotiated" (Bhabha 1990: 4). The danger of arguments such as Bhabha's in encouraging a reading of nationhood as free-floating liminal spaces is that critics will let the meaning of being female and Scottish remain forever untheorised and forever deferred. Instead I argue that, far from wishing a definite signification to be laid on the words "female Scot", it is nonetheless surely a good idea if we pay full attention to what our muted nineteenth-century Scottish women writers have to offer on the subject. The academic community may continue to foreground male constructions of nationhood, but the fact of the matter is that, in the words of Margaret Oliphant, "woman is half the world" (Oliphant 1855), and despite Scottish women's muted history and forgotten writing, women are half the Scottish nation too – or is that too hard to imagine?

---

[6] In *A Room of One's Own* Woolf argues that the male sentence is "unsuited for a woman's use" but fails to pinpoint exactly what she means by a female sentence preferring instead to state that this difficult question "lies in the twilight of the future" (Woolf 1967: 77-78).

Bibliography

Abel, Hirsch and Langland (eds). 1983. *The Voyage In: Fictions of Female Develop-ment*. Anover and London: University of New England Press.

Anderson. Benedict. 1983. *Imagined Communities: Reflections on the Origins and Spread of Nationalism*. London: Verso.

Bhabha, Homi (ed.). 1990. *Nation and Narration*. London and New York: Routledge.

Calder, Jenni. 1992. *Margaret Oliphant*. Edinburgh: Scottish Academic Press.

Colby, Robert and Vineta Colby. 1966. *The Equivocal Virtue: Mrs Oliphant and the Victorian Literary Marketplace*. Hamden, Conn.: Archon.

Drescher, Horst. 1985. "Introduction" in Drescher, Horst and Joachim Schwend (eds) *Studies in Scottish Fiction: Nineteenth Century*. Frankfurt am Main: Peter Lang. 7-13.

Dunn, Douglas. 1994. "The Representation of Women in Scottish Literature" in *Scot-lands* 2: 1-23.

Fielding, Penny. 1996. *Writing and Orality: Nationality, Culture and Nineteenth-Century Scottish Fiction*. Oxford: Clarendon Press.

Gifford, Douglas and Dorothy MacMillan (eds). 1997. *A History of Scottish Women's Writing*. Edinburgh: Edinburgh University Press.

Gifford, Douglas, Sarah Dunnigan and Alan MacGillivray (eds). 2002. *Scottish Lit-erature in English and Scots*. Edinburgh: Edinburgh University Press.

Hendry, Joy. 1987. "Double Knot in the Peeny" in Chester, Gail and Sigrid Nielson (eds) *In Other Words: Writing as a Feminist*. London: Century Hutchinson. 32-43.

Jay, Elizabeth.1995. *Mrs Oliphant: A Fiction to Herself*. Oxford: Clarendon Press.

Kamper, Birgit. 2001. *Margaret Oliphant's Carlingsford Series: An Original Contri-bution to the Debate on Religion, Class and Gender in the 1860s and 70s*. Frankfurt am Main: Peter Lang.

Locke, John. 2002. *Two Treatises of Government*. Cambridge: Cambridge University Press.

McClintock, Anne. 1997. "No Longer in a Future Heaven: Gender, Race and Nation-alism" in McClintock, Anne, Aamir Mufti and Ellen Shohat (eds) *Dangerous Liaisons: Gender, Nation and Postcolonial Perspectives*. Minneapolis and Lon-don: University of Minnesota Press. 89-112.

McCrone, David. 1992. *Understanding Scotland: The Sociology of a Stateless Nation*. London and New York: Routledge.

Manlove, Colin. 1994. *Scottish Fantasy Literature: A Critical Survey*. Edinburgh: Canongate Academic.

Norquay, Glenda. 1998. "Welcome Oh Mine Old Rugged Scotland" in Paul Hullah (ed.) *Romanticism and Wild Places*. Edinburgh: Quadriga. 176-99.

Oliphant, Margaret. 1860. "Scottish National Character" in *Blackwood's Magazine*, June. National Library of Scotland. Volume LXXXVII. Shelfmark: Mf.SP.Ser 3.

—. 1855. "Modern Novelists – Great and Small" in *Blackwood's Magazine*, May. National Library of Scotland. Shelfmark: mf.SP.Ser 3.

—. 1984. *Kirsteen: The Story of a Scotch Family Seventy Years Ago*. London and Melbourne: Dent.

Pateman, Carole. 1988. *The Sexual Contract*. Cambridge: Polity Press.

Rich, Adrienne. 1995. *On Lies, Secrets and Silence: Selected Prose 1966-1978*. New York and London: Norton.

Rubik, Margaret. 1994. *The Novels of Mrs Oliphant: A Subversive View of Traditional Themes*. New York and Bern: Peter Lang.

Russ, Joanna. 1997. "Anomalousness" in Warhol and Herndl (eds) *Feminisms: An Anthology of Literary Theory and Criticism*. Basingstoke: Macmillan. 97-105.

Showalter, Elaine (ed.). 1986. *The New Feminist Criticism: Essays on Women, Literature and Theory*. London: Virago.

Trela, D.J. 1995. *Margaret Oliphant: Critical Essays on a Gentle Subversive*. Selinsgrove and London: Associated University Press.

Whyte, Christopher (ed.). 1995. *Gendering the Nation: Studies in Modern Scottish Literature*. Edinburgh: Edinburgh University Press.

Williams, Merryn. 1986. *Margaret Oliphant: A Critical Biography*. London: Macmillan.

Woolf, Virginia. 1967. *A Room of One's Own*. Harmondsworth: Penguin.

—. 1992. *Three Guineas*. Oxford and New York: Oxford University Press.

Yufal Davis, Nira. 1997. *Gender and Nation*. London and New Delhi: Sage Publications.

Scottish Fighting Men: Big and Wee

Kasia Boddy

Depictions of boxing in Scottish literature and culture interlink masculinity, violence, aggression, sexual desire and national identity. From Walter Scott to William McIlvanney, the varying meanings of the boxer's body provide an unofficial emblem of Scottish national identity.
Keywords: Hugh McIlvanney, Benny Lynch, Walter Scott, William McIlvanney, masculinity, sexuality, unconscious desire, national identity.

The first part of my title is borrowed from that of an essay by the Scottish sportswriter Hugh McIlvanney, first published in the American magazine, *Sports Illustrated*, in 1971. I will also borrow his opening lines:

Anyone who suggests that the Scots are infatuated with their own image as fighting men has failed to distinguish between infatuation and the real thing. On the corner of any one of a thousand grey streets from Wick to Berwick-upon-Tweed you are in danger of finding people who will earnestly ponder the question of whether it will take one or two Scottish regiments to cope with the Red Army and who will argue persuasively that Benny Lynch, if caught on a sober night, would have floored Muhammad Ali mid-shuffle. (McIlvanney 1982: 97)

The humour of McIlvanney's piece relies on knowing that Benny Lynch, fine boxer, though he was, fought as a flyweight, and Muhammad Ali, of course, as a heavyweight. Scottish boxers are wee men who like to take on big men. It is not so much that they are Davids faced with Goliaths, more that they seem unaware of the discrepancy between size and sense. McIlvanney tells another story, about the time that the American heavyweight Sonny Liston demanded that Peter Keenan, bantamweight (and "archetypal Glaswegian") put out his cigar: "'Listen,' said Keenan, glaring up from the level of Sonny's chest, 'you may be the heavyweight champion, but I have never lost a fight in the street in my life. If anything is going out it's not the cigar.'" Sonny, we are told, backed down, and Keenan could soon be found sitting on his knee "like a ventriloquist's doll" (McIlvanney 1982: 97).

McIlvanney tries to locate the origin of "the Scottish capacity for personalised aggression" in Scottish history. He concludes that a variety of ethnic, environmental, religious and economic factors are relevant, but that rather than weighing up their individual impact, he suggests, we should simply recognise that "their combined effect is to produce an identifiable paranoia":

To most Scots, especially to those who inhabit the urban areas of the Central Lowlands, turning the other cheek is the ultimate heresy. They are a small race (there has never been a Scottish heavyweight boxer who could be guaranteed to hit a door if he held it by the handle), but their violence is not a petulant expression of frustration. Their problem is less a suspicion of inferiority than a conviction that the world is conspiring to conceal how remarkable they are. (McIlvanney 1982: 98)

In this chapter, I want to consider what McIlvanney so elegantly calls "the Scottish capacity for personalized aggression", and its inherent "identifiable paranoia", in some stories about boxing. In works from Walter Scott's "The Two Drovers" (perhaps the first story featuring a Scotsman boxing), to *The Big Man*, by Hugh's brother, William McIlvanney, size does seem to matter. But is it a matter of gender or sexual identity, or one of national identity; or are these all related?

1. The Two Drovers

Walter Scott's short story "The Two Drovers" (1827) presents a conflict between two friends – a Highlander, Robin Oig and an Englishman, Harry Wakefield – and two different forms of combat – the sword and the fists. Oig and Wakefield, both drovers (men who drive livestock to market), are physically very different. Robin Oig, we are told, was "small of stature, as the epithet Oig implies, and not very strongly limbed"; on the other hand, he "was as light and alert as one of the deer of his mountains" (Scott 1990: 4). Harry Wakefield

was nearly six feet high, gallantly formed to keep the rounds at Smithfield, or maintain the ring at a wrestling match; and although he might have been overmatched, perhaps, among the regular professors of the Fancy, yet, as a yokel or a rustic, or a chance customer, he was able to give a bellyful to any amateur of the pugilistic art. (Scott 1990: 8)[1]

The men quarrel over who has the rights to rest his sheep in a particular field, just on the English side of the Border:

"This will never do, Robin. We must have a turn-up, or we shall be the talk of the country side. I'll be d----d if I hurt thee – I'll put the gloves gin thou like. Come, stand forward like a man."

"To be beaten like a dog," said Robin; "is there any reason in that? If you think I have done you wrong, I'll go before your judge, though I know neither his law nor his language."

A general cry of "No, no – no law, no lawyer! a bellyful and be friends," was echoed by the bystanders.

"But," continued Robin, "if I am to fight, I have no skill to fight like a jacka-napes, with hands and nails."

"How would you fight then?" said his antagonist; "though I am thinking it would be hard to bring you to the scratch anyhow."

"I would fight with broadswords, and sink point on the first blood drawn – like gentlemans [*sic*]." (Scott 1990: 16)

Neither men are "gentlemans", but both are anxious to claim that status – Robin by evoking the Highland and European traditions of sword fighting; Harry with the newly fashionable English "pugilistic art". They start with Harry's game, in which he beats Robin "with as much ease as a boy bowls down a ninepin". In victory, Harry offers dubious consolation to his friend:

"'Tis not thy fault, man, that not having the luck to be born an Englishman, thou canst not fight more than a school-girl."

"I *can* fight," answered Robin Oig sternly, but calmly, "and you shall know it. You, Harry Wakefield, showed me to-day how the Saxon churls fight – I show you now how the Highland Dunniewassal fights."

He seconded the word with the action, and plunged the dagger, which he sud-denly displayed, into the broad breast of the English yeoman, with such fatal certainty and force, that the hilt made a hollow sound against the breast-bone, and the double-edged point split the very heart of his victim. (Scott 1990: 22)

The English game ended with a handshake; the Highland game with "the very heart" of the victim split in two. Is it obvious which is better

---

[1] For a full discussion of the story's pugilistic context, see Johnson 1995.

in this tale of the Borders? The story ends with Robin Oig on trial, and with the judge pointing out the relativity of codes of honour.

The story is set in the 1780s, a time when boxing was coming to be seen as a particularly English sport.[2] During the Napoleonic Wars pugilism's association with English nationalism was further strengthened.[3] Thomas Moore, for example, in his "Epistle from Tom Cribb to Big Ben concerning some 'Foul Play' in a Late Transaction" (1818) satirically compares the conduct of the allies in exiling Napoleon to St Helena to kicking a man when he is down; in other words, "Foul Play" (Heinz 1961: 300). Meanwhile Pierce Egan, the foremost boxing writer of the day, set forth in *Boxiana: Sketches of Ancient and Modern Pugilism*, "a dispassionate review of those countries where Pugilism is unknown". In those countries, he concludes:

We find, that, upon the most trifling misunderstanding, the life of the individual is in danger. In Holland the long knife decides too frequently; scarcely any person in Italy is without the stiletto; and France and Germany are not particular about using stones, sticks, &c. to gratify revenge; but, in England, the FIST only is used, where malice is not suffered to engender and poison the composition, and induce the inhabitants to the commission of deeds which their souls abhor and shudder at – but an immediate appeal to Boxing – the bystanders make a ring, and where no unfair advantage is suffered to be taken of each other. The fight done, the hand is given, in token of peace; resentment vanishes; and the cause generally buried in oblivion. (Egan 1971: 13-14)

Pugilism injected manliness as well as honour into English nationalism. Fighting with knives in particular was seen not only as foreign but as unmanly – Robin's lack of pugilistic skill makes him "a school-girl" in Tom's eyes. Robin in turn characterises boxing as fighting "with hands and nails", a form of fighting, in other words,

---

[2] Boxing did infiltrate lowland society with some academies set up in Scotland – notably under George Cooper who had fought the champion Tom Molineaux in Lanarkshire in 1815. Scott's familiarity with boxing culture emerges in surprising places. For example, in an 1803 letter to George Ellis, he begins by announcing, "My conscience has been thumping me as hard as if it had studied under Mendoza" (Grierson 1932: 196). Boxing's role in defining Englishness can be seen as early as 1749 in Henry Fielding's *Tom Jones*. See Johnson 1996: 331-51.
[3] Peter Bailey notes that "in the mythology of the Ring, the fist was England's national weapon and the skilful and courageous wielding of it in public kept alive the spirit of Waterloo" (Bailey 1987: 36).

that is unseemly, even animalistic, in its intimate physicality.[4] The first fight ends, as we have seen, with a clasping of hands, and the rivals moving away from each other. Robin's later plunge of the dirk into his friend's heart might be read as a more complete consummation of their relationship.

2. A Short Life

On 9 September 1935, 20,000 people crowded into Glasgow's city centre to welcome home Scotland's first world champion boxer. The flyweight Benny Lynch had beaten Manchester's Jackie Brown, knocking him down eight times before the referee stopped the fight in the second round. The *Evening Times* newspaper responded in verse:

Glasgow at last with flag unfurled
Sits right atop the cockeyed world.
Our Wee Men may honk their klaxon
Since one of them has laid low the Saxon. (Burrowes 1982: 174)

Lynch's last fight took place in 1937, when he defeated Peter Kane for the world championship, in what was widely thought of as the most exciting flyweight bout of all time (Odd 1948: 24-34). By the time of his next defence, however, his drinking had taken its toll and after weighing in over the limit, he was stripped of his title. As Thomas Healey put it, "Lynch lost his title on the scales" (Healy 1996: 116). The subtitle of Bill Bryden's play about Lynch, *Benny Lynch: Scenes from a Short Life*, can thus be read as a pun: Lynch died in 1946 at the age of 33, but he was also known as "the wee man", fighting at eight stones. Bryden has Lynch complain that "I spend hauf ma life weighin masel". The play ends nostalgically with an acknowledgment that "the National Health Service killed all the flyweights" (Bryden 1975: 97).[5]

---

[4] That the boxer was an attractive figure to other men in this period is made clear in Robert Fergusson's account of a drunken bruiser "wi broken lines" and his groupies or "macaronis" in his 1773 poem *Auld Reekie*. See Morgan 1995: 208-9.
[5] The last Scot to hold the flyweight title was Walter McGowan in 1966. Scots boxers, nevertheless, continued to flourish in the lower divisions. Lightweight (9 stones 9 pounds) champions include Ken Buchanan and Jim Watt.

Benny's 1930s wee-ness was very different from Robin Oig's 1780s wee-ness. By the early twentieth century, boxing had lost its "gentlemanly" connotations and had become a professional sport of the working-classes. Since the late nineteenth century it had also been a predominantly American sport. Lynch's championship victory was not therefore simply one over "the Saxon", but one which aligned him with the popular American fighters of the day – both in the ring, and on the screen.

Benny Lynch was frequently compared both to the reigning American heavyweight champion of the day – he was known as the "Jack Dempsey of the small men" – and to the reigning movie champion – James Cagney (Burrowes 1982: 199).[6] Robert Sklar argues that, in the 1930s, Cagney

established a new cultural type on the American screen and in the world's imagination. It was the urban tough guy – small, wiry, savvy, and street-smart, a figure out of the immigrant ghettoes and ethnic neighbourhoods of Chicago and New York. (Sklar 1992: 12)

The small, wiry, urban tough guy was also very much at home in the Gorbals. When Lynch won in 1934, one of his seconds reputedly expressed his admiration by saying, "Christ Benny, you were Jimmy Cagney in *White Heat* there the night" (Burrowes 1982: 151).[7] A debate about the relative skills (and ferocity) of Cagney and Lynch then ensued.

If there is less concern with homoerotic play in descriptions of Lynch's fights than we found in Scott's description of the Oig vs Wakefield bout, it is not wholly absent. Most importantly, national manliness (defeating the Saxon, emulating the American) requires staying away from women. In Bryden's play, Puggy, Lynch's manager tells him, "Train a' day an' shag a' night – net result – an absolute standstill. Wan cancels oot the other" (Burrowes 1982: 27). But if sex with women, and indeed the company of women at all, is

---

[6] Joyce Carol Oates notes that Dempsey's ring style, "swift, pitiless, always direct and percussive [...] changed American boxing forever" (Oates 1988: 88).
[7] Cagney appears as a boxer in several films including *The Irish in Us* (1935) and *City for Conquest* (1940). The "boxer-made-good" story (often featuring a priest) was a staple of Hollywood Depression output.

seen to be feminising, boxing is not exactly a world in which feminine values are absent.[8] The play presents Lynch's longest and closest relationship as being with his coach – Lynch fondly describes Puggy as "a terrible oul' sweetie-wife", while Nick and Johnny are his "nurse-maids" (Burrowes 1982: 80).

3. The Missing Link

Brian Donald's history of *The Fight Game in Scotland* includes a chapter on heavyweight boxing which he entitles "the missing link". The chapter begins:

Ever since that great patron of heavyweight boxing the Duke of Cumberland butchered the brawny pride of Highland manhood at the Battle of Culloden in 1746, Scotland's association with heavyweight boxing has generally been an unhappy one. (Donald 1988: 66)

In fact, it is not much of an association at all. On the chapter's first page, Donald tells us that John L. Sullivan's toughest opponent in 1886 was a Scots emigrant called Duncan McDonald, and that Jack Dempsey and Max Baer laid claim to some Scottish ancestry, but that is about it (Donald 1988: 66). The remainder of the chapter examines why (with a few brave exceptions) this is so. Donald gives four main reasons which interestingly mix the social and the geographical. First, "the descendants of the wild charges at Prestonpans and Culloden tended to go into the armed forces or the police, normally for long engagements" (Donald 1988: 67), and neither organisation would allow its members to moonlight as a professional fighter. Secondly, the inhabitants of the Borders ("another region of Scotland famed for the brawniness of its manhood" (Donald 1988: 67)) have historically been more interested in rugby than boxing. Thirdly, the working-class population of the places where boxing has been popular – the cities – tended to be small (and the larger middle-classes tended to be uninter-

---

[8] Although Joyce Carol Oates, on the contrary, argues that boxing is "the obverse of the feminine, the denial of the feminine-in-man that has its ambiguous attraction for all men" (Oates 1998: 76-77).

ested). Finally, whenever a heavyweight prospect did appear, he found it impossible to find opponents. Donald's explanation of the Scots' lack of heavyweight success seems quite measured and precise, yet by the end of the chapter he moves on to a more general (and familiar) claim about "all Scottish history":

> The story of Scottish heavyweight boxing is hardly an inspiring one, yet in a sense it is a microcosm of all Scottish history. Scots seem to take a perverse pride in defeat as in victory – Flodden, Culloden, the Darien Scheme are as widely remembered as Bannockburn and Jim Baxter sitting on the ball at Wembley in 1967. (Donald 1988: 76)

But there is more to the story of Scotland's big fighting men than pride in defeat. To recall McIlvanney's analysis (with which we began), the issue is "less a suspicion of inferiority than a conviction that the world is conspiring to conceal how remarkable they are". Referring back to Donald's earlier analysis, we can see that the conspiracy (the true "missing link") includes, for starters, the police, the army, rugby, poor nutrition, and public schools.

Conspiracy theories, and the suspicion of inferiority, also battle it out in Thomas Healey's highly acclaimed memoir, *A Hurting Business*, a work that explicitly connects size, sexuality, fighting and nationhood. Healy, himself 6 feet 2 inches, describes growing up in the Gorbals in the 1950s. In a "nation of midget folk", where "you could be sure a *wee* person was truly wee", he felt himself "a fucking giraffe" (Healy 1996: 41-42). This is perhaps why Healy is, as he freely admits, obsessed with other big men. The telling of his life story is intertwined with the story of heavyweight triumphs and defeats. If boxers generally are to be admired because "they put their manhood, it is the *only* word, on the line", heavyweights are "the epitome of manhood" (Healy 1996: 18). Healy's aspiration to heavyweight boxing prowess is unequivocally bound up with his sexual aspirations (but which is primary is not always clear). So we hear of his seduction of the school tough girl, Brenda Kane, after watching a film of Dempsey pulverizing Willard, his acquisition of a New York Jewish girlfriend, Norma (her main appeal is sharing a name with Rocky Graziano's girlfriend), and finally his coming to terms with the fact that he'll never be a heavyweight champion. But that admission is immediately

followed by the thought that if he can't be one himself, perhaps he can
father one:

It would be going too far – or *would* it? – to say that I began to cast about for a big
strong woman, and that it crossed my mind, for stronger blood, that I should go to
Africa. Such was my obsession: that I did not want a son, but rather a heavyweight
boxer. (Healy 1996: 101)

Unlike many writers about boxing, Healy is unembarrassed about ex-
ploring the homoerotic element in all this.[9] First, he tells us that
"[Sonny] Liston was a real man, and I was half in love with him. In a
manly way" (Healy 1996: 63). Next we learn of his admiration for
Cassius Clay's legs – Clay, supposedly, has "better legs than Betty
Grable" (Healy 1996: 72). Finally, he admits to being "in love with a
boy, and this was a blow to me and my manly aspirations": "A
strange, dual life. I was beating up on the heavyweights but sucking
on a phallus. There was no escaping that one. The musk and hair and
tilt and throb and it was all a contradiction" (Healy 1996: 81).

   In aspiring to be a heavyweight champion, Healy is not only aspiring to "the epitome of manhood" in (ambiguous) sexual terms. He
is also aspiring to the "epitome of manhood" in national terms. All the
great heavyweights that he mentions are American, most of them are
black. He cannot be American and black; he cannot, when it comes
down to it, sire a black American child. So what does he do? He as-
pires to take on the American writer whose persona was most closely
modelled on that of a heavyweight boxer, Norman Mailer. Mailer, he
says, is "the man to beat for the men who punch out words" (Healy

---

[9] Compare, for example, Barry Graham's *The Champion's New Clothes*, a novel full
of sexual anxiety – for example, the boxer-protagonist says of a friend, "we were still
as close as two men can be without bottoms becoming involved" – and disgust – (of
his opponent's girlfriend) "I knew Liz doted on him. She'd have used his shit for
toothpaste" (Graham 1991: 33, 36). A test case for Norman Mailer's claim that "the
accusation of homosexuality arouses a major passion in many men; they spend their
lives resisting it with a biological force" (Mailer 1964: 243) can be found in Ken
Buchanan's autobiography. By far the most violent scene in the book depicts
Buchanan, practically unconscious after taking sleeping pills, finding a man in his
bed. In order to rouse himself, he headbutts the wall. Buchanan details, but does not
explain, the "rage like I've never felt before" (Buchanan 2000: 211-14).

1996: 173).[10] In the early 1980s Healy tries to write a Glasgow boxing novel, but fails: "The plot seemed too unlikely"; "Had I gone for a more modest hero – a lightweight champion – it might have worked, only I did not want a lightweight" (Healy 1996: 174). (Healy's bitterness at this outcome immediately gives him a reason to compare himself to the then, also undervalued, heavyweight champion, Larry Holmes.) Soon afterwards, some of his *short* stories are accepted, but this is merely a lightweight solution, and so he proceeds with the novel. Healy compares his editing to "butcher work", getting rid of "chunks of prose", a process paralleled, during the same period, by the butchering of rival "chunks of meat" by heavyweight stylist Mike Tyson (Healy 1996: 195). Healy's *It Might Have Been Jerusalem* was published in 1991, when, however, not Tyson but Evander Holyfield was world champion. Healy tells us that Holyfield had beaten Douglas who had, in turn, beaten Tyson, and that Tyson admitted he had lost his title "to a bum". For once, Healy does not connect events in his life to the holder of the heavyweight crown. Does he fear that having achieved heavyweight status at last (by publishing a novel) he has nevertheless not quite made it into the first rank of heavyweights? Does he worry that he is only a Holyfield, dependant on luck and someone else's misfortune? Again, America figures largely in twentieth-century Scots' ambitions and measurements. If Lynch was praised as the "Jack Dempsey of the small men", then Healy hopes to be the Norman Mailer of "the midget folk". At 6 feet 2 inches tall, he may be a big man, but he cannot forget that he is a big man from a wee country.

4. Big Men, Hardmen, and New Men

The relativity of size is a lesson that Dan Scoular also learns in William McIlvanney's 1985 novel, *The Big Man*. Dan Scoular is "the big man" in the wee town of Thornbank ("the kind of place people get a fix on by association with the nearest big town"):

---

[10] Compare Max Apple's story "Inside Norman Mailer", which imagines the writer taking on Mailer with the critics as cornermen (Apple 1986: 49-60).

Their name for him was, perhaps, a clue. They called him "the big man". It was an expression used of other men in the town, of course. But if the words were used out of any explanatory context, they meant Dan Scoular. Though he was six-feet-one, the implications were more than physical. They meant stature in some less definable sense. (McIlvanney 1986: 18)

But Scoular fears that the name is false – "his stature didn't fit". In order to try to make it fit, he agrees to fight bare-knuckled for a fee, a gesture of "small rebellion" which will give a town full of desperate unemployed men "a small sense of itself" (McIlvanney 1986: 108-9). Although the training process brings him "the closest he had ever come to finding an external set of circumstances that matched the vague blueprint he had of himself" (McIlvanney 1986: 86), the fight itself is ultimately revealed as a sham. The real "big men" are the gangsters who live in big houses in the big city and whose score is being settled by proxy – Dan and his opponent, Cutty Dawson, are their dupes – and beyond them, those who have closed the mines, the "dark and uncontrollable forces to which everyone was subject, and some were more subject than others" (McIlvanney 1986: 18). The "heroic stances" of Dan and Cutty are really "gestures of despair" (McIlvanney 1986: 214), gestures which echo those of "all those self-defeating brave men of his boyhood":

Dan seemed to himself to be fighting all those working-class hardmen who had formed the pantheon of his youth, men who in thinking they defied the injustice of their lives had been acquiescing in it because they compounded the injustice by unloading their weakness on to someone else, making him carry it. (McIlvanney 1986: 186)

In rejecting the smallness of heroic stances and gestures, Scoular (and McIlvanney) do not, however, embrace large systemic change – when, for example, socialist Vince suggests changing the system, Dan merely reflects that "it was as though ideas were his element, not air" (McIlvanney 1986: 269). Rather "true heroism" lies in a different kind of small gesture, "the commonplace white magic" performed by working-class women like his mother and wife (McIlvanney 1986: 157). By the novel's end, Dan has become a kind of New Man, no longer "infatuated" with his own image as a "big man" or "a fighting man" (to recall Hugh McIlvanney's formulation). Instead, in proudly

taking on the epithet "Betty's man", he embraces his own vulnerability, and his need for the solidarity of his own wee town
(McIlvanney 1986: 263).

5. Scottish Fighting Men: Big or Wee?

Over the last twenty years the work of historians such as Eric Hobsbawm and Benedict Anderson has redirected the study of nationalism
away from political philosophy and ruling élites toward the wider society, and the broader culture. National formations of literature, sport
and gender – to name only my concerns here – have become as much
objects of study as government and law. National memory, as Benedict Anderson has argued, is shared by people who have never met yet
who regard themselves as having a common history. Modern nations
are therefore in Anderson's words, "imagined communities" (Anderson 1983: 12-13). More than this, however, they are communities with
imagined psychologies and pathologies, responding to history with
what Tom Nairn identifies as a shared "mechanism of adjustment and
compensation" (Nairn 1977: 332-41). I have considered some instances in which the figure of the boxer becomes a national
representative of this process, in more than simply the colours that he
wears. According to Joyce Carol Oates, "a boxer 'is' his body, and is
totally identified with it. And (more than other sports) the body is
identified with a certain weight" (Oates 1988: 5). If we want to posit a
national body, then Robin Oig represents an early nineteenth-century
Scotland that is wee, and fast, and fierce, and perhaps a little in love
with its English rival. Benny Lynch represents a Scotland that is wee,
and fast, and fierce, and more than a little in love with an imaginary
American identity. Both these "wee Scotlands" are "identifiably paranoid"; both end badly. In the late twentieth century, Thomas Healy
and Dan Scoular are still exceptional in being Big Men. While Healy
is irredeemably in love with bigness, he cannot escape the suspicion
that he will never be big enough; never, perhaps, American enough.
Dan Scoular, on the other hand, even more aware of conspiracy, finally recognises the irrelevance of the Big Man to the wee place.

In his discussion of the ways in which national traditions are invented, Eric Hobsbawm considers what he calls "the personification of 'the nation' in symbol or image". Such personifications can be officially sanctioned "as with Marianne and France" or emerge unofficially "as in the cartoon stereotypes of John Bull, the lean Yankee Uncle Sam and the 'German Michel'" (Hobsbawm and Ranger 1983: 1-15). In Scotland's case, it is hard to pinpoint a single personification, and I am suggesting that both wee men and big men could be said to represent both a paranoid conviction of the world's hostile conspiracy, *and* a genuine suspicion of inferiority.[11] In his glossary of Glasgow dialect, *The Patter*, Michael Munro straightforwardly defines "wee man" as "an affectionate title or form of address for a small individual", and "big man" as "a friendly term of address used to someone the speaker regards as being taller than himself" (Munro 2001:17).[12] When addressing Scottish fighting men, and indeed Scotland itself, as "big" or "wee", we may, however, be saying a wee bit more.

---

[11] The fact that I am considering only masculine personifications here, does not suggest that feminine ones do not exist. They are not always very different. A.L. Kennedy's *On Bullfighting*, for example, can usefully be read alongside Healy's memoir as another Scottish response to American writing (represented by both Hemingway's *Death in the Afternoon* and his female challenger Joyce Carol Oates, whose *On Boxing* I rely on here).

[12] Many thanks to my parents for giving me this book, and for their own extensive, and much appreciated, research into Glasgow usages of "big man" and "wee man".

Bibliography

Anderson, Benedict. 1983. *Imagined Communities: Reflections on the Origins and Spread of Nationalism*. London: Verso.

Apple, Max. 1986. *The Oranging of America*. London: Faber.

Bailey, Peter. 1987. *Leisure and Class in Victorian England: National Recreation and the Contest for Control, 1830-1885*. London: Methuen.

Bryden, Bill. 1975. *Benny Lynch: Scenes from a Short Life*. Edinburgh: Southside.

Buchanan, Ken. 2000. *The Tartan Legend: The Autobiography*. London: Headline Books.

Burrowes, John. 1982. *Benny: The Life and Times of a Fighting Legend*. Edinburgh: Mainstream.

Donald, Brian. 1988. *The Fight Game in Scotland*. Edinburgh: Mainstream.

Egan, Pierce, 1971. *Boxiana: Sketches of Ancient and Modern Pugilism*. Leicester: Vance Harvey.

Graham, Barry. 1991. *The Champion's New Clothes*. London: Bloomsbury.

Grierson, H.J.C. (ed.). 1932. *The Letters of Sir Walter Scott, 1787-1807, Vol.1*. London: Constable.

Healy, Thomas. 1991. *It Might Have Been Jerusalem*. Edinburgh: Polygon.

—. 1996. *A Hurting Business*. London: Picador.

Heinz, W.C. (ed.). 1961. *The Fireside Book of Boxing*. New York: Simon and Schuster.

Hobsbawm, Eric and Ranger, Terence (eds). 1983. *The Invention of Tradition*. Cambridge: Cambridge University Press.

Johnson, Christopher. 1995. "Anti-Pugilism: Violence and Justice in Scott's 'The Two Drovers'" in *Scottish Literary Journal* 22(1): 46-60.

—. 1996. "British Championism: Early Pugilism and the Works of Fielding" in *Review of English Studies* 47(187): 331-51.

Kennedy, A.L. 1999. *On Bullfighting*. London: Yellow Jersey Press.

McIlvanney, Hugh. 1982. *McIlvanney on Boxing*. London: Stanley Paul.

McIlvanney, William. 1986. *The Big Man*. London: Sceptre.

Mailer, Norman. 1964. *The Presidential Papers*. London: Andre Deutsch.

—. 1968. *The Armies of the Night*. Harmondsworth: Penguin.

Morgan, Edwin. 1995. "A Scottish Trawl" in Whyte, Christopher (ed.) *Gendering the Nation: Essays in Modern Scottish Literature*. Edinburgh: Edinburgh University Press. 205-22.

Munro, Michael. 2001. *The Patter*. Edinburgh: Berlinn.

Nairn, Tom. 1977. *The Break-Up of Britain: Crisis and Neo-Nationalism*. London: New Left Books.

Oates, Joyce Carol. 1988. *On Boxing*. London: Pan Books.

Odd, Gilbert E. 1948. *Ring Battles of the Century*. London: Nicholson and Watson.

Scott, Walter. 1990. "The Two Drovers". Pontypridd: Biddulph.

Sklar, Robert. 1992. *City Boys: Cagney, Bogart, Garfield*. Princeton: Princeton University Press.

"Persuade without convincing … represent without reasoning": the Inferiorist Mythology of the Scots Language

Gavin Miller

Franz Fanon's concept of "inferiorism" has an application beyond Scottish intellectual life. Scots-language poetry (and criticism) are caught up in inferiorist binary thinking. The Scots speaker or writer supposedly possesses a magical language which communicates through direct sound-sense connections. This linguistic mythology merely continues the familiar colonial opposition between English intellectualism and Scots sensuality.
Keywords: Craig Beveridge, Ronald Turnbull, Derrick McClure, Franz Fanon, Alfred Adler, Hugh MacDiarmid, inferiorism, Scots poetry, phonaesthesia.

In *The Eclipse of Scottish Culture*, Craig Beveridge and Ronald Turnbull bring to bear upon contemporary Scotland a post-colonial analysis in which the terms "inferiorism" and "inferiorisation" are central:

we rely on the concept of inferiorisation, which was developed by Frantz Fanon in his account of the psycho-cultural dimensions of national subordination in the Third World. Fanon argues that the native comes to internalise the message that local customs are inferior to the culture of the coloniser. (Beveridge and Turnbull 1989: 1)

Beveridge and Turnbull argue that, in a Scottish context,

inferiorism is then expressed […] in the adoption of discourses which portray Scotland as a dark and backward corner of the land, and in the severe distrust of Scottish traditions and precedents displayed by the intellectuals. (Fanon 1986: 30)

For Beveridge and Turnbull, this distrust is due to the transformation of Scottish universities during the nineteenth and twentieth centuries by English institutional practices. The generalist approach (later identified by George Davie in *The Democratic Intellect*) was consequently replaced by a technocratic approach hostile to the philosophical investigation of first principles.

Beveridge and Turnbull convincingly refute the notion that
Scotland was enlightened only by an increasing union with England.
Their analysis of inferiorisation, however, is primarily political and
institutional. Fanon's theory, though, is directly concerned with the
psyche of the colonised: "What I want to do", says Fanon, "is to help
the black man to free himself of the arsenal of complexes that has
been developed by the colonial environment" (Fanon 1986: 30). He
believes that, for "every people in whose soul an inferiority complex
has been created by the death and burial of its local cultural original-
ity" (Fanon 1986: 42), there arises "that feeling of inferiority or that
Adlerian exaltation, that overcompensation, which seem to be the in-
dices of the black *Weltanschauung*" (Fanon 1986: 42). In this essay, I
argue that a fuller comprehension of the term "inferiorism" is useful to
the analysis of Scottish culture. In particular, I contend that the discourse which surrounds and pervades Scots-language poetry espouses
the inferiorist idea that Scots is a naturally expressive primitive dialect
of English.

Fanon's term refers directly to the psychiatrist Alfred Adler's
notion of an "inferiority complex" in the psyche of an individual.
Those who use this concept – or its derivatives – may assume that it
refers to a soul plagued by a sense of inadequacy and worthlessness.
In fact, though, the possessor of an inferiority complex leads an inner
life based around a rigid conviction of his own (eventual) superiority.
Adler's central argument (which would later be picked up in Jacques
Lacan's account of the "mirror stage") is that, in order to withstand
the anxieties of childhood, the individual

can only obtain security by striving towards a fixed point where he sees himself
greater and stronger, where he finds himself rid of the helplessness of infancy. The
symbolic and logical nature of our process of thinking permits the construction of this
future changed personality in the image of the father, the mother, of an elder brother
or sister, or teacher or some professional man, or hero, or animal or God. (Adler 1918:
53)

For a perfect individual, this self-ideal would have no harmful im-
pingement on waking life:

His uncertainty is sufficient to make him set up a fantastic goal for the purpose of
orientation in the world, but it is not so great as to make him deprive reality of its

value and to assert dogmatically the reality of this guiding model, as is the case in the psychoses. (Adler 1918: 54)

However, the less confident the individual, the more he is possessed by this fiction: "the neurotic keeps before his eye his God, his idol, his ideal of personality and clings to his guiding principle, losing sight in the meanwhile of reality" (Adler 1918: 66). Furthermore, the more marked this imaginary life, the greater the tendency to binary modes of thinking: "the neurotic [...] holds the possibilities of experience constantly before him arranged dogmatically and in sharply antithetical groups according to the Scheme 'Triumph – Defeat'" (Adler 1918: 86). This may, for example, be expressed in the "'antithesis' of 'man-woman' so that the feeling of inferiority, uncertainty, lowliness, effeminacy, falls on one side of the table, the antithesis of certainty, superiority, self-esteem, manliness, on the other" (Adler 1918: 99).

Adler's theory provides a useful way for Fanon to explain the mentality of the coloniser. The colonial attitude of superiority, the sharp distinction between white and black, and the myths which stubbornly surround this relationship, extend an everyday neurotic attitude which now takes "race" as its material. To the "white", the "black" therefore exists on the same side as that which is alien to the guiding fiction of omnipotence: "For the white man The Other is perceived on the level of the body image, absolutely as the not-self – that is, the unidentifiable, the unassimilable" (Fanon 1986: 161). The imaginary Negro superimposed upon the real coloured person is a projection of the inner needs which threaten the coloniser's ego-ideal:

The civilized white man retains an irrational longing for unusual eras of sexual license, of orgiastic scenes, of unpunished rapes, of unrepressed incest. [...] Projecting his own desires onto the Negro, the white man behaves "as if" the Negro really had them [...]. The Negro is fixated at the genital; or at any rate he has been fixated there. (Fanon 1986: 165)

Fanon's ultimate aim, though, is to explain the mentality of the colonised. To his Adlerian basis he therefore adds an argument from Sartre to explain their psychic condition. Sartre implicates emotions in our existence for others: "It is shame or pride which reveals to me the Other's look and myself at the end of that look. It is the shame or

pride which makes me *live*, not *know* the situation of being looked at"
(Sartre 1957: 261). The neurotic gaze of the coloniser, for Fanon,
therefore has a profound effect upon the colonised, whose "inferiority
comes into being through the other" (Fanon 1986: 110) via the cry
"'Dirty nigger'. Or simply 'Look, a Negro!'" (Fanon 1986: 109).
Fanon describes his own experience of being submerged by this
imaginary symbolism, of having "to wear the livery that the white
man has sewed for him" (Fanon 1986: 34): "I discovered my blackness, my ethnic characteristics; and I was battered down by tom-toms,
cannibalism, intellectual deficiency, fetichism [*sic*], [and] racial
defects" (Fanon 1986: 112). This encounter explains why "a normal
Negro child, having grown up within a normal family, will become
abnormal on the slightest contact with the white world" (Fanon 1986:
143).

Fanon further recognises that speech as well as appearance is an
instance of such contact. The colonial encounter with the native dialect is far different from that with a non-inferiorised group:

> I meet a Russian or a German who speaks French badly. With gestures I try to
> give him the information that he requests, but at the same time I can hardly forget that
> he has a language of his own, a country, and that perhaps he is a lawyer or an engineer
> [...].
>   When it comes to the case of the Negro, nothing of the kind. He has no culture,
> no civilization, no "long historical past". (Fanon 1986: 34)

The application to Scottish culture of Fanon's theory of the vocal encounter may therefore seem self-evident. Scottish literature is pep-
pered with scenes where Scottish children are convinced of their
innate stupidity by a sadistic schoolmaster who detests their dialect.
Here is a typical example from Alasdair Gray's *1982 Janine*:

> "The antonym of *blunt*, Anderson, is not *jaggy*. The antonym of *blunt* is *sharp*. You
> have heard the word *sharp* before? Of course you have. So your employment of local
> slang is either a conscious or unconscious effort to destroy communication between
> the provinces of a once mighty empire. Are you a linguistic saboteur or are you an
> idiot?" (Gray 1984: 83-84)

What value can there be, then, in bringing Fanon to bear upon a
culture which seems already to understand the colonial dimensions of

the suppression of dialect? We must remember, though, that the real mark of an inferiority complex is a secret conviction of superiority. The normal response of the colonised is to copy the inferiority complex of the coloniser – Fanon observes this, for example, in the desire to be white. An alternative response is to assert the advantages of the imaginary Negro identity:

> I had rationalized the world and the world had rejected me on the basis of color prejudice. Since no agreement was possible on the level of reason, I threw myself back towards unreason. […] Out of the necessities of my struggle I had chosen the method of regression. (Fanon 1986: 123)

"Yes", exclaims Fanon ironically, "we are – we Negroes – backward, simple, free in our behavior" (Fanon 1986: 126). This attitude is one of secret superiority to the colonial master:

> The soul of the white man was corrupted, and, as I was told by a friend who was a teacher in the United States, "The presence of the Negroes beside the whites is in a way an insurance policy on humanness. When the whites feel they have become too mechanized, they turn to the men of color and ask them for a little human sustenance." (Fanon 1986: 129)

There exists an analogous position in Scottish culture. In his pamphlet, *Why Scots Matters*, the linguist J. Derrick McClure, a respected expert on the Scots language, argues (quite reasonably) against the idea that Scots is a dialect naturally inferior to Standard English. Yet, there is also in his work a curious strand of argument which asserts the *superiority* of the Scots language. Standard English is inferior to Scots because the former is the language of public life:

> the [English] language, in its spoken and written forms, is increasingly limited to its simplest, least imaginative and least challenging registers. Its utilitarian use as a language of technology, commerce, tourism and mass entertainment has undermined its status as a vehicle for work of literary and intellectual distinction. (McClure 1988: 59)

On the other hand, argues McClure, there is in Scots a "vitality" which could potentially "exert a beneficial influence on the entire English-speaking world" (McClure 1988: 60). He hints as to the nature of this vigour when he asserts that "Scots exploits the possibilities of phonaesthetic expression (i.e. the emotive power of the actual *sounds* of the words) to an extent that has no parallel in Western European languages" (McClure 1988: 54-55). This assumed direct relation between sound and meaning, for McClure, means that Scots is a "most onomatopoeic of languages [which] speaks for itself in accents that can appeal to the ear of anybody not suffering from the self-inflicted deafness of prejudice" (McClure 1988: 56). To McClure, Scots is a linguistic resource opposed to the humdrum technical rationality of the Anglo-Saxons. Like Fanon's "simple, free" Negro, McClure's Scotsman offers, via a specially emotive and imitative language, another kind of "insurance policy on humanness".

This account of the Scots language as "phonaesthetic", McClure notes in a later work, *Language, Poetry, and Nationhood*, is central to the Scots Renaissance. In the work of MacDiarmid, for example,

even rare and obsolete words spring to a vibrant new life in his poems. No doubt readers who are prepared to take the trouble to discover their meanings will arrive at a clearer appreciation of the poems than those who are not; but a passage in *Gairmscoile* expresses the clear realisation that even readers who have not the words in their own active or passive vocabularies can share his imaginative response:

It's soon', no' sense, that faddoms the herts o' men,
And by my sangs the rouch auld Scots I ken
E'en herts that ha'e nae Scots'll dirl thro'
As nocht else could – for here's a language rings
Wi' datchie sesames, and names for nameless things. (McClure 2000: 93)

For MacDiarmid and McClure, to read Scots poetry it is only minimally necessary to have a previous knowledge of the meanings of the words – the miraculous phonaesthetic power of Scots is sufficient to fill in the gaps.

However, a brief consideration of the passage from MacDiarmid undermines the idea that our comprehension relies on phonaesthesia. Firstly, this passage uses apostrophes to show the English orthography for a word that, on sound alone, might prove confusing in English. The apostrophe in "soon'", for example, reminds us that the English equivalent is "sound". Furthermore, many other seemingly unfamiliar words involve only minor and predictable differences from Standard English – thus "rouch" instead of "rough". Even those words which are completely different are quite easy to understand. Take, for example, "datchie" which, for this reader, was quite unknown before reading the poem. From the form and position of this word, it may be inferred that it is probably an adjective, and that, from context, it probably means something like "apt", or "fitting". Consultation of Jamieson's *Dictionary of the Scottish Language*, which provides MacDiarmid with so many of his words, produces the following:

DATCHIE, *adj.* 1. Penetrating; applied to intellectual power, Ayrs.
2. Sly, cunning, […].
3. Hidden, secret. (Jamieson 1880, 2: 19)

The phrase "datchie sesames" implies a direct, if occult, relation between the Scots language and the world. The process by which we interpret this phrase, however, is anything but magical.

MacDiarmid's work is, in fact, very similar to Victorian nonsense poetry. Consider this passage from Lewis Carroll's "Jabberwocky":

The Jabberwock, with eyes of flame,
Came whiffling through the tulgey wood,
And burbled as it came!

One, two! One, two! And through and through
The vorpal blade went snicker-snack!
He left it dead, and with its head
He went galumphing back.

"And hast thou slain the Jabberwock?
Come to my arms, my beamish boy!
O frabjous day! Callooh! Callay!" (Carroll 1982: 142)

Some words – "burbled", "snicker-snack" – are indeed onomatopoeic. Words such as "beamish" and "frabjous" we know by their form and position to be adjectives, and clearly positive in tone. Others, such as "vorpal" and "tulgey" we give a meaning from context: a "vorpal" blade must be sharp if it can sever the Jabberwocky's head, and a "tulgey" wood is unlikely to be a happy glade if it is home to a monster with eyes of flame.

To compare MacDiarmid with Carroll is useful because there are no oppressed speakers of Looking-Glass English intent on asserting the mystical vitality of their tongue. We understand that Carroll's verse, like that of MacDiarmid, simply forces the reader to intensify his or her usual hermeneutic strategies. When faced with puzzling elements in a text which is understood as a whole, we look for clues which can help us make sense of these individual parts. What can we tell from the position and form of the unknown words? What is their general sense from the context? Are there any etymological clues? Is there any possibility of onomatopoeia? We certain need not conclude that comprehension of Carroll and MacDiarmid relies upon a language of direct sound-sense connections which magically resonate through the mind.

This, however, is exactly what McClure appears to assume in relation to the Scots language. He declares, for example, that "there are a number of Scots words which convey the physical or emotional force of an event more powerfully than any English words could (*gralloch, dwam, fuff, breinge, blinter*)" (McClure 2000: 203). This leads him to complain that the poet Tom Hubbard's Scots, "despite its virtues, is not intoxicating"; there is "an ominous hint [...] of an English underlay" (McClure 2000: 201). For McClure, the aim of poetry, to which Scots is supposedly most effective, and which the use of English vitiates, is to convey sensory and imaginative experience as vividly and directly as possible. He prefers the work of Harvey Holton because "to a much greater extent than Hubbard [...] he uses words not only as units in the expression of a sequence of thoughts but for their phonaesthetic and sensory power as individual elements" (McClure 2000: 201).

"Phonaesthesia", though, is a far more obscure phenomenon than onomatopoeia. Here is a standard dictionary definition (with, happily, another reference to "Jabberwocky"): phonaesthesia (or "synaesthesia") is "a direct association between the form and the meaning of language. For example, the *sl-* sound combination is often felt to express unpleasantness (cf. *slimy, slither,* etc., – and Lewis Carroll's *slithy*)" (Crystal 1997: 375). Yet, apart from clear instances of onomatopoeia, such sound-sense connections are unlikely to be in any way imitative or iconic. As C.L. Barber argues, in English we find initial *fl-* in a number of words connected with fire and light (eg. *flame, flare, flash*) and in an even larger number of words connected with a flying or waving kind of motion (e.g. *flail, flap, flaunt, flay, flicker, flog, fluctuate, flurry, flutter*). But it is difficult to see any *inherent* appropriateness in the *fl-* sound for expressing ideas of flame or flickering motion: the sense of appropriateness surely arises from the fact that it occurs in all these words, not vice versa. And once a group of words like this exists in the language, new words may be coined on the same model (as perhaps happened with *flash* and *flap*), and words of similar form may develop new meanings on analogy with the members of the group (as perhaps has happened with *flourish*). (Barber 1972: 28-29)

Phonaesthesia would seem, at best, to allow us some capacity to create neologisms which may be understood by their similarity to existing (but contingent) associations. Outside of a few familiar correlations, though, phonaesthesia has no real existence. This may explain why McClure's perceptions of phonaesthesia seem more than a little fanciful. He remarks, for example, on a line from Hubbard: "'I am o grugous gyres the gurliest', where clearly the excessive emphasis on [g] is designed to emphasise the grotesque quality of the image" (McClure 2000: 198). This phonaesthetic association of [g] with the "grotesque" seems rather unlikely – compare Tony, the grinning cartoon tiger, whose groovy growl announces that the breakfast cereal Kellog's *Frosties* are "grrrrrrreat!".

McClure portrays Scots as a magical language which is directly connected to the world of things, feelings, and actions – a language in which one can directly hear meaning. In so doing, he grafts the technical discourse of linguistics into the realm of imaginary Scots-English binaries. This is perfectly clear in his discussion of the work of Robert Crawford:

A trick unique to him of printing some poems with facing-page English prose translations (after the manner of many contemporary Gaelic poets) has complex implications. On the most obvious level, it underwrites the status of Scots and English as mutually foreign languages: for monolingual Anglophones, the suggestion is, even a glossary would not give access to a full understanding of Crawford's poetry. It also has the more unexpected effect of undercutting English as a medium for imaginative literary expression. (McClure 2000: 209)

That the language of Shakespeare, Milton, Eliot, and Auden (amongst others) should be so innately unsuited to poetry seems extraordinary.

A more impartial commentator might think that the facing-page English "translation" is simply a piece of clumsy English prose. Here is an example from Crawford's "The Herr-Knit Bunnett":

> I grope in the dark like a cloud among high mountains, attempting the trial of strength in trying to raise the heavy caber of Scotland: utter worldliness, stubbornness, ingrained devils, abortionists' plants that kill the foetus in the womb are just severe passing showers as far as God is concerned. (Crawford and Herbert 1990: 85)

McClure's true agenda appears in his subsequent commentary on the Scots original:

> If this passage is compared with the English version, the combination of over-inflated rhetoric and flaccid sentence-construction of the latter reveals, ironically, the futility of trying to express the same idea in English: the semantic conciseness and rhythmic control achieved by the use of richly-loaded Scots words is essential if the thought is to be expressed with any degree of force. (McClure 2000: 210)

McClure's remarks convert language into a metaphor for the secret superiority of the sensual Scot over the cerebral Englishman. The language of the latter is both "over-inflated" and "flaccid" – a reflection, no doubt, of his flatulence and impotence.

In the poetic tradition started by MacDiarmid, continued by Crawford, and analysed by McClure, the discourse of the Scot is presented as inherently vivid, forceful, emotive, vigorous and embodied – as an antidote, in short, to the supposed intellectual detachment of the English. Yet what seems to be an act of resistance to English cultural domination is little more than acquiescence in the imaginary binaries of inferiorism. The colonisers have already declared themselves to be rational, thoughtful, and cultured, in opposition to the colonised who are irrational, passionate, and primitive. Beveridge and Turnbull draw up a list of such binarisms, where we find that Scotland is "dark", "backwards", "fanatical" and "violent", whereas England is "enlightened", "advanced", "reasonable" and "decent" (Beveridge and Turnbull 1989: 7). The discourse surrounding Scots-language poetry employs such binary thinking, but simply valorises the attributes assigned to the Scots. They are not dark, backward, fanatical, and violent; they are sensual, emotional, impassioned and vigorous. These latter characteristics are readily apparent in their language, an especially expressive and imitative tongue which reflects their immediate engagement with feeling and reality.

Such myths are by no means confined to discussions of the Scots language. Rousseau advances this kind of argument in his *Essay on the Origin of Languages*. A primitive language, Rousseau tells us, would entirely bypass rational thought: "It would persuade without convincing, and would represent without reasoning" (Rousseau 1966: 15). Poetry, supposes Rousseau, preserves the original phonaesthetic properties of such a language:

For moving a young heart, or repelling an unjust aggressor, nature dictates accents, cries, lamentations, [...] and that is why the first languages were singable and passionate before they became simple and methodical. (Rousseau 1966: 12)

For Rousseau, it is axiomatic that the strange tongues of the East are primitive languages:

The genesis of oriental languages, the oldest known, absolutely refutes the assumption of a didactic progression in their development. These languages are not at all systematic or rational. They are vital and figurative. The language of the first men is represented to us as the tongues of geometers, but we see that they were the tongues of poets. (Rousseau 1966: 11)

Vital, figurative, passionate, unreasoning: these are much the characteristics which Scotland has internalised as peculiar to its own dialect of English. In this mythology, the Scots are everyday poets whose primitive national language is both alien and superior to the rational discourse of their Southern neighbours. For McClure, this language was supposedly rediscovered by that "Scots Renaissance [which] is still in vigorous life" (McClure 2000: 197); it was formerly arrayed amongst "the vast magical powers wielded by poets in the ancient Celtic world – to which, of course, contemporary Scotland is linked by direct descent" (McClure 2000: 198).

Such an ideology invites immunity from rational accountability. The true Scot, we are told, employs a language which projects sense and feeling into words – a musical language which dispenses with concepts, and instead directly conveys the immediacy of life via a synaesthetic expression of outer reality and inner feeling. Such a language implies a form of life in which, as Rousseau rightly indicates, the world is only represented, never analysed, and in which conviction proceeds from persuasion, not argument. The capacity to abstract, speculate, and hypothesise is absent. A person who employed this kind of language (were it indeed to exist) would move in a closed world where thought could have no purchase upon immediate "gut" certainties. This worldview contrasts with that of the rational man, who, as Sartre reminds us,

groans as he gropes for the truth; he know that his reasoning is no more than tentative, that other considerations may supervene to cast doubt on it. He never sees clearly where he is going; he is "open", he may even appear to be hesitant. But there are people who are attracted by the durability of a stone. They wish to be massive and impenetrable; they wish not to change. Where, indeed, would change take them? (Sartre 1948: 18-19)

If Scotland is to change, then it must abandon its inferiorist ideas about its own language – in particular, the myth which insists that the truest Scot is one incapable of rational thought.

A comprehensive debunking of the inferiorist mythology which surrounds Scots would require a much longer and more thorough investigation. In particular, it would be necessary to gather a larger body of material on the Scots language and its alleged powers. Furthermore, a thorough analysis of phonaesthesia would be required in order to define and explain this rather shadowy phenomenon. Nonetheless, this chapter can at least challenge the complacency within Scottish studies over the status of the Scots language. In their eagerness to throw off the myth of Scots as substandard, broken English, Scottish writers and critics have tended to substitute a new, and equally inferiorist, mythology – that of Scots as a primitive language which is naturally expressive of feelings, and naturally imitative of things.

Bibliography

Adler, Alfred. 1918. *The Neurotic Constitution: Outlines of a Comparative Individualistic Psychology and Psychotherapy* (tr. Bernard Glueck and John E. Lind). London: Kegan Paul, Trench, Trubner, and co.

Barber, C.L. 1972. *The Story of Language*. London: Pan.

Beveridge, Craig and Ronald Turnbull. 1989. *The Eclipse of Scottish Culture: Inferiorism and the Intellectuals*. Edinburgh: Polygon.

Carroll, Lewis. 1982. "Jabberwocky" in *Through The Looking-Glass* in *The Penguin Complete Lewis Carroll*. Harmondsworth, Middlesex: Penguin. 140-42.

Crawford, Robert and W.N. Herbert. 1990. *Sharawaggi: Poems in Scots*. Edinburgh: Polygon.

Crystal, David (ed.). 1997. *A Dictionary of Linguistics and Phonetics*. Oxford, England and Cambridge, Mass.: Blackwell.

Fanon, Frantz. 1986. *Black Skins, White Masks* (tr. Charles Lam Markmann). London: Pluto.

Gray, Alasdair. 1984. *1982 Janine*. London: Jonathan Cape.

Jamieson, John (ed.). 1880. *An Etymological Dictionary of The Scottish Language*. 4 vols. Paisley: Alexander Gardner.

McClure, J. Derrick. 1988. *Why Scots Matters*. Edinburgh: Saltire Society in association with The Scots Language Society.

—. 2000. *Language, Poetry and Nationhood: Scots as a Poetic language from 1878 to the Present*. East Linton, Scotland: Tuckwell.

Rousseau, Jean-Jacques. 1966. *Essay on the Origin of Languages which treats of Melody and Musical Imitation* in *On the Origin of Language* (tr. John H. Moran). Chicago and London: University of Chicago. 1-74.

Sartre, Jean-Paul. 1948. *Anti-Semite and Jew* (tr. George J. Becker). New York: Schocken.

—. 1957. *Being and Nothingness* (tr. Hazel E. Barnes). London: Methuen.

Philosophy, Tradition, Nation

Laurence Nicoll

Beveridge and Turnbull's *Eclipse of Scottish Culture* prescribes a particular identity to philosophy conducted in Scotland. Not only does this stipulation restrict individual cultural and intellectual freedom, it also mistakenly assumes that there can be radically distinct national traditions of philosophy. Like the terms "Anglo-American" and "Continental" philosophy, "Scottish philosophy" is merely a projection of political geography onto intellectual life.
Keywords: Craig Beveridge, Ronald Turnbull, George Davie, Alasdair MacIntyre, John Haldane, inferiorism, democratic intellect, Scottish philosophy.

In both *The Eclipse of Scottish Culture* and *Scotland After Enlightenment*, Craig Beveridge and Ronald Turnbull engage with and expand substantially upon those issues and themes familiar from George Davie's influential thesis, *The Democratic Intellect*. Beveridge and Turnbull adopt Davie's apocalyptic vocabulary of cultural crisis and intellectual collapse, and they follow Davie too in advancing an impassioned argument that should philosophy recover and re-occupy its former position of pedagogical centrality. There is much in both books to elicit sympathy and at times easy agreement – in particular the resistance to the conversion of tertiary education into a form of professional training, whereby universities merely become vocational kindergärten, preparing students, "customers", for the needs of the business world. So too with the attempt to recuperate philosophy, a discipline and practice fundamentally inimical to the kind of thinking which equates value with a crass notion of graduate employability. However, there are a number of difficulties in their position and it is to these difficulties that I wish to attend. Here I want to argue that a number of problems are engendered by Beveridge and Turnbull's reliance upon a framework, a premise, that is not itself argued for – nation – and that their unquestioned acceptance of a necessary connection between nation and culture, together with the use to which this is put, reveals and results in a number of confusions. This in turn affects, or constricts, their reading of philosophy, of what counts as tradition, and has, as its tacit consequence, a presumably unintentional replication of the colonising processes that they rightly seek to eliminate.

In *The Eclipse of Scottish Culture*, Turnbull and Beveridge aim to "analyse cultural oppression in the Scottish context" and to do so, they rely upon Fanon's concept of "inferiorisation":

Fanon argues that the native comes to internalise the message that local customs are inferior to the culture of the coloniser, a theme which runs through cultural production in the colony [...] The inferiorist reflex is also expressed in an inability to respond to Scottish practices which are not sanctioned by metropolitan culture. The fate of Scottish approaches to philosophy is viewed as a consequence of this paralysis. (Beveridge and Turnbull 1989: 1-2)

Philosophy in particular is seen as a matter of considerable cultural importance as it becomes both an index and a prominent site of a fundamental cultural contest. Native, that is "Scottish", intellectual and philosophical practice has been effaced, discarded and usurped by what Beveridge and Turnbull term "English" thought-models:

English intellectual life is expressed in and moulded by a specialist and empiricist philosophical tradition; the establishment of the English approach to philosophical studies in Scottish universities is therefore a significant modality of English cultural power. (Beveridge and Turnbull 1989: 3)

Philosophy departments in Scottish universities have become mere outposts of Anglo-American philosophy; and our intelligentsia seem entirely ignorant of Scottish philosophers who have resisted the specialising tendencies of this tradition, its break with philosophy in the Continental style, and its retreat to concern with issues remote from social and political life. A central task of cultural nationalism is the recovery of Scottish cultural practices (like those native philosophical traditions) which have been submerged by the intelligentsia's adoption of English cultural modes. (Beveridge and Turnbull 1989: 15)

Discard for a moment the hint of question-begging (they assume that Scotland is intellectually oppressed and then look for the evidence), discard the implication of the locution "cultural production" (does this not work against the idea of tradition as a passing on?), discard too the question of whether or not Fanon's model is adequate or appropriate in a "Scottish context" (surely part of the colonial process that Fanon seeks to diagnose and combat is based upon the perceived superiority and inferiority attaching to crude notions of "race" and skin colour rather than simply intellectual practice). Consider, instead, what these passages rely upon and set into play. Firstly, philosophy and nationality are somehow conjoined; secondly, "Scottish" philosophy and "English" philosophy are both clearly distinguishable and fundamentally inimical; and, thirdly, unlike "Scottish" philosophy, "English" philosophy is insensitive to, and dismissive of, "Continental" philosophy. Let us treat these issues in order.

1. Philosophy and Nationality

In their book, *Scotland After Enlightenment*, Beveridge and Turnbull make considerable use of the position advanced by Alasdair MacIntyre in *Whose Justice? Which Rationality?* Here, MacIntyre proposes that the continuity of Scottish thought "in which the fundamental concerns of philosophy, Scots Law, and Presbyterian theology [are] inseparable" is subverted – "Anglicised" – by the philosophy of David Hume. For MacIntyre, Hume

consistently discarded everything distinctively Scottish in matters of intellectual attitude and belief, while with equal consistency he retained and developed the warmest personal ties with his family, with early friends, and with a variety of figures prominent in Scottish life. His published work presented a series of the profoundest challenges to and ruptures with the fundamental convictions which had been embodied in the dominant Scottish tradition. (MacIntyre 1988: 281)

However, as Cairns Craig points out in *The Modern Scottish Novel*, there are three principal difficulties with MacIntyre's account of philosophy and its relation to both culture and tradition within Scotland. Firstly, in the quotation above the use of "dominant" seems to be indicative of other traditions, but of these the reader is left unaware, for MacIntyre does not examine or discuss any rival, antecedent, or contemporaneous thought-models. Through this occlusion, Scottish philosophy is collapsed into a single monolithic tradition: the indefinite article "a", becomes the definite article "the" (and though Craig does not say this, a similar charge, *mutatis mutandis*, may be levelled at George Davie). Craig's second point is that MacIntyre's depiction of Hume's philosophy as an embodiment and representation of *English* values is, by MacIntyre's own account, mistaken. Surprisingly, for a thinker whom Craig rightly identifies as "residually marxist", MacIntyre fails to note that what Hume actually adopts is a set of *class* values. Craig argues that these class values are not simply English, but the product of a cultural commingling produced by and productive of a nascent "Britishness":

The property values of the upper classes which, if MacIntyre is right, are at the centre of Hume's moral philosophy are thus the expression not of Hume's commitment to English culture but of his commitment to the new British culture which, at this early stage in its formation, was only beginning to develop a language in which to express itself. (Craig 1999: 28)

Concomitantly, and this is Craig's last point, anglicising is not a state but a process, and moreover a process only possible within a culture that is *not yet* English: anglicising is a form of becoming which operates *within* Scottish culture (contrast this with Beveridge and Turnbull who treat anglicising as an *externally* imposed quasi-imperial act). Through these criticisms, Craig identifies a paradox at the core of MacIntyre's account of Scottish thought: "having provided the tools by which it is possible to identify and valorise the significance of Scottish tradition, he then negates the tradition by denying that its greatest mind has any place within it" (Craig 1999: 27). So, in accepting MacIntyre's version of Hume, the authors who excoriate T.C. Smout for failing to sufficiently valorise James Clerk Maxwell, opt to relegate a philosopher routinely described as not simply the finest mind Scotland has produced, but the finest philosophical mind in the English language and cast him instead as a progenitor of "the now culturally hegemonic discourse of management and marketing" (Beveridge and Turbull 1997: 110). Seen in these terms, MacIntyre, and by implication Turnbull and Beveridge, proffer a mutation of the no-true-Scotsman argument. Scottish philosophy, so the argument goes, is composed of certain identifiable features and all and only all of Scottish philosophers display these qualities. Thus, to the critic who replies, "But Hume is a Scottish philosopher and he does not display these properties," the reply comes "He is not a *true* Scottish philosopher."

It is possible to augment Craig's argument, for Hume's philosophy is a *critical* philosophy – to the point of self-criticism – and therefore one which cannot merely accept the ready-made tradition(s) in which it finds itself. In a letter held in the National Library of Scotland, Hume points to independent and wide-ranging post-university study as the basis of his critical thought:

As our College Education in Scotland, extending little further than the Languages, ends commonly when we are about 14 or 15 Years of Age, I was after that left to my own Choice in my Reading, & found it to incline me almost equally to Books of Reasoning & Philosophy, & to Poetry & the Polite Authors. [...] Upon examination of these, I found a certain Boldness of Temper, growing in me, which was not enclin'd to submit to any Authority in these subjects, but led me to seek out some new Medium, by which Truth might be establisht. (Cited in Norton 1993: 346)

The traditions and authorities against which this thought is directed are not then simply Scottish, they are philosophical, for Hume is as much concerned with identifying and overcoming the problems within (putatively) foundational Cartesian/Rationalist epistemologies as he is with overturning or developing the thought of any "Scottish" thinker, such as the Irishman Hutcheson. Those readers of Hume who seek to align or consign his thought to a single tradition ought to bear in mind David Fate Norton's admonition:

no single writer or philosophical tradition can be relied upon to provide a comprehensive key to [Hume's] thought. Readers of Hume should be wary of those commentators who engage in the kind of historical reductivism that claims to unlock the secrets of Hume's thought by reference to one or two authors or one intellectual tradition. (Norton 1993: 3)

It can also be argued that Hume is merely being consistent with his own ontology. The Humean conception of personal identity, the bundle theory, would seem to suggest that there is no essential self which can be either Scottish, English, nor indeed anglicised, for there is no enduring property, no enduring self across time, to which such predicates can be permanently and securely attached (Hume 1978: 252). However, crucially, even were we to accept MacIntyre's account, it is surely not Hume's putative Englishness that is problematic. Rather, the problem is with the philosophical approach which Englishness purportedly represents. So, we might ask what *philosophical* work is "English" doing here? For presumably, MacIntyre wants to argue against a morality based upon individual property-rights simply because it is a morality based upon individual property-rights rather than because it is, contingently, the morality of the English, or as Craig has it, the British, upper-classes.

With this last point we arrive at an equivocation, one which becomes perspicuous in Beveridge and Turnbull. For in both their books, there is a tendency to conflate the proposition, *p* and *q*, with the proposition, if *p*, therefore *q*, that is, to conflate: (1) *X* is a valuable method of philosophical practice *and* it is "Scottish" with (2) *X* is a valuable method of philosophical enquiry *because* it is "Scottish". The first is acceptable but contains a component which is philosophically trivial; the second merely an instance of prejudice. In the first proposition, the phrase "and it is Scottish" does not impact upon the philosophical validity of "is a valuable method of philosophical practice" – it is simply a secondary fact. Therefore, Hume's "Scottishness", "Englishness", or lack thereof impinges not a whit on the status of his philosophy *qua* philosophy, anymore than the colour or country of origin of my car impinges upon its ability to negotiate a steep gradient. Even if, *pace* MacIntyre, Hume adopted a certain conception of philosophy because it happened to be (contingently) popular with the (contingent) cultural dominance of England/Britain, then this is simply a socio-economic, or worse, a psychological epiphenomenon. It says precisely nothing about the *philosophical* value of Hume's metaphysics, his view of personal identity or his conception of morality, just as Beveridge and Turnbull identifying linguistic analysis as an "Oxbridge" method of philosophical inquiry neither adds to nor subtracts from the value of this practice.

The principal difficulty here is that Turnbull and Beveridge attach philosophy to nationality in some mystical, mystifying quasi-Hegelian way – a way through which philosophy becomes both an expression of national culture and something that is expressed by national culture. This leads them to the conclusion that to adopt or reject a particular philosophy is to somehow adopt or reject a particular national identity. But, as Allan Bloom writes:

Greek and French philosophy were universalistic in intention and fact. They appealed
to the use of a faculty potentially possessed by all men everywhere at all times. The
proper noun in *Greek* philosophy is only an inessential tag, as it is in *French*
Enlightenment. (The same is true of *Italian* Renaissance, a rebirth that is proof of the
accidental character of nations and of the universality of Greek thinkers.) The good
life and just regime they taught knew no limits of race, nation, religion or climate.
This relation of man to man was the very definition of philosophy. We are aware of
this when we speak of science, and no one seriously talks of German, Italian or
English physics. (Bloom 1988: 153)

This last sentence is not strictly accurate for of course, the Nobel
Laureate Phillip Lenard supported Hitler's claim to save German
universities from "un-German" science (quantum theory and
relativity) but Bloom's central point – that "Greek" thinkers did not
conceive themselves as doing "Greek" philosophy – is what is
valuable here. So, whilst we might want to agree with Beveridge and
Turnbull that philosophy is of considerable cultural importance, this
tells us nothing about *philosophical* importance. For what is
philosophically important is, simply, philosophical efficacy, and
philosophical efficacy is determined by the analysis, the testing, the
proposing, the revising of philosophical arguments. The efficacy and
value of a particular philosophy cannot be tested by, as it were,
examining the passport of its proponent: Aristotle is not a profound
thinker because he is "Greek". Similarly, the limitations, and there are
many, of logical positivism do not proceed from A.J. Ayer's
"Englishness" (an ascription that is, incidentally, factually inaccurate
given that he was half Dutch/Jewish, half French/Swiss), but from the
problems obtaining within logical positivism. These problems only
become apparent through analysis of the proffered arguments.

Furthermore, by attempting to render philosophy an essential
aspect of nation, Beveridge and Turnbull simply fail to see, or fail to
accept, that within any given country, any given community, any
given university, an individual or a group of individuals might adopt a
particular conception of philosophical enquiry purely because it is felt,
or more likely reasoned, to be a better conceptual or explanatory tool
or to offer a more convincing depiction of the good life. Instead, they
suggest that if an "English" thought-model is adopted then this is an
instance of "cultural colonialism" (Beveridge and Turnbull 1989: 41);
if a "Continental" thought-model is adopted then this is an example of

fruitful conversation and mutually enriching intellectual interplay. Thus they operate a philosophical customs' point where a crude check – Continental equals "good"; English equals "bad" – determines what philosophies may be happily admitted into Scotland. Crucially however this performs at an individual level what it seeks to combat at a national level, for it colonises. It colonises, for it restricts individual intellectual and cultural freedom by calling for that individual to adopt, maintain, and valorise a pre-cast "national" form. In seeking, therefore, to make identity a product of purely national difference, Beveridge and Turnbull obliviate difference at the level of the individual: nations are – supposedly – culturally different, but the individuals within them, in order to be "authentic", should all exhibit and seek to maintain this supposedly homogenous culture. This amounts to the assertion that an individual ought to adopt a cultural practice simply because he or she is contingently born within the contingent borders of the contingent geographical space in which these contingent cultural practices arose or came to dominate. Reasserting "the practices which define our own culture" (Beveridge and Turnbull 1999: 15) simply replaces Anglicisation with "Scotticisation", a move which is, I would suggest, neither democratic, nor particularly intellectual.

2. Radically distinct communities: Scottish philosophy and English philosophy

For MacIntyre it is a condition of philosophical discourse that it has no presuppositionless point of departure and he deploys this condition to ward off charges that his accounts of philosophy and its relation to culture are contaminated by a potentially disabling question-begging. What matters, he argues, is what comes after the initial presupposition: "What vindicates this or that starting point is what comes next, the enquiry thus generated and its outcome in the achievement of some particular kind of understanding of some subject matter" (MacIntyre 1999: 77). One presupposition that Beveridge and Turnbull rely upon is a notion – common to the thought of both MacIntyre and George Davie – that cultures and the philosophies they putatively engender, or putatively reflect, are somehow radically distinct. Acceptance of this position in turn generates a suspicion of both the universalism inherent in Enlightenment thought, and also of any philosophy which takes the individual as its point of departure: like MacIntyre, Beveridge and Turnbull are notably and noticeably hostile to any form of philosophical individualism.

In discussing those philosophies and thought-models to which they are opposed, Beveridge and Turnbull practise a number of un-satisfactory conflations. Opponents of the kind of communitarian and nationalist culture-model they outline and evidently favour are lumped together as either Enlightenment-liberals or Enlightenment-modernists and so we find that some altogether curious bedfellows – Kantians and Utilitarians, Freudians and those sympathetic to Nietzsche – are, bizarrely, forced together. These modernists are in turn joined by that other catch-all, the postmodernists, among whom they number one of their critics, David McCrone. Against these varied and competing an-tagonists, Beveridge and Turnbull propose the aim of their self-professed "cultural nationalism" to be the "reconstruction of an autonomous intellectual culture" (Beveridge and Turnbull 1989: 70). Notice again that what is in question is a *single* culture and notice too that to reconstruct implies that whatever constitutes intellectual auton-omy is to be found in the past. This retrospective movement is, for R.D. Anderson, characteristic of those for whom George Davie is, in Anderson's words, a "cult figure":

For it is a well-known feature of Scottish educational discourse that it commonly includes an appeal to the past, or at least to an idealised version of it. In disputes over recent government legislation, it is striking how both sides have felt it necessary to claim the sanction of tradition, and to repudiate any "anglicisation" of the Scottish system. Historians who have scrutinised this use of the past as myth have tended to observe that the myth's content has changed radically over the years, the one constant being that whatever distinguishes Scotland from England at any one time is regarded as traditional, even when the differences are quite recent. (Anderson 1992: 67)

Anderson is valuable because he identifies a number of problems within Davie's commonly accepted account of Scottish education. For Beveridge and Turnbull, Davie "has laid the groundwork for a de-colonised understanding of Scotland" (Beveridge and Turnbull 1989: 112); for Anderson he has laid the groundwork for a number of misunderstandings of Scotland. Anderson argues that when analysed closely, Davie's account of the "crises" in Scottish education tend "to come apart in the historian's hands" (Anderson 1987: 3). One of Davie's most oft-repeated and approvingly quoted assertions, the pedagogical centrality of philosophy, is, Anderson argues, somewhat misleading. Within the general MA, Davie seems to suggest that philosophy alone was deemed compulsory, but as Anderson demonstrates, *every* subject in the general MA was compulsory. Davie tends also to treat tertiary education as if it were (pre- and post- "crisis") a single, homogenous tradition, the composition of which was a matter of consensus. This is a significant oversimplification, for as Anderson shows, no such consensus existed:

it is important to note the central role of mathematics in general education in the nineteenth century. And many professors, not least in Aberdeen, saw the classics rather than philosophy as the heart of the Scottish tradition. Latin was the subject which linked universities and parish schools, while Greek remained a compulsory part of the uniform MA curriculum down to 1892. (Anderson 1992: 74)

Anderson quotes Hugh MacDiarmid as insisting that the "true Scottish tradition" was in fact freedom of choice (Anderson 1987: 3), a quotation which once again returns us to the question of individual intellectual freedom, for as Anderson suggests, were one to adopt and accept the position argued for by Davie and Beveridge and Turnbull, then this intellectual freedom would be curtailed: "to maintain the Scottish character of universities means not only keeping them different from English ones, but also keeping them more like each other, and restraining divergent enthusiasms" (Anderson 1992: 74). What is at stake is considerably more than the restraining of "divergent enthusiasms", it is the restriction of intellectual freedom, a notion and principle of operation absolutely vital to any university. Anderson further suggests that the notion of educational difference so central to followers of Davie is less stark then is routinely suggested. To an outsider, the differences between Scottish and English education are less significant than the features which distinguish the British system as a whole. Consequently, if one wishes to make philosophy a compulsory and primary part of tertiary education, one needs to advance an argument which does not appeal to *the* Scottish tradition, for no such tradition existed.

If Davie provides a by no means certain taxonomy of philosophical and cultural difference, then perhaps MacIntyre, the other key architect of Beveridge and Turnbull's "cultural nationalism" can be more successful. A sequence of challenges from John Haldane tends to suggest otherwise. Haldane is a sensitive but nonetheless critical reader of MacIntyre, and the criticisms at which Haldane arrives are apposite here for they impinge upon the conceptual bases, the presuppositions and operational assumptions of many of Beveridge and Turnbull's own arguments. Firstly, Haldane questions the validity of the notion of radically distinct communities, the notion of alien traditions, and thus implicitly questions the notion of disjunctive national cultures. He does so initially by asking what are the criteria of identity for cultures and societies. Now this seems to be merely the stock rejoinder to those who accept that there are such things as national cultures (and it is no less effective for being so), but Haldane couples this question to another – "Where do *we* stop and *others* begin?":

Certainly, geography and time may separate communities but this empirical fact is, in itself, philosophically trivial. What has to be shown is that there are points of separation beyond these spatio-temporal ones which constitute incommensurable differences. A line of reasoning familiar from Wittgenstein and Davidson suggests that this may not be possible. MacIntyre is dismissive of Davidson's interpretative argument but yet invokes a linguistic criterion of difference: roughly, a culture is distinct from one's own to the extent that understanding what speakers belonging to it are saying involves learning the meaning of their words as terms in a second language. But, this suggestion invites a reapplication of the Davidsonian argument: either such learning involves translations of terms from one language into those of another or it does not. If it does, then in what sense did the foreign language represent an incommensurable difference, as opposed to an interesting variant of common human culture? If it does not, then how does one know what one is saying, or indeed that one is saying anything coherent at all? (Haldane 1994: 95)

The piece by Donald Davidson to which Haldane refers and makes use of, "On the Very Idea of a Conceptual Scheme" (Davidson 1984), attacks a central premise of MacIntyrean thought namely that there are languages, traditions, "conceptual schemes", which cannot be translated one into another. Now, if one were to persist with the notion that there are untranslatable cultures, then one would have to ask Beveridge and Turnbull how it is possible for them to reach a position from which to criticise a supposedly fundamentally alien English culture. For if rationality, the capacity which permits and shapes criticism, is a historically and culturally conditioned reflex, one which can only exist *within* a tradition, then what enables anyone within tradition *A* to criticise those holding another position, tradition *B*? Simply, if Scottish culture is so radically other, then how can those who both belong to and are shaped by this Scottish culture even recognise, let alone translate or criticise, English culture? Or, as Haldane asks, how can any socially constituted rational order be judged superior to any other? Haldane is thus suspicious that MacIntyre's position entails and contains a relativism to which it is ostensibly hostile, and furthermore that the alternative to this relativism is a non-rationalism equally at odds with MacIntyre's project.

Haldane notes that in *Whose Justice? Which Rationality?*, MacIntyre describes a person yet to give themselves to a tradition of rational enquiry. Enquirer *X*, currently outwith all traditions, faces a number of competing and divergent choices, but, if rationality only obtains *within* a tradition then it is unclear how enquirer *X* can make any choice.

It would seem that his or her choice must either be rooted in reason or else be non-rational. But the former is excluded if rational norms are only available to a participant within a coherent tradition, for, *ex hypothesi*, the addressee is a complete outsider. If the latter, however, then one may be hesitant to speak of a "choice" as having been made, and certainly it could not be seen as other than arbitrary viewed from *all* rational perspectives. [...] We are prohibited from saying that the rootless addressee can choose on the basis of transcendent norms of practical reason, so that excludes a realist resolution. This returns us to the thought that all choosing is from within a tradition, but if so there is after all nothing to be said to such a person, and *a fortiori* he cannot make a rational choice. (Haldane 1994: 96-97)

Later, MacIntyre suggests that this position, that of the traditionless outsider seeking a method of enquiry, is actually unavailable. MacIntyre states that to be outside of all traditions "is to be a stranger to enquiry; it is to be in a state of intellectual and moral destitution", a position with which Beveridge and Turnbull concur (1989: 132). But as Haldane argues, this contradicts the suggestion that such a person stands to be helped by what MacIntyre has to say:

A rational enquirer finds himself confronted by rival accounts of *moral* reasoning between which it is said to be impossible for him to make a rational choice. This suggests either that the rival accounts lack any kind of rationality, or that their rationality is internal to them, Thus we arrive at either non-rationalism or relativism. (Haldane 1994: 97)

Beveridge and Turnbull recognise some of these difficulties and attempt to obviate them, but they do not quite succeed. They criticise, among others, the modern liberal for being a traditionless isolate, but their adherence to MacIntyre's position entails the absorption of a contradiction: if all enquiry is necessarily from within a tradition then how does one find oneself outwith all tradition; how is it possible to be traditionless? Secondly, and as Haldane indicates, in order that his account not leave tradition as something fixed and final, MacIntyre's notion of progress within tradition proposes that traditions can alter and recognise internal weaknesses by undergoing periods of crisis. These crises prompt tradition *A* into reassessing itself and through such reassessment come to recognise that another tradition, tradition *B*, may offer a solution, but, crucially, a solution intelligible to and in some measure consistent with the practices and procedures of tradition *A*. But, as Haldane records, the crises within Thomism, which after all MacIntyre sees as the best method of enquiry, have not followed the course which MacIntyre describes. These crises have led to Thomism being supplanted – ironically – by the genealogical tradition to which it is supposedly superior. Thomism has "lost out to Nietzsche" in North American universities and colleges, and to phenomenology, Gadamer, Levinas and Derrida in Europe. MacIntyre, and Beveridge and Turnbull (if they accept the validity of this model), need to explain how.

There is, however, a more fundamental challenge which suggests that the very notion of historically or socially mediated progress within a tradition is deeply problematic.

Clearly it is a matter of some contention whether the work of an author represents advance or confusion in the development of an enquiry, and such matters are not resolvable without reference to a *philosophical* investigation of the issues and arguments. But that casts doubt on the very idea that history or narrative can, of themselves, play a major part in determining the standing of a tradition. [...] What need to be assessed [...] are arguments and concepts considered in their own right and largely independently of their role in any recorded sequence of debates. This thought prompts worries about the historical conception and methods of enquiry which constitute the framework of MacIntyre's project. (Haldane 1994: 103)

The same, of course, may be said regarding the framework of Beveridge and Turnbull. Thus, we arrive back at the issues that I mentioned above in connection with Hume, where disputes about philosophy can only be resolved in terms of philosophy. Moreover, if you characterise philosophy as a truth-seeking activity then this conjures a further difficulty, for as Haldane argues, MacIntyre's immanentism cannot by itself give an account of truth. MacIntyre's notion of progress within tradition-constituted rationality can only provide examples of something being better (traditions recognise and resolve difficulties); it cannot, as it stands, give examples of something being true. Though Haldane does not say so, this absence of the possibility of tradition-transcendent truth begins to resemble the Nietzschean position that MacIntyre and Beveridge and Turnbull seek to resist.[1]

We might, however, question the governing assumption as it appears in Beveridge and Turnbull, that to be outwith *the* Scottish tradition is to be somehow culturally indigent. As Cairns Craig has argued, far from constituting an impediment, the absence of a single monolithic, national tradition has in fact been a considerable cultural propellant:

As the sweep of modernisation took in more and more of the world, and as the wars of the twentieth century broke down and reconstructed the "nations" of the world, [the] model of a homogenous nation shaped within a homogenous cultural and linguistic tradition became more and more irrelevant not only to the reality of people's experience, but to any possible projection of what nations were ever likely to be [...] the inheritance of a diversity of fragmented traditions were to be the source of creativity rather than its inhibition in the second half of the 20th [century], and Scotland ceased to have to measure itself against the false "norm", psychological as well as cultural, of the unified national tradition. (Craig 1987: 7)

---

[1] Alexander Nehamas suggests further points of convergence as well as identifying problems with MacIntyre's understanding of Nietzsche (Nehamas 1996).

Instead then, of functioning as a restriction, the absence of a single unified and unifying national tradition actually opens up avenues of creative freedom. Equally, far from evidencing a cultural backwardness, this absence, this lack of a false and falsifying norm, prefigures a number of positions loosely codified as "postmodern" or "multicultural". Now regardless of whether one accepts that postmodernity or multiculturalism are usefully productive terms, it is unnecessary to accept Beveridge and Turnbull's rather biblical injunction that to eschew the single coherent tradition they outline equates to some kind of cultural damnation. For Beveridge and Turnbull, *anything* other than tradition-based rationality must, per force, result in "personal impoverishment" – "impoverishment" because where a single philosophy should be "there is instead a clutter of unrelated and unrelatable postures, a rag-bag of assorted superficialities" (Beveridge and Turnbull 1997: 132). The language here is deliberately contoured, but the conclusion to which these words frog-march the reader is moot and circular: tradition-dependent culture is best because it is tradition-dependent culture. It also involves an appeal to consequences: you do not wish *P* to be true, therefore *P* is false. The weighted language they employ suggests that a society or polity in such a state just is a bad thing, and it is a bad thing because it is not tradition-dependent. This is by no means so, for it is possible to argue that a society in which cultural flux does not obtain is an ossified society. Stuart Hampshire suggests that dynamism and acceptable intellectual conflict and competition are not only unavoidable but eminently desirable.

We should look in society not for consensus, but for ineliminable and acceptable conflicts, and for rationally controlled hostilities, as the normal condition of mankind; not only normal, but also the best condition of mankind from the moral point of view, both between states and within states. This was Heraclitus's vision: that life, and liveliness, within the soul and within society, consists in perpetual conflicts between rival impulses and ideals [...] Harmony and inner consensus come with death [...] In pursuing its changing conceptions of the good, the life of the soul is a series of compromise formations, which are evidently unstable and transient, just as every successive state of society is evidently unstable and transient. (Hampshire 1989: 189)

It is, therefore, perfectly possible to live a confident, productive, perhaps even good, life without the comfort-blanket of consensus, of a homogenous national identity, or a homogenous tradition – by Beveridge and Turnbull's own concession this is the predominant state in a liberal society. Moreover, in claiming that "we" – whatever the referents of this troublesome pronoun – *ought* to readopt certain practices, Beveridge and Turnbull necessarily commit themselves to the claim that "we" *can* readopt these practices. But, like any other modern polity, Scotland contains and is the site of a number of fluid, divergent and competing conceptions of identity. For Beveridge and Turnbull though, fluidity and multiplicity result in the "Pick 'n' Mix" identity discussed by David McCrone (1992: 195). Beveridge and Turnbull are sharply critical of McCrone, yet fail to see that their principal criticism – McCrone does not consider the negative implications of his position – is precisely the criticism that their own position invites. Beveridge and Turnbull simply do not see that the notion of identity sketched out by McCrone, one which by declining the ascription of any ontological essence leaves individual freedom intact, may actually be construed as a positive.

3. Anglo-American philosophy and/or Continental philosophy

The last issue I wish to examine is the supposed isolation of "English" and "Anglo-American" philosophy. Beveridge and Turnbull repeat Davie's view that "Scottish" philosophy was/is open to "Continental" influence (by which Davie usually means France), and that this serves as a method of contrast and a token of separation from "English" philosophy. Again, this supposed polarity is produced by a conflation. As Simon Critchley writes,

> questions of the identity of philosophical tradition become totally enmeshed in the obfuscatory ideological prejudice of a political geography. In my view, the conflation of philosophical tradition with political geography tends to the ideological stereotyping and distortion that can be found in such labels as "British empiricism", "French rationalism", and "German metaphysics", labels which only seek to widen the gulf between philosophical traditions and block the possibility of dialogue. (Critchley 1998: 4)

Perhaps too, the same may be said of Davie's "empirical England" and "metaphysical Scotland" (Davie 1999: xii). Beveridge and Turnbull single out Scottish theologians for practising a very "un-English" Germanophilia; a puzzling and characteristically conflationary claim. Coleridge utilised German thought to such an extent that he was accused by, among others, Ferrier, of plagiarising Kant and Schlegel; George Eliot translated Feuerbach; Oscar Wilde's notebooks kept while a student at Oxford demonstrate what the editors term "the powerful influence of the Oxford Hegelians" William Wallace and Benjamin Jowett (Wilde 1989: 17); both D.H. Lawrence and Thomas Hardy were steeped in the thought of Schopenhauer.[2] Going further back and moving outwith Germany, Hobbes and Descartes met and exchanged letters; Locke, greatly influential in France, read Gassendi and studied Malebranche. The *Weiner Kreis*, the Vienna Circle, together with Wittgenstein greatly influenced the shape, scope and development of analytical philosophy in the first part of the twentieth century – and we might point out, that the largest Continental philosophy departments in Britain are all in England. Indeed, an excellent recent example of the dialogue which Critchley urges and praises is Gregory McCulloch's book on Sartre (McCulloch 1994). As Bernard Williams (an "analytical" philosopher who takes Nietzsche seriously) famously suggests, the division between analytic and Continental further involves "a quite bizarre conflation of the methodological and the topographical, as though one classified cars into front-wheel drive and Japanese" (Williams 1995: 66).[3] Given all of which, it is by no means clear how "we" are to return to philosophy in the "Continental style". Which "Continental style"? Frege's idea of philosophy is not that of Heidegger; Sartre's idea of philosophy is not that of Derrida. Moreover, it is the adoption of these "Continental" thinkers such as Derrida and Foucault that Allan Bloom – whose defence of the traditional against relativism, Beveridge and Turnbull cite approvingly – takes to be partly responsible for the closing of the American mind, and that David Lehman takes as being symptomatic of a sorry sign of the intellectual times. For the latter, it is Derridean

---

[2] For details of Coleridge see his *Biographia Literaria* and also Holmes 1998. For Schopenhauer's influence on creative artists see Magee 1997.
[3] In an interview for *Cogito*, Williams places Nietzsche among the half-dozen or so books of moral philosophy worth reading. See Pyle 1999: 143.

deconstruction that "has aspired to supplant philosophy as the discipline of highest thought in the university":

> The impulse of deconstruction is profoundly inimical to art (which it subordinates to theory), to biography and history (whose relevance it denies), to conventional methods of critical analysis (which it considers retrograde), and to any philosophy of action (since existential choices are always transmuted into linguistic predicaments). (Lehman 1991: 132)

So, lest they welcome in the means of their own de(con)struction, Beveridge and Turnbull need to specify exactly what they take "Continental style" to mean. Whilst we might welcome a great deal of what they have to say, and they certainly contribute to the kind of liveliness that Stuart Hampshire commends, their nationalistically inspired account of philosophy, tradition and culture is, nonetheless, flawed. For if there are no fixed monolithic traditions, if there are no radically distinct communities, if the distinction between "Continental" philosophy and "English" philosophy is problematic and not altogether stable, then the cultural nationalism which they propose, and upon which they base these assumptions, becomes increasingly to resemble a cure for which there is no known disease.

Bibliography

Anderson, Robert. 1987. "Democracy and Intellect" in *Cencrastus* (Spring 1987): 3-4.
—. 1992. "The Scottish University Tradition: Past and Future" in Carter, Jennifer J. and Donald J. Withrington (eds) *Scottish Universities: Distinctiveness and Diversity*. Edinburgh: John Donald. 67-78.
Beveridge, Craig and Ronald Turnbull. 1989. *The Eclipse of Scottish Culture: Inferiorism and the Intellectuals*. Edinburgh: Polygon.
—. 1997. *Scotland After Enlightenment: Image and Tradition in Modern Scottish Culture*. Edinburgh: Polygon.
Bloom, Allan. 1988. *The Closing of the American Mind*. New York: Simon and Schuster.
Craig, Cairns. 1987. "Twentieth-Century Scottish Literature: An Introduction" in Craig, Cairns (general ed.) *The History of Scottish Literature*. 4 vols. Aberdeen: Aberdeen University Press. 4: 1-9.
—. 1999. *The Modern Scottish Novel: Narrative and the National Imagination*. Edinburgh: Edinburgh University Press.
Critchley, Simon. 1998. "Introduction: what is Continental philosophy?" in Critchley, Simon and William R Schroeder (eds) *A Companion to Continental Philosophy*. Oxford: Blackwell. 1-17.
Davidson, Donald. 1984. "On the Very Idea of a Conceptual Scheme" in Davidson, Donald *Inquiries into Truth and Interpretation*. Oxford: Clarendon Press. 183-98.
Davie, George. 1999. *The Democratic Intellect: Scotland and her Universities in the Nineteenth Century*. Edinburgh: Edinburgh University Press.
Haldane, John. 1994. "MacIntyre's Thomist Revival: What Next?" in Horton, John and Susan Mendus (eds) *Critical Perspectives on the Work of Alasdair MacIntyre*. London: Polity. 91-107.
Hampshire, Stuart. 1989. *Innocence and Experience*. Harmondsworth: Penguin.
Holmes, Richard. 1998. *Coleridge: Darker Reflections*. London: Harper Collins.
Hume, David. 1978. *A Treatise of Human Nature* (ed. L.A. Selby-Bigge). Oxford: Clarendon Press.
Lehman, David. 1991. *Signs of the Times: Deconstruction and the Fall of Paul de Man*. London: André Deutsch.
McCrone, David. 1992. *Understanding Scotland: The Sociology of a Stateless Nation*. London: Routledge.
McCulloch, Gregory. 1994. *Using Sartre: An Analytical Introduction to Early Sartrean Themes*. London: Routledge.
MacIntyre, Alasdair. 1988. *Whose Justice? Which Rationality?* London: Duckworth.
—. 1999. *Dependent Rational Animals: Why Human Beings Need the Virtues*. London: Duckworth.
Magee, Bryan. 1997. *The Philosophy of Schopenhauer*. Oxford: Oxford University Press.

Nehamas, Alexander. 1996. "Nietzsche, modernity, aestheticism" in Magnus, Bernd
    and Kathleen M. Higgins (eds) *The Cambridge Companion to Nietzsche*.
    Cambridge: Cambridge University Press. 223-51.
Norton, David Fate (ed.). 1993. *The Cambridge Companion to Hume*. Cambridge:
    Cambridge University Press.
Pyle, Andrew (ed.). 1999. *Key Philosophers in Conversation: The Cogito Interviews*.
    London: Routledge.
Wilde, Oscar. 1989. *Oscar Wilde's Oxford Notebooks: a Portrait of Mind in the
    Making* (eds Philip E. Smith II and Michael S. Helfland). Oxford: Oxford Uni-
    versity Press.
Williams, Bernard. 1995. "Nietzsche's minimalist moral psychology" in Williams,
    Bernard *Making Sense of Humanity and other Philosophical Papers 1982-1993*.
    Cambridge: Cambridge University Press. 65-76.

The Existence of Scotland

Thomas Docherty

The *Bildungsroman* of Walter Scott's *Waverley* may seem to present an essentially ahistorical vision. However, if Scotland is not to be conceived of as a historically passive object, then we must use this text to develop the notion of Scotland as "theoretical possibility".
Keywords: Theodor Adorno, Max Horkheimer, Frankfurt School, Cairns Craig, Walter Scott, democratic intellect, Giorgio Agamben.

In their critique of the culture industry, originally written in 1944 while the authors were exiled in America from the Nazi terror, Theodor Adorno and Max Horkheimer complain about what we might call a specific kind of "reality-effect" in mass culture. They argue in *Dialectic of Enlightenment* that there is a clear tendency in mass culture to advance the notion of the world as unchangeable, and that the corollary of this idea is the impossibility of history and of historical change. A further corollary is the impossibility of criticism making any substantive change to the way in which we conceptualise the world, for what is now of interest is not the condition of the world but rather its mere (unchangeable) existence. They point out first that, in the "transition to the administered life" that they are diagnosing, there is a "conversion of enlightenment into positivism" and the rise of a concomitant "myth of things as they actually are". That combination establishes the ostensibly dismal pointlessness of critique; and, for those who remain uncritical of this state of affairs, the task facing us is not how to *change* the world but rather how to *manage* it as it is. As they put it:

The new ideology has as its objects the world as such. It makes use of the worship of facts by no more than elevating a disagreeable existence into the world of facts in representing it meticulously. This transference makes existence itself a substitute for meaning and right. Whatever the camera reproduces is beautiful. [...] Not Italy is offered, but evidence that it exists. (Adorno and Horkheimer 1979: 148)

In this – a description that in some way matches a prevalent under-standing of the postmodern as a media age – there is what Fredric Jameson characterises as a "waning of affect" (Jameson 1991: 10-16). The "massification" of information and its dissemination in various media leads to a state of affairs in which the world is too much with us, and the superfluity of information and "knowledge" leads to the demise of that *pathos* on which the possibility of motivated human agency has traditionally been thought to rest.

Gianni Vattimo in *The Transparent Society* explores the hy-pothesis that in our technocratic age, when mass-media are capable of offering us "real-time" history (as when we watch history unfolding "live" on television), we might have reached a moment of an ostensi-ble total transparency in history and knowledge (Vattimo 1992). That is to say, it looks as if we have reached the stage in which the Hege-lian Absolute Spirit has fully realised itself, in that there is now no "mediation/knowledge" to come *between* the subject and her or his history. This, however, is for Vattimo a too simplistic view; he argues that the massification of the media has in fact established a state of affairs in which there is no longer any belief in "history-as-such". The multiplication of media leads us to take the view that there is not one history unfolding at all, but rather that there are multiple histories, many of them overlapping, all of them "situated", and all vying for position with regard to truth-claims.

"Scotland", in this view, is both the site of a local history that takes its place amidst a crowd of other, no less viable, histories (that of "England", that of "France", that of "India" and so on, in a series of contestations with ostensibly "external" histories), and also the site that *contains* a multiplicity of internal dissonant and dissident histories (that of the "Highlands", say, against that of the "Lowlands"; that of "metropolitan" Glasgow or Edinburgh against that of the rural Gram-pians; and so on in a series of ostensibly internal conflicts and crises that shape the class and sometimes frankly sectarian or tribal struc-tures of the modern nation). Far from offering "transparency" and immediacy (the perfect cohabitation of epistemology with ontology), mass culture is more mediated than ever; and one likely consequence is that we start to give up on belief in any single and unified reality at all. Like the victims of mass culture that Adorno and Horkheimer saw us becoming, we give up on the real thing, having in our hands something even better than the real thing – even better in that it is an administratively graspable, "manageable" proof that the real thing exists. That "proof" is always based upon a mythic, or, more generally, simply an "imagined", version of the essence of the thing whose existence is supposedly proved; and such a proof allows for an administering of the real thing (a taxonomy of its components, an analysis of its intrinsic structure, a description of its form, such as that I gave above in my characterisation of Scotland as riven by other internal and external histories), while the reality itself (the component parts that are taxonomised, the relation of its intrinsic structure to a world outside of it, a description of its content) escapes everything except its administration. The question to be posed here is a simple one: in the devolved age (when, ostensibly at least, Scotland has regained some control over aspects of the administration of Scotland), is it the case that "not Scotland is offered, but merely evidence that Scotland exists"? In short, do we have a Scotland *in theory*, "merely"?[1]

In what follows, I shall explore the question of the realisation or self-articulation of Scotland. I aim to show that while Scotland exists, it does so in what I shall call a mode of theoretical potentiality. I shall contend that arguments about whether we should regard Scotland in "essentialist" terms, or "Scotlands" as constructions, or Scotland as a deconstruction of nationhood, and so on, are all arguments that, while interesting, are strangely beside at least one central point. The real issue is whether we prioritise *Scotland* (in which case we see it simply as a theoretical possibility rather than as a material fact) or, on the other hand, whether we prioritise the *existence* of Scotland (in which case we see it as material fact, devoid of further ontological possibilities, and thus, paradoxically denied the very history that its supposed existence claims in the first place). Scotland as theoretical potentiality is no less "real" than any of these other variant and conflicting definitions; and, indeed, I shall argue that it is *only* by regarding Scotland as just such a theoretical possibility that Scotland, rather than just the evidence that it exists, can be offered. At stake in

---

[1] "Merely" here means not simply "only", but also "purely"; it has a positive inflection rather than the negative that the word often implies.

this is the question of how (and, indeed, if) Scotland might be an agent of both its own history and that of others.[2]

1. On cynicism; or, on going to the dogs

Nineteenth-century critics such as George Saintsbury famously argued, that, with *Waverley* in 1814, Walter Scott effectively "invented" the historical novel, and gave it a form that would be imitated right across Europe.[3] However, this position is one that takes the optimistic view of "history-as-such" that has come to be regarded as problematic, especially in relation to the question of the particularities, even the very essence, of Scotland's history. In his reading of Scott, Cairns Craig has astutely argued that the text of *Waverley* contains a paradoxical *elision* of history, in that the question of history as a temporal structure cedes place to a question of geography, where the text sets up oppositions that are determined according to a place-logic: "What Scott does in *Waverley* is to make a division in geography equivalent to a division in history: to cross the Highland boundary is effectively to step into the past" (Craig 1996: 70). In an expert gloss on this that serves to explain the huge popularity and success of this kind of writing, Craig goes on:

> For Scott, history, geography and psychology form a triptych whose terms are mutually interchangeable [...] his heroes can stand on both sides of a *historical* divide precisely because they can travel across a *geographical* boundary and in so doing experience the changes in history at a *psychological* level. (Craig 1996: 70-71)

The argument here is something akin to Franco Moretti's description of the European form of the *Bildungsroman* (Moretti

---

[2] For an excellent meditation on the question of such autonomy from an entirely different point of view, see Paterson 1994.

[3] For a sense of the impact of this on world literature, see the catalogue of names advanced by Andrew Hook as the followers of this new form of historical novel in his "Introduction" to his Penguin Classics edition of Sir Walter Scott, *Waverley* (Scott 1985: 10).

1987).[4] In *The Way of the World*, Moretti argues that the *Bildungsroman*, while ostensibly dominated entirely by history, is actually shaped by a vision of society as inimical to historical change. The central character of the *Bildungsroman* starts as an outsider of sorts in her or his social formation, usually because she or he is youthful and not fully versed in the ways of her or his society. It is precisely those ways – the norms that constitute a normative and value-laden ideology – that the character has to learn; and indeed, in internalising them, the character finds that she or he can be fully inserted into the very heart of the society, legitimised and authorised by it now as an independent adult[5] precisely in the same instant that, in circular fashion, they legitimise the society by an endorsement and espousal (literally, since they marry) of its ideology. Historical development becomes, at most, a psychological question (the question of the individual growing into adulthood, accepting fatalistically that "experience" shows their youthful aspirations to be idealistic).[6] Material history, those forces that are larger than any single individual, are rendered as if constant, eternal and immutable. In this way, ostensibly denying the possibility of critique of the society that it represents, the text of the *Bildungsroman* legitimises the very ideology that its central, youthful character had seemed to question on behalf of its reader. While that youth, and that reader, might have thought that it was possible to change the world by an engagement with it that would set history and all its open possibilities going, the text serves to defuse that possibility by effectively domesticating the possibility of historical revolt or criticism.

Craig's view differs from this slightly in seeing the central character – in this instance Edward Waverley – not as one entirely de-

---

[4] In relation to Scott's *Waverley* and how space becomes time "only in the proximity of the internal border" in historical novels, see also Moretti 1999: 38ff.

[5] Their adulthood is typically signified by a supposedly freely chosen marriage, based upon affective individualism, to one who was always already a fully legitimised member of the society's insider-class. On "affective individualism" as the ground of a supposed free autonomy in the making of marriage-allegiances, see Stone 1982.

[6] For a fuller consideration of the question of "experience", its relation to history and to material practice in the sphere of the aesthetic, see my "Aesthetics and the Demise of Experience", in Joughin (Forthcoming). Key figures in the question of experience are Benjamin, Agamben and Leavis.

feated by ideology, but rather as one who mediates between two worlds. One world is historical and shaped by Enlightenment ideas of the possibility of progress (that is, the possibility of getting history going; "progress" in this case represented by England, though England as a psychological state of affairs and not a place). The other is a world entirely "out of history" and shaped by its exclusion from the centres of power that shape historical being itself (thus effectively becoming an *object* of historical progress, and its potential victim; in this case, Scotland is, psychologically, such an "object"-world). For Craig, the character of Edward becomes a vehicle for the reader's own imaginings, both of the possibility of progress (in which the reader is the *agent* of history) and of the thwarting of any such idea (in which the reader is effectively paralysed, the passive recipient – the *patient* – of a history that is beyond her or his grasp).

For my present argument, this has a particular importance when Edward gets his first impressions of Scotland as a place, for here we have Scott mediating a kind of foundational view of Scotland for us, and one that carries a particular weight of legitimacy and authority precisely because it is the view of the naïve, innocent, youthful outsider. It thus pretends to a condition of some "objectivity" (the word usually means simply "neutrality"; but here it should be charged with the idea that Scotland is purely the *object* of this imaginative view). Having arrived at, and spent some time in, his military quarters in Dundee, Edward Waverley decides to get out and see something of Scotland during a requested leave of absence. In this visit to Baron Bradwardine's village-home of Tully-Veolan, he is effectively making his first proper engagement with the ostensible "reality" of Scotland. The place stands outside of the "official" Scotland, the Scotland presented to the military officer class; and it is here, therefore, that Waverley gets his first opportunity of seeing "real" Scottish people.

The first image that we are offered of the Scots here is that of an impoverished, violent, savagely physical people. Their houses are "miserable in the extreme, especially to an eye accustomed to the smiling neatness of English cottages"; they are buildings that straggle their way irregularly along unpaved streets, "where children, almost in a primitive state of nakedness, lay sprawling". The children lie exposed to the danger of being crushed by passing horses; and, even when the aged women of the place want to rescue the children from such danger, they do so in a fashion that shows savage force, as some

watchful old grandam [...] snatching up her own charge from among the sunburnt loiterers, saluted him with a sound cuff, and transported him back to his dungeon, the little white-headed varlet screaming all the while. (Scott 1985: 74)

Most important in this description, however, is the next characteristic. The place is a bedlam of confused noise; and these people live among dogs:

Another part in this concert was sustained by the incessant yelping of a score of idle useless curs, which followed, snarling, barking, howling, and snapping at the horses heels; a nuisance at that time so common in Scotland, that a French tourist who, like other travellers, longed to find a good and rational reason for everything he saw, has recorded, as one of his memorabilia of Caledonia, that the state maintained in each village a relay of curs, called *collies*, whose duty it was to chase the *chevaux de poste* [...] from one hamlet to another. (Scott 1985: 74)

First, here is Scotland as, literally, *cynical*: like ancient Diogenes of Sinope, follower of Antisthenes – called "the cynic" after the ancient Greek for "dog" (*kuon*) and reputed to live among the stray curs of Sinop (in modern-day Turkey) – the Scot has gone to the dogs. The non-cynical outsider (the French tourist), in an effort to understand or contain this cynicism, rationalises it as part of a national communications service. Scott here legitimises the view of the outsider who sees Scottish *communications* – the basis of Scottish society as such – as grounded in, indeed dependent upon, a fundamentally inhospitable and anti-social cynicism. The consequence of this representation is not only a view of Scotland as cynical and inhospitable, but also a view of the people as incapable of forming a society: here, there is no such thing as society.[7]

This figure of the cynical "dogged" Scot recurs in the narrative, on a day singled out for its "rationality", in Chapter Thirteen ("A

---

[7] Famously, both Margaret Thatcher and, in a rather different way, Jean Baudrillard, both questioned the existence of society. Thatcher's view (so roundly rejected in contemporary Scotland, of course) was precisely akin to the view proffered here via Scott, paradoxically. "Society" as I use the term here refers also to "official" society, the *haut-monde*.

Day More Rational than the Last"). When Bradwardine takes Edward
out hunting, they are surrounded not only by the hunting dogs but also
by the "gillie-wet-foots", the impoverished young lads who want to
join the hunt, working as beaters alongside (we might even say beneath) the hunting dogs. On the hunt itself, Bradwardine and Edward,
on horseback, *mediate* or live "between" cynicism (the gillie-wet-
foots) and killing (the hunt itself). Importantly, they live also between
two discourses. The *language* of the gillie-wet-foots goes unrepre-
sented here (all we are told is that their usual mode of greeting Davie
Gellatley is "daft Davie" except when they want to go on the hunt,
when it's "Maister Gellatley"), while the language of the hunt appears,
and is a polyglot mixture including English, French and some Scottish: the Baron flays the dead animal "(which, he observed, was called
by the French chasseurs *faire la curee*) with his own baronial *couteau
de chasse*", and, when he tells in this same passage of his literary
tastes there is a highly distinctive Scottish flavour (Scott 1985: 107-
8).[8] After the hunt, Bradwardine takes Edward on a circuitous route
home, effectively offering a tour that yields many historical anecdotes
(the details of which Scott does not reveal, thus allowing the terrain to
be passed over in a kind of silence for the reader) about the villages
through which they pass. Here, the Baron gives each local habitation a
specific local history which, because local, is restricted to the level of
the anecdote; but Edward's romantic mind enlarges the anecdotes into
tales that reveal more general *character*, becoming thereby *illustrative*
and exemplary tales whose purchase goes well beyond the local and
precise fact. This hunt and this trip home cements a bond between
Edward and Bradwardine who, though differing in almost every
respect, nonetheless find their point of communion through the day's
outing. Their communion depends upon that union of Bradwardine's
recounting of history as a tale of bare but precise facts with Edward's
romanticising glosses that adorn those facts and give them a more
general applicability. Here, in the hospitable discovery of the possibility of an intimacy between two who are radically opposed as characters, one finds the alleged "rationality" of the day (reason operating
here as a combination of sense and sensibility).

---

[8] On this multilingualism see also Crawford 1992: 124-31.

We might call this, then, a form of "cynical reason", in that the social intimacy that they establish is *grounded* in the dogs whose local condition they transcend (and whose noise or language they effectively silence). Bradwardine achieves this intimacy through his command of different languages, Waverley through his luxuriating command of the language of romance. In their union with each other, they transcend their local condition; and they do so by the processes or possibilities of translation: they say one thing; but they mean many things by it; and that plurality of sense opens communication to the realm of *possibility*, characterising it as the site of multiple sense, multiple meaning, mutable history; and this is preferable to a view that reduces communication to a simple transfer of information (the postal service).

It is important that this cynicism, on which the openness of communication-as-possibility rests, remains itself largely inarticulate; or, rather, that it has its own modes of discourse. The cynicism becomes thus the *means* of communication and not the communication itself; the Scottish lads, and, with them, Davie Gellatley, become the *medium* through whom Edward and Bradwardine are able to establish their "rational" society; it thus establishes the form but not the content of communication (and thus, by extension, the form and not the content of the substance of the possibilities of their being a Scottish people or nation). This cynicism though itself inarticulate nonetheless operates at the level of the linguistic: in itself, it is a reduction of language *either* to the mindless and incoherent barking of dogs *or* to the ostensibly senseless but actually oddly rational songs of Davie; but it is more important for what it facilitates than for what it is in itself.

Davie Gellatley becomes a key figure in this. Supposedly the son of a witch and brother of a now-dead poet, Gellatley seems almost permanently to live among dogs: whenever we see him, his dogs are not far away. He is less a fool than an idler, using his reputation as simple-minded in order to do little work except that which he himself wants to do. He is using his status as mere object – in what Baudrillard will much later identify as a "fatal strategy" – in order to assert a subjectivity.[9] Hovering always as he does between folly and privileged insight (if not total knowledge), he is described explicitly in the terms that cast him as the original cynic. On the morning of the initial *creagh* on Tully-Veolan, Edward is trying to work out what is going on, and he comes upon Gellatley who "was also seen in the group, idle as Diogenes at Sinope, while his country men were preparing for a siege" (Scott 1985: 123).[10]

This version of Scotland as informed by cynicism or by cynical reason is important. Cynicism, distrustful of "civilisation", which it sees as an artificial graft that harms our natural condition of independence, effectively advocates precisely a stepping "out of history" (to misapply Craig's terms here). Cynicism (like Adorno and Horkheimer; and, in different ways, like Rousseau and Freud) is troubled by the subsuming of real material conditions of human society beneath the regularities and norms of a society that sees its realities in the administratively established rules and norms that give the society its existence. In *Waverley*'s "more rational day", however, we see what can be founded upon such cynicism. We do not get a "real" Scotland; rather, what we get is the establishment of the possibility of human communicability, friendship, or pleasure. Such friendship or allegiance rests not upon transparent communication of a message between two individuals (as in one version of the postal service); rather, it rests upon the fact that communication establishes itself merely as the *possibility of communication* and as the *communication of possibility*. "Scotland" is the name that the text offers for this position in which language is the condition of translatability and of mutable uncertainty. Scotland is thus the site of *possibility*, and it is in this possibility that the cynic, out of history, can be brought back into history as the very ground of history's possibilities.

To be out of history in the way described by Craig is, however, to be cynical in a different way; and, in the end, this way aligns us not

---

[9] See Baudrillard 1979, where he first advocated a "fatal strategy" for feminism, advising women that the road to power lay, counter-intuitively, in "going over to the side of the objects"; and Baudrillard 1983, where he generalised this hypothesis more widely.
[10] Gellatley, it might be said in passing, owes much to the character of Thersites in Shakespeare's *Troilus and Cressida*, though with the bitterness of spirit withdrawn.

with those who will make history (the Edwards, the Bradwardines) but rather with the cynic herself in her silencing. There is a structural limitation in this form – a weaker form – of the cynicism that I discuss here. Craig's argument, of course, is the twofold thesis that, first, Scotland is *constructed* as being out of history, by such as Scott; and second, that history – by which he means official history, the kind that gets written – happens elsewhere; and so Scotland's attempts at writing its own history fall, of necessity, into imagination, into fiction. This is cleverly argued by Craig (1996: 67-72); yet the terms in which he makes the case oppose history to barbarism. The case rests on the assumption of a common (if not a universal) history, bracketed at one end by progress, modernity and the civilised future and, at the other end by regressive and barbaric imaginings or primitivism. Such a view of history leads inexorably to the story that Craig tells (in this accurately representing Scott, let it be said) in which history is a neo-Hegelian tale of victors and victims; and, in this, if one is not a victor, the only position left to assume is that of victim. The position that Craig offers us is either that of the little boy in the streets of Tully-Veolan, surrounded by dogs and threatened constantly with being trampled, or the position of Davie Gellatley, the "critic" as licensed or knowledgeable fool.[11] In short, the version of history assumed by Craig is one in which progress must be based upon a "fatal strategy" (at best) grounded in a logic of victimhood. In this, there is little possibility of Scotland *ever* escaping such a condition, which becomes instead ingrained, leading to the weak sarcasms of a little Scotlandism.

My contention here is, rather, that the logic of cynicism offers a different way of considering the question; and one in which we find a better or more useful opposition, this time between history on one hand and potentiality or theory on the other. In Craig's terms, the opposition that is established seems to be of necessity backward-looking because it thematises the division between progress and barbarism – between being the agent and being the victim of history – as an opposition grounded in 1707 and thus as an opposition between England

---

[11] That position is one that became favoured under the influence of Bakhtin in recent times. For a useful consideration of the position, see Eagleton 1986, where he relates it to pastoralism.

and a supposedly autonomous Scotland. Such a ground is indeed available in Scott; and it is to that that we can now turn.

2. Scotland as possibility

Near the start of *Waverley*, there is a definition advanced of Scottish scholarship, as evidenced in the figure of the Baron of Bradwardine:

He was of a very ancient family, and somewhat embarrassed fortune; a scholar, according to the scholarship of Scotchmen, that is, his learning was more diffuse than accurate, and he was rather a reader than a grammarian. (Scott 1985: 65-66)

Scott characterises Bradwardine at this point with a story that he claims, in one of his authorial notes, is derived from historical fact. Bradwardine is bookish to the extent that he trades his freedom for the reading of Livy. Having escaped imprisonment, he ventured back towards his captors in an effort to pick up the copy of Livy that he had been reading. Scott's own note grounds this in non-fiction, in factual history:

The attachment to this classic [Livy] was, it is said, actually displayed, in the manner mentioned in the text, by an unfortunate Jacobite in that unhappy period. He escaped from the jail in which he was confined for a hasty trial and certain condemnation, and was retaken as he hovered around the place in which he had been imprisoned, for which he could give no better reason than the hope of recovering his favourite *Titus Livius*. I am sorry to add, that the simplicity of such a character was found to form no apology for his guilt as a rebel, and that he was condemned and executed. (Scott 1985: 495)

Bradwardine, on the other hand, gets away with it, due to the fact that his guard, who recaptures him, is of a similarly bookish disposition, favouring Livy almost as much as Bradwardine; and, having found a kindred spirit, the guard pleads on Bradwardine's behalf, and so softens the charge against him, that he gets off scot-free.

We should remark here the oddity of Scott's note, however. The point of the note is to claim historical veracity for his tale. Yet, in the opening sentence of the note, there is that discomforting interjection, "it is said". In other words, the testimony for the verity of this passage is not historical fact, but rather mere anecdote. It is not true, but possible; and Scott sees precisely such possibility as the ground for the legitimisation of his tale. As Nietzsche would later have it, "in the end the true world becomes a fable" (Nietzsche 1968: 12).

The truth becomes possibility. Why might this be important? It is important here because the text offers us, in its opening section after the historical backdrop and genealogy, another specific view of Scotland, this time based on an idea of Scottish learning or "scholarship"; and it is a version that is picked up some one hundred and fifty years later by George Davie, in his characterisation of a Scottish educational system as one that fosters "the democratic intellect" (Davie 1982).[12] Davie's argument is straightforward, if far-reaching and consequential: due to historical and political circumstances (which relate to a colonial situation in the nineteenth century), a Scottish tradition of generalist education gave way to an English mode in which early specialisation in specific disciplines narrows the critical range of the student, giving knowledge without cleverness, as it were. The Scottish tradition was more democratic, it is claimed, not just because Scotland had more universities, but also – and primarily – because the Scottish student was being trained philosophically in how to find the general or *theoretical* case that lay behind the particular. While the English student might be able to translate a particular term from ancient Greek into nineteenth-century English, he would have no knowledge of a general semantics, of the historicity of meaning, of the problems of translation between cultures, and so on. The English tradition is practical; the Scottish tradition is abstract: the English solves problems in their particularity, the Scottish sees the general problem that shapes the particular; and so on. The Scottish mode, thus, is more democratic because it is more foundationalist, more *theoretical*, and it is in this way that its beneficiaries can participate fully and autonomously – *critically* – in their history.

This "Scottish learning", that is characterised as being "more diffuse than accurate", is what Davie will later identify as the "generalist tradition" of education as practised in the Scottish universities; and, in Davie (as in Scott), it is set against the rather mechanical "knowledge"

---

[12] For a fuller account of the stakes of the argument that I shall advance here, see Docherty 1999.

of technical particularity. Let us here call it, simply, "Scotland *as* theory". Yet in *Waverley*, an odd inversion is at work. In the "more rational day" of the hunt discussed above, it is Bradwardine, the Scot, who professes "mere" or factual historical knowledge, so that the young Englishman, Waverley himself, can be represented as "imaginative" and romantic. In all the anecdotes that Bradwardine relates, he restricts himself to the bare knowledge of the particular facts: "the Baron, indeed, only cumbered his memory with matters of fact – the cold, dry, hard outlines which history delineates" (Scott 1985: 109). On the other hand, Edward "loved to fill up and round the sketch with the colouring of a warm and vivid imagination, which gives light and life to the actors and speakers in the drama of past ages" (Scott 1985: 109).

What follows from my argument above, however, is that it is an error to read this in simple allegorical terms, the terms that would be given to us by the kind of "place-logic" so ably described by Craig, Crawford, and, in a different context, Moretti. It is not the case that Edward is England, Bradwardine Scotland. Scotland is neither one nor another character at all, not even one or another location; rather, it is the site in which communication between these characters, locations, and histories is established as the site of theoretical possibility. By this, I do not mean to signal just that Scotland makes communication possible; but, more forcefully and more radically, that Scotland transforms communication into the communication of possibility, and that it establishes communication as a rather uncertain communication-as-the-possibility-of-communication itself. With this mode of communication, Scotland is more *possibility* than it is *theory*. Scotland might thus be seen as analogous to the condition that Keats had in mind as the negative capability that allows for Shakespeare's plays to have their particular reality and vitality.

In this "more rational day", we have not just the *means* of communication being represented, but also the *fact* of it (though it remains a fact devoid of precise detail); and the result is not only society but also the indulgence of pleasure. In this, we see a resolution of the hypothetical conflict between particularity and generality, between "English" and "Scottish" (indeed, "Scotland" is the name for such an "irresolute resolution"); and, importantly, the figure who resolves theory into practice is womanly, first Rose and then Flora: "Shortly after dinner," we are told, "the Baron, as if to show that his temperament was not entirely theoretical, proposed a visit to Rose's apartment, or, as he termed it, her *Troisieme Etage*" (Scott 1985: 109). There we find Rose, conversant in French and Italian, able to sing and to recite poetry. In this image of a European multilingual culture, we have the prefiguration of the more romantic shape of Flora Mac-Ivor, another woman who can exist in the social precisely by her capacities for translation.

Flora shares these same "accomplishments" but, living in a more isolated situation, she has added to them her knowledge of the local customs and language too. However, the text suggests that there are at least two ways in which one can come to such an engagement with the local. Flora differs from her brother, Fergus:

> When settled in the lonely regions of Glennaquoich, she found that her resources in French, English, and Italian literature, were likely to be few and interrupted; and, in order to fill up the vacant time, she bestowed a part of it upon the music and poetical traditions of the Highlanders, and began really to feel the pleasure in the pursuit, which her brother, whose perceptions of literary merit were more blunt, rather affected for the sake of popularity than actually experienced. (Scott 1985: 169).

Fergus, to return to the terms that began this essay, is concerned with the *existence* of Scotland; Flora (and Rose both before and after her) is the person concerned with *Scotland*. She is interrupted in her translation of the Gaelic song in which Edward had heard his name mentioned.[13] The incompleteness leaves him in a state of irresolution and uncertainty still; but it is precisely such uncertainty that enables the condition of sociability – it is such uncertainty (or, better, openness to possibility) that is Scotland. Scotland here is the word for such irresolution; and Edward is left in a state of uncertainty; but he nonetheless remains in a state of *society*, for the text situates Edward uncertainly between Rose and Flora (between an "English" flower and a more general floweriness); and that condition – the condition of possibility – is Scotland, for us every bit as much as for Waverley.

---

[13] It will be remembered, in passing, that it is actually the arrival of Fergus's dog that arrests the translation.

The question of the existence of Scotland, then, as Keats would have known, has something of the Hamlet about it: "to be or not to be, that is the question". When A.C. Bradley, lecturing in Glasgow University at the turn of the twentieth century, analysed the character of Hamlet, he found his presiding force to be a moral melancholy (Bradley 1976: 86). Certainly, he argued, this play, like *Julius Caesar,* is a tragedy of intellect (though passion – his other kind of tragedy – is present here too). Yet Hamlet's prevarications have little to do with excessive "theorising", according to Bradley (complicit in this with a logic of the fatal strategy that is victimhood), and everything to do with the melancholy into which he is thrown by the precipitate behaviour of his mother. Hamlet is entirely the victim of circumstance; and, as a victim, it becomes unclear as to whether he can effect any serious agency, whether, simply, he can act.

This, however, is the point, especially regarding the existence of Scotland. In Hamlet's most famous soliloquy we can see, by analogy, an address to the question of the existence of Scotland. My claim here is that Scotland is, in a peculiar sense, "the undiscovered country". In Hamlet's speech, that country is one that lies beyond death, and in the realm of the spectral or ghostly. However, it is not definitively a place to which there is only a one-way street or one-way ticket; to go there is to go to another place without the promise of return but most certainly, as the Ghost shows (and as Hamlet understands in this most famous soliloquy), with the *possibility* of return. Moreover, the undiscovered country might not even be there anyway. Its mode of existence is, we might say, pure potentiality.

I borrow the term "potentiality" from Giorgio Agamben (Agamben 1999).[14] There are two kinds of potential, he argues, following Aristotle. The first is a potential that exhausts itself in kinetic realisation (the child with the potential to become an adult, say, who stops being a child as soon as she reaches maturity). The second is of a different order, and Agamben explains it through the examples of the writer or the architect. The architect has the potential to build, certainly; but she does not exhaust that potential in its realisation, when she builds a building. The potential remains, even after the fact.

---

[14] For a fuller account of Agamben, dealing with his work as a whole, see Docherty (Forthcoming).

This kind of potential is not to be set against realisation; rather it is to be understood as a potential that is kept in existence *even when it is not being articulated*. This kind of potential for some state of affairs to come about depends, paradoxically, upon the maintenance of the potential for that same state of affairs *not* to come about. Potentiality is aligned with impotentiality; or, as Hamlet has it, "to be or not to be?" This question is best understood as one that does not pose a choice between two mutually exclusive opposites, but rather as an inclusive state of affairs that conditions Hamlet's being as pure potentiality. As with Hamlet, so also with Scotland: devolved, not independent – and therefore always as *possibility*.

Only among those who see themselves as empowered by their victimhood (in a fatal strategy of an inverted autonomy) does such a state of affairs provoke the moral melancholy described by Bradley during his time teaching in Glasgow. A genuine autonomy – one that is predicated upon the more important issue of freedom, and thus one that is political and not merely psychological – would be one that is not dependent on the master-slave dialectics of Hegel, and thus not dependent upon the logic of inverting one's own self-constructed inferiority. A free Scotland – the only Scotland worth considering – is the endless perpetuation of its own possibility. *Then* we would have Scotland, and not just formal proof of its existence.

Bibliography

Adorno, Theodor and Max Horkheimer. 1979. *Dialectic of Enlightenment* (tr. John Cumming). London: Verso.

Agamben, Giorgio. 1999. *Potentialities* (tr. Daniel Heller-Roazen). Stanford: Stanford University Press.

Baudrillard, Jean. 1979. *De la seduction*. Paris: Denoel.

—. 1983. *Les Strategies fatales*. Paris: Grasset.

Bradley, A.C. 1976. *Shakespearean Tragedy*. London: Macmillan.

Craig, Cairns. 1996. *Out of History*. Edinburgh: Polygon.

Crawford, Robert. 1992. *Devolving English Literature*. Oxford: Oxford University Press.

Davie, George. 1982. *The Democratic Intellect*. Edinburgh: Edinburgh University Press.

Docherty, Thomas. 1999. *Criticism and Modernity: Aesthetics, Literature and Nations in Europe and its Academies*. Oxford: Oxford University Press.

—. Forthcoming. "Potential European Democracy" in *Paragraph*.

Eagleton, Terry. 1986. *Against the Grain*. London: Verso.

Jameson, Fredric. 1991. *Postmodernism, or, the Cultural Logic of Late Capitalism*. London: Verso.

Joughin, John (ed.). Forthcoming. *The New Aestheticism*. Manchester: Manchester University Press.

Moretti, Franco. 1987. *The Way of the World* (tr. Albert Sbraggia). London: Verso.

—. 1999. *Atlas of the European Novel: 1800-1900*. London: Verso.

Nietzsche, Friedrich. 1968. *Twilight of the Idols* (tr. R.J. Hollingdale). Harmondsworth: Penguin.

Paterson, Lindsay. 1994. *The Autonomy of Modern Scotland*. Edinburgh: Edinburgh University Press.

Scott, Walter. 1985. *Waverley*. Harmondsworth, Penguin.

Stone, Lawrence. 1982. *The Family, Sex and Marriage in England 1500-1800*. Harmondsworth: Penguin.

Vattimo, Gianni, 1992. *The Transparent Society*. Cambridge: Polity Press.

Beyond Reason – Hume, Seth, Macmurray and Scotland's Postmodernity

Cairns Craig

Scottish literature has a long tradition of presciently "postmodern" devices and techniques. This is puzzling for contemporary theory, which locates postmodern literature
and thought in a post-Kantian context. Scotland, however, has its own postmodern
tradition in philosophers whose response to Hume is more plausible than Kant's phe-
nomenalism. Their distinctive Scottish philosophy of the self as social agent is the
foundation of Scotland's truly postmodern literary tradition.
Keywords: J. Hutchison Stirling, Immanuel Kant, David Hume, Jean-Francois Lyotard, John Macmurray, Andrew Seth Pringle-Pattison, postmodernism, postmodernity,
sublime.

1.

At the Walter Scott conference in Oregon in 1999, Jerome McGann
pronounced Scott to be the first postmodernist, a judgment based on
Scott's use of various metafictional techniques and his ironic combination of contradictory genres (McGann 1999, forthcoming). The
proposal was less surprising (to some, at any rate) than it might have
been, given how regularly another Scottish novel of the early nineteenth century – James Hogg's *Confessions of a Justified Sinner* – is
cited as prophetic of postmodernism in its use of multiple and conflicting narratives. Taken together, the implications of these prescient
texts might suggest that there is something inherently postmodern
about Scottish culture, or something in Scottish culture which leads its
writers to exploit narrative strategies that we now identify as typical of
postmodernism.

   This possibility is substantially endorsed by Scotland's
twentieth-century literary history, since many of the earliest examples
of recognisably "postmodern" writing in Britain were produced by
Scots. Hugh MacDiarmid's *In Memoriam James Joyce,* for instance,
first published in 1955, celebrates a poetry

[…] beyond all that is heteropeoic, holophrastic,
Macaronic, philomathic, psychopetal,
Jerqueing every idioticon,
Comes this supreme paraleipsis,
Full of potential song as a humming bird
Is full of potential motion,
When, as we race along with kingfisher brilliance,
Seeking always for that which "being known
Everything else becomes known,"
That which we can only know
By allowing it to know itself in us,
Since "determinatio est negatio,"
Suddenly "chaos falls silent in the dazzled abyss." (MacDiarmid 1955: 47)

The extravagant use of quotation and paraphrase in MacDiarmid's late poems, which produces a palimpsest of re-iterations and re-inscriptions of previous language, undermines, as thoroughly as poststructuralist theorists such as Jacques Derrida or Roland Barthes could have wished, any notion of the author as source and origin of the text. In the same year, W.S. Graham's *The Nightfishing* was published, inaugurating a poetry constructed around the self-referentiality that was to become typical of postmodernist texts. Brian McHale has argued that the historical development of postmodernism involved the replacement of modernist concerns with epistemology by postmodern concerns with ontology (McHale 1987). Graham may have been the first British poet to make that transition. In poems such as "The Constructed Space", alternative ontological levels interact in the "being" of the poem:

I say this silence, or, better, construct this space
So that somehow something may move across
The caught habits of language to you and me. (Graham 1979: 153)

The "I" hovers between the "I" of the poet who wrote, the "I" of the reader in the process of reading, and the semantic "I" that exists only in language itself. As rigorously as Derrida, Graham turns saying into writing and turns the implied origin of a presence in speech into the necessary absence of the speaker from writing. Graham's poetry is often, as here, a commentary upon its own formal attributes and upon the endless deferral of meaning that it enacts.

What Graham was doing in poetry, however, was being done just as radically for the novel by Muriel Spark. In Spark's earliest novel, *The Comforters*, published in 1957, Caroline, the central character, is constantly aware of a typewriter and of voices that anticipate the events of her own life: "'But the typewriter and the voices – it is as if a writer on another plane of existence was writing a story about us' As soon as she had said these words, Caroline knew that she had hit on the truth" (Spark 1963: 63). *The Comforters*, which gestures in the name of one of its central characters – Mrs Hogg – to its connection with *Confessions of a Justified Sinner*, conforms to McHale's conception of conflicting ontological levels. Others of Spark's novels, such as *The Prime of Miss Jean Brodie*, "play" with conceptions of history and of fictionality in ways that fit with Linda Hutcheon's famous definition of the postmodern as "historiographic metafiction" (Hutcheon 1988). If we can say that Scottish writers were very early entrants into the styles that were to become typical of postmodernism, the centrality of those techniques to the representation of modern Scottish experience was established by Alasdair Gray's groundbreaking novel, *Lanark*, in 1981. In its (con)fusion of realism, fantasy and science fiction, *Lanark* both fulfilled the postmodernist use of "popular" genres for serious purposes and set a pattern that many other Scottish writers – from Iain Banks's *The Bridge* to A.L. Kennedy's *And so I am Glad* and James Robertson's *The Fanatic* – have followed in their representations of modern Scotland.

The characteristics typical of much postmodernist literature, in other words, fit with key elements of the Scottish literary tradition, and do so from long before the invention of "postmodernism" as a critical term. Alex Clunas's article on Robert Louis Stevenson's "postmodernity", for example, reveals a truth that goes far wider than its ostensible subject (Clunas 1982). Indeed, given postmodernism's obsession with varieties of literary illusion, one could argue that Scottish writing was postmodernist from the moment that James Macpherson presented a poem of his own construction as a translation of a Gaelic epic, and attributed it to an ancient bard by the name of Ossian. The complexities of authorial origin, historical status and generic uncertainty that bedevilled Macpherson's Ossianic poems, even while the vogue for them was sweeping Europe, were perhaps only symptoms of a radical uncertainty about literary forms which post-modernism, two hundred years later, came to replicate – thereby, perhaps, "authenticating" as its precursor a work whose lack of authenticity has always been held to be a sign of its literary failure.

The source of such prescient postmodernity might be traced to Scotland's tangential relationship to the grand narratives of history whose foundering was, according to Jean-Francois Lyotard's seminal *The Postmodern Condition*, the necessary prelude to the postmodern. For Lyotard, the grand narratives of the past, whether religious, philosophical or ideological, provided the totalising context in which the events of ordinary life could find their justification, whereas postmodernity is underpinned by what he describes "as incredulity toward metanarratives" (Lyotard 1984: xxiv). Such scepticism is the product of mid twentieth-century economic changes – especially the "redeployment of advanced liberal capitalism" that has "eliminated the communist alternative and valorized the individual enjoyment of goods and services" (Lyotard 1984: 37-38). However, in an Appendix to *The Postmodern Condition*, Lyotard holds out an alternative to this *historical* development of the postmodern by suggesting that, in art at least, postmodernity does not develop out of modernity but is, rather, the inherent *ground* of the modern: "A work can become modern only if it is first postmodern. Postmodernism thus understood is not modernism at its end but in the nascent state, and this state is constant" (Lyotard 1984: 79). Scotland may be postmodernism's "nascent state", precisely because, as a stateless nation, it never fully entered into the world of modernity. If, as Benedict Anderson has suggested, nationalism was the necessary adjunct of secular modernity (Anderson 1991), then Scotland's noted lack of a nationalist movement in the nineteenth century made it a place without a metanarrative of the kind that other "modern" nations were developing. In that situation, "incredulity toward metanarrative" was not only possible but became one of the defining features of Scottish culture. The use of "postmodernist" techniques by Scottish writers may reflect, therefore, a situation which was prescient of the more recent collapse of metanarrative, and which produced precisely those multiple narratives and differentiations of ontological levels typical of late twentieth-century writing.

The fit between Lyotard's conception of postmodernism and the way in which Scottish culture developed from the eighteenth century is underlined by the fact that at least three different versions of Scotland's loss of historical metanarrative have been advanced by Scottish critics since the 1970s. The first is Tom Nairn's in *The Break-Up of Britain* (1979), which suggests that Scottish culture was profoundly flawed by Scotland's good fortune to have crossed the divide into modernity before the onset of the era of nationalism. As a result, Scotland, like the Britain of which it was a part, remained a *pre-modern* culture, and its failure to conform to the metanarrative of modern history – which for Nairn is fundamentally a Marxist one – produced a necessarily deformed version of the real "modern" cultures developing in the rest of Europe.

The second analysis is Colin Kidd's in *Subverting Scotland's Past* (1993): Kidd argues that Scotland's culture imploded as a result of the sceptical demolition of the myths of its own history upon which its claim to separate identity from England had depended. As the historical past of Scotland was revealed to be a series of forgeries (the Fergusian line of kings which underpinned Scotland's ancient independence) or was challenged as having no political relevance to modern society (the Buchananite conception of kingship), Scotland's independent conception of its own historical trajectory was supplanted by conceptions of English history, producing an "Anglo-Scottish" ideology which could never find any relevance in its own national past to the political realities of its new national context. Since Scottish historiography had been revealed to be merely fictional, the Scots were thrust early into the arena of historiographic metafiction.

The third version is my own, and is presented in *Out of History*, published in book form in 1996, though originally appearing as articles in the 1980s (Craig 1982, 1983). While arguing, like Kidd, that the narrative of Scottish history had been displaced by the narrative of English history, leaving Scotland in a kind of historical limbo, I suggested a less pessimistic outcome than either Nairn or Kidd. Cast into the rapid development of its new commercial, technological and industrial world, and made aware by the Jacobite Rebellions of the distinction between the "primitive" culture of the Highlands and the "modern" culture of the Lowlands, eighteenth-century Scotland was

forced to consider the nature of history – how did it develop, what im-
pelled it, what values were promoted or destroyed by it? The Scottish
Enlightenment's enormous contribution to European thought was, in
many respects, to develop answers to such questions. But as Scotland
was incorporated into a British history of which Scots could never be
fully a part, the effect, I suggested, was that Scottish thinkers shifted
to questions about what was before, beyond or outside of the boundaries of history. Being "out of history", Scots could question the very
nature and value of history, and could initiate the search for the foundations on which history itself was erected, a search that would
culminate in the encyclopaedic anthropology of J.G. Frazer's *The
Golden Bough*.

Though each of these arguments interprets differently Scotland's
loss of metanarrative, what they confirm is a crisis which, by opening
up competing and contradictory historical narratives, undermined the
possibility that any single narrative could claim "metanarrative" status
as representative of the nation as a whole. Such "incredulity towards
metanarrative" is, arguably, what underlies Scottish literature's famous engagement with doubles and *döppelgangers* (Miller 1985,
Gifford 1988) that dramatise the conflict between alternative origins
for Scotland's social world and alternative teleologies defining the
ends to which that history is directed. In this context, Scotland's most
important contribution to nineteenth-century literature, Walter Scott's
invention of the "historical novel", can be seen to rest not in the origi-
nality of the means by which he represented the *reality* of the past,[1]
but by his evocation of competing historical narratives, each of which
is, in anticipation, equally "real" but only some of which will survive
the trial of history. Postmodernist theorists such as Hayden White
have argued that all history writing is actually shaped by literary genres and that the "truth" which the historian seeks is always structured
according to the dictates of fiction (White 1973). Scott's historical
fictions, on the other hand, invoke "real" histories but set those histories in generic conflict with one another, so that in *Waverley*, for
instance, the Jacobite cause is an ironic tragedy and the Hanoverian an
accidental comedy. Postmodernists like White, who are deeply scepti-

---

[1] The revitalisation of Scott's reputation since the 1960s was largely based on such
"realist" readings of his historical novels, pioneered in Lukacs 1969.

cal of our ability to *know* the past because of the necessary rhetorical or imaginative procedures through which it has to be reproduced, read history as though it were historical fiction, thus making Scott's historical fiction the precursor of postmodernist theory. Indeed, the foundation of Scottish Enlightenment historiography on which Scott drew for his fiction was the notion of "conjectural history", which is defined by Dugald Stewart as allowing that,

In want of [...] direct evidence, we are under a necessity of supplying the place of fact by conjecture; and when we are unable to ascertain how men have actually conducted themselves upon particular occasions, of considering in what manner they are likely to have proceeded, from the principles of their nature, and the circumstances of their external situation. (Stewart 1980: 293)

Stewart, like his mentor Adam Smith, thinks such conjecture can be well-founded; postmodernists regard them as inevitably vitiating the truthfulness of history: both, however, agree that all history is a necessarily imaginative creation in which the "real" is infused with fictional constructions.

As Arthur Herman's book *The Scottish Enlightenment* confirms, it has become commonplace to view eighteenth-century Scotland as the foundation of the modern world (Herman 2002) – which means, if we follow Lyotard, that it must also be the cradle of "nascent postmodernism", and that the crisis of historical that is central to both should be reflected in other aspects of intellectual life. The similarities are equally striking, for instance, if we look at theories of language and aesthetics. Postmodern theory relies heavily on decoupling the "signifier" of a sign (the sign's sonic or graphic medium) from the "signified" (the concept which the sign embodies)[2] so that meaning may develop along the multifarious relations of the former rather than being determined by the fixity of the latter. This is particularly crucial to the ways in which literary texts are both composed and read. Roland Barthes, for instance, proposes the following notion of the "text" (which acts on the axis of the signifier) as opposed to the "work" (which acts on the axis of the signified):

---

[2] See, for instance, Ermarth 1992.

The Text, on the contrary, practises the infinite deferment of the signified, is dilatory; its field is that of the signifier and the signifier must not be conceived as "the first stage of meaning", its material vestibule, but, in complete opposition to this, as its *deferred action*. Similarly, the *infinity* of the signifier refers not to some idea of the ineffable (the unnameable signified) but to that of *playing* […] The logic regulating the Text is not comprehensive (define "what the work means") but metonymic; the activity of associations, contiguities, carryings-over coincides with a liberation of symbolic energy. (Barthes 1977: 158).

Such a text "without closure", a text which is "an explosion, a dissemination" of meaning, is precisely the kind of text which was defined by Scottish thinkers influenced by Hume's conception of the mind as a complex process of association. Even the terminology of Barthes – associations, contiguities – echoes those Scottish theorists such as Archibald Alison for whom, equally, the text explodes along the processes of association invoked by the signifier. For Alison, aesthetic experiences

seem often, indeed, to have but a very distant relation to the object that at first excited them; and the object itself appears only to serve as a hint, to awaken the imagination, and to lead it through every analogous idea that has a place in the memory. It is then, indeed, in this powerless state of reverie, when we are carried on by our conceptions, not guiding them, that the deepest emotions of beauty and sublimity are felt; that our hearts swell with feelings which language is too weak to express; and that, in the depth of silence and astonishment, we pay to the charm that enthralls us, the most flattering mark of our applause. (Alison 1811: 46)

In Alison, as in the other Scottish aestheticians of the eighteenth and nineteenth century whose associationist principles derive from Hume, the work of art is only the starting point for the kind of "dissemination" of uncontrollable possibilities of meaning that postmodernist theory presents as a new revelation of the possibilities of literature. The features that Barthes takes to be characteristic of postmodern literature's destruction of "meta-language" (Barthes 1977: 164) are already present, in other words, in Scottish Enlightenment theories of literature.

The displacement of "meta-meaning" which applies to both historiography and to literary language is equally evident in another profound displacement that connects the postmodern to the Scottish Enlightenment – the dissolution of the autonomous self as symbolised by Descartes' *cogito ergo sum*. For postmodernists, the Cartesian ego is both the foundation for, and the consequence of, conceptions of history and language as hierarchically ordered and providing ultimate, transcendent truths upon which the rest of our knowledge can be based. The self in this traditional form cannot survive a situation in which the history of which it is a part and the language through which it is expressed are beyond both knowledge and control. The ousting of "western man" as thus defined is often associated with Michel Foucault, for whom notions of the "soul" and "self" are simply the fictions of a coherent identity to which none of us can actually aspire:

Where the soul pretends unification or the self fabricates a coherent identity, the genealogist sets out to study the beginning – numberless beginnings whose faint traces and hints of color are readily seen by an historical eye. The analysis of descent permits the dissociation of the self, its recognition and displacement as an empty synthesis, in liberating a profusion of lost events. (Foucault 1977: 145-46)

The very terms – "unification", "fabricates", "dissociation" – point back, however, to Hume's famous dissolution of the unity of the self into the sequence of its associations, associations from which a unitary identity can only be a fabrication. For Hume, the "identity, which we ascribe to the mind of man, is a fictitious one" (Hume 1888: 259) because it is only

on these three relations of resemblance, contiguity and causation, that identity depends; and as the very essence of these relations consists in their producing an easy transition of ideas; it follows, that our notions of personal identity, proceed entirely from the smooth and uninterrupted progress of the thought along a train of connected ideas. (Hume 1888: 260)

The associationism which transforms the work of art into the multiple possible interconnections generated by the signifier equally dissolves the bonds that we usually believe to unite the self in its personal identity. If the disaggregated self of a modern genealogist like Foucault repeats a key element in eighteenth-century Scotland's reduction of the self to its associations, then Scotland's role as that of a "nascent postmodernism" seems even more compelling.

Such stylistic and conceptual similarities between the Scottish tradition and postmodernism have, however, to be balanced against the fact that many of the recent Scottish writers who are most clearly identifiable as "postmodern" in their practice are in fact deeply antagonistic to the world-view which has come to be identified with postmodernism. If we take Lyotard's *Postmodern Condition* as the defining text, then the condition of postmodernity is one in which

> the State and/or company must abandon the idealist and humanist narratives of legitimation in order to justify the new goal: in the discourse of today's financial backers of research, the only credible goal is power. (Lyotard 1984: 46).

Postmodernism, in this sense, has come to be identified not as a generic or stylistic issue but as the cultural expression of the changing nature of modern capitalism. As such, postmodernism is nothing other than the power relations of capitalism which function, in the contemporary world, through the processes of Americanisation and globalisation – two words which are, unfortunately, almost synonymous. As Fredric Jameson puts it:

> What has happened is that aesthetic production today has become integrated into commodity production generally: the frantic economic urgency of producing fresh waves of ever more novel-seeming goods (from clothing to airplanes) at ever greater rates of turnover, now assigns an increasingly essential structural function and position to aesthetic innovation and experimentation. (Jameson 1991: 4-5)

Postmodern aesthetics can thus be argued to be simply the transfer to the cultural realm of the requirements of contemporary capitalism, just as contemporary capitalism has adopted aesthetics – the aesthetics of the "new", the "innovative", the "challenging" – as the means of fulfilling its economic ends.

However, Scottish writers such as Muriel Spark (a Catholic convert), or Alasdair Gray (who declares himself to be anachronistically in favour of a Scottish Co-operative Workers Republic), are hardly likely to see their own use of postmodernist techniques as implying commitment to such conceptions of the world. We can integrate this opposition into a theory of the postmodern by suggesting, as Linda Hutcheon does in *The Politics of Postmodernism*, that the postmodern condition (globalising capitalism) is not identical with postmodernism in art, which actually develops as a resistance to the former. For

Hutcheon, "critique is as important as complicity in the response of cultural postmodernism to the philosophic and socio-economic realities of postmodernity" (Hutcheon 1989: 26), thereby allowing writers like Spark or Gray to be postmodern*ist* in their opposition to postmodern*ism*. On the other hand, it might be better to say that their style is peculiarly Scottish – rooted in stylistic devices which happen to have become typically post-modernist – and that their resistance is to a world system which sees small and marginal cultures as irrelevant to its logic. And yet, within Lyotard's conception of postmodernism, it is precisely the privilege conferred by the decay of grand narratives that the local can be asserted and celebrated. In which case, the resistant – indeed, national or nationalist – postmodernism would represent the real fulfilment of the postmodern condition. Could it be that Scotland's long maturation of the postmodern was preparation for the fulfilment of its national identity? This defiance of the world's apparent unification into a single, globalised culture would have been made possible by the postmodern decay of grand narratives.

2.

"Postmodernism", no doubt, has become as resistant to a single definition as "Romanticism", another stylistic and historical denominator.[3] Oddly, there is a recurrent element in discussions of the postmodern which is itself a continuation of Romantic aesthetics – the concept of the "sublime". In an Appendix to *The Postmodern Condition*, Lyotard appeals to the "sublime" as the ultimate explanation of the development of modernist and postmodernist art. The definition of the sublime that he adopts is that offered by Kant, who is, according to Lyotard's essay on "The Sign of History", both the "the epilogue to modernity" and "also a prologue to postmodernity" (Lyotard 1989: 394). Kant's "prologue" involves the first assertion of what has come to be a commonplace in postmodernism: that the world we know is a world which is entirely constructed by the human mind; that it is im-

---

[3] Arthur Lovejoy's essay on "On the Discrimination of Romanticisms" has become the *locus classicus* of all such dissolutions of period descriptors (Lovejoy 1924).

possible for us to encounter the world as it *really* is because the world is always already structured and shaped by the categories imposed on it by our own consciousness. Kant's "Copernican revolution" in philosophy required that we can only ever know the *phenomena* of our own sensory experience and never the *noumenon* of the world-in-itself. Poststructuralism has transformed this into the assertion that we can never know anything but the world as it is structured by our language (or by the categories of narrative). The consequence, though, is the same: rather than living in a world where consciousness is in touch with the reality of nature, we are forever trapped within a world whose reality is constituted by the nature of our own consciousness.

In Lyotard's version of this argument, we have come to recognise that we are all necessarily involved in "language games" and that "truth" is not the discovery of the "real" out there in the world but the construction of the world according to the rules of a particular game.

It is useful to make the following three observations about language games. The first is that their rules do not carry within themselves their own legitimation, but are the object of a contract, explicit or not, between players (which is not to say that the players invent the rules). The second is that if there are no rules, there is no game, that even an infinitesimal modification of one rule alters the nature of the game, that a "move" or utterance that does not satisfy the rules does not belong to the game they define. The third remark is suggested by what has just been said: every utterance should be thought of as a "move" in a game. (Lyotard 1984: 10)

Since the "social bond is linguistic, but is not woven with a single thread", producing "at least two (and in reality an indeterminate number of) language games" (Lyotard 1984: 40), there can be "no possibility that language games can be unified or totalised in any metadiscourse" (Lyotard 1984: 36). The postmodern conditions of knowledge as language games may first have been formulated by Wittgenstein, but "the exploding of language into families of heteronomous language-games is the theme that Wittgenstein, whether he knew it or not, took from Kant" (Lyotard 1989: 410).

The problem that haunted the Kantian project – how could there be a responsible moral act if all events in the world are necessarily structured by the category of cause and effect? – is precisely paralleled in the problem that haunts the Lyotardian scheme: how can one be responsible for one's statements in the language-game in which one is playing if all language games define in advance their own terms of validity? That we can posit a noumenon lying beyond the phenomena of experience is not enough; we must have some mode of access to it that justifies our belief that we are not simply products of a causality that we cannot escape: equally, there must be some means of escaping from the entrapments of language games, some means of switching between them or transforming them that is not simply another move in another language game. The sublime is important because it is the one instance in experience when the mechanism of the Kantian categories fails to operate and by failing thereby confirms the "beyond" upon which Kant's whole metaphysic depends.

For Kant, of course, the key issue was not the sublime – which he regarded as less philosophically significant than the beautiful – but the freedom of moral decision-making, in which we step from being creatures of the world of cause and effect into the noumenal world in which we are both free and immortal. Since this convoluted escape from the world of causal necessity cost even Kant some doubts, later thinkers have elevated the sublime, rather than moral decision-making, as the experience in which we discover that the categories that normally structure our thought fail, and thereby provide an insight into the unbounded universe that otherwise must always lie beyond the world constructed for us by consciousness. Lyotard takes this failure of categorical understanding to be crucial in the sublime, and central to modernist and postmodernist art: real art challenges us precisely because there is no rule to which it adheres; no understanding of previous art that can be mapped on to it to make sense of it; and by breaking the rules it launches us into the experience of the sublime as an assertion of freedom against the constraining limits of the existing categories of understanding. We can appeal only to the sublime as a guarantor of our ability to escape from the net of causal and categorical necessity. For Lyotard, the aesthetics of modernism fulfil precisely the Kantian sublime to the extent that the latter aims "to present the fact that the unpresentable exists. To make visible that there is something which can be conceived and which can neither be seen nor made visible: this is what is at stake in modern painting" (Lyotard 1984: 78). In this perspective, the aesthetics of literary or pictorial modern-

ism is the precursor of a freedom which only postmodernism can
fulfil:

> Here, then, lies the difference: modern aesthetics is an aesthetic of the sublime,
> though a nostalgic one. It allows the unpresentable to be put forward only as the
> missing contents; but the form, because of its recognizable consistency, continues to
> offer to the reader or viewer matter for solace and pleasure. Yet these sentiments do
> not constitute the real sublime sentiment, which is in an intrinsic combination of
> pleasure and pain: the pleasure that reason should exceed all presentation, the pain
> that imagination or sensibility should not be equal to the concept.
>
> The postmodern would be that which, in the modern, puts forward the unpre-
> sentable in presentation itself, that which denies itself the solace of good forms, the
> consensus of a taste which would make it possible to share collectively the nostalgia
> for the unattainable; that which searches for new presentations, not in order to enjoy
> them but in order to impart a stronger sense of the unpresentable. A postmodern artist
> or writer is in the position of a philosopher: the text he writes, the work he produces
> are not in principle governed by pre-established rules, and they cannot be judged ac-
> cording to a determining judgment, by applying familiar categories to the text or to
> the work. Those rules and categories are what the work of art itself is looking for. The
> artist and the writer, then, are working without rules in order to formulate the rules of
> what will have been done. (Lyotard 1984: 81)

Lyotard's postmodern is the fulfilment of the Kantian sublime as the
escape from a rule-bound universe, the moment when "reason" cannot
provide a category for the imagined or when the imagined cannot find
an explanation through the understanding. Like Kant, Lyotard demands a rule-bound world in all its determinacy while maintaining, as
the basis of our real humanity, a freedom that can defy those rules.

This potential for defying a deterministic universe has made the
sublime so significant in postmodernism: it maintains a freedom that
would otherwise dissolve into the banality of digressing from one
rule-bound system into another. Fredric Jameson invokes this sense of
the postmodern sublime in *Postmodernism or the Cultural Logic of
Late Capitalism*: the truly postmodern, for Jameson, involves "the
sense that beyond all thematics or content the work seems somehow to
tap the networks of the reproductive process and thereby to afford us
some glimpse into the postmodern or technological sublime", a
glimpse which gives us back our freedom by revealing in their "dis-
torted figuration" the "whole world system of present-day
multinational capitalism" (Jameson 1991: 37). The sublime, for Kant,

allows us to escape the determinations of the categories; the sublime, for Lyotard, allows us to defy the existing categories that determine general taste; the sublime, for Jameson, allows us to see – and therefore, at least potentially, to challenge – the economic categories by which we are determined. The sublime haunts the postmodern as the last possibility of real freedom in a world where freedom, as we generally understand it, is an illusion; a world where, as postmodernists like Foucault suggest, all change is caused not by the actions of free agents but by the historical equivalents of Kantian categories – "epistemes" which define and delimit all thought and therefore all action (Foucault 1970). Postmodernism, in other words, is a late twentieth-century replay of some of the key elements of Kantianism, replacing Kant's transcendental "categories" with historically-based or linguistically-based determinants of consciousness. Baudrillard's "simulacra", for instance, are little more than a technological version of Kant's "phenomena" (Baudrillard 1993): both ensure that human beings live in a world which is necessarily constructed – either physically or mentally – by the structures which shape the world for them and which shut them out forever from any contact with the "real". A typical example of this renewed Kantianism is Elizabeth Ermarth's assertion that "the imperial Subject, like the imperial History it founds, exists to sustain a one-world hypothesis: the idea that everything submits to a single system of measurement" and that postmodern identity "can appear only as the sequence of specifications of the available rule regimens" (Ermarth 2001: 47).

Kant's project was inspired by his effort to answer Hume's scepticism, which had "awakened him from his dogmatic slumbers",[4] and postmodernism's adoption of a Kantian perspective on the nature of knowledge suggests that Kant did indeed answer Hume. As long ago, however, as 1884, J. Hutchison Stirling, the Scottish philosopher responsible for introducing Hegel to a British audience through his study, *The Secret of Hegel* (1865), argued in the journal *Mind*, that "Kant has *not* answered Hume" (Hutchison Stirling 1884, 1885). Hutchison Stirling's case was based precisely on the issue which has required the prominence of the sublime in contemporary theory – the

---

[4] See Kuehn 1983 for a contextualisation of Kant's famous comment on his relationship to Hume. See also Kuehn 1987: chapter 9.

issue of "necessity" in the causal relations which Hume had put in doubt by claiming that we could never know that one thing was the cause of another. For Kant, causality was "necessary" because it was a category by which the human mind perceived the world: the necessity that Hume sought, in other words, was already implicit in the very perceptual framework which he had to use in order to ask the question about the nature of causality, and so could not be doubted. What Hutchison Stirling pointed out, however, was that the Kantian category of causation was involved in a profound self-contradiction. For Hume, succession could never be proved to be causality because it was possible that one thing which had always been perceived to follow from another might *not* occur in the future (the sun might not rise; flame might not produce heat). For Kant the opposite was true, and causality could never be distinguished from succession, since the category of causality was the inevitable template with which the human mind structured the world that it experienced. However, if mere succession – it rains, a particular tune is played on the radio – is to be distinguished from causal succession, then the category of causality must be able to distinguish a difference inherent in the successive objects it is experiencing – in which case, the necessity of causality is not in the category but in the objects themselves, and we are back in Hume's original (and unresolved) problem:

That rule, law, order, necessity itself, must already exist in the elements of sense even *for* the categories – that was an afterthought. This after-thought – But how, then, do the categories find their cues ? – coming suddenly upon him in the end, with all his vast labour behind him, must have appalled him like the apparition of a ghost. Ah yes, law can be the product of the understanding alone, no repetition can make this clearer; but then sense itself must have one necessary order under causality, and quite another necessary order under reciprocity, or how could these categories themselves act without mutual interference and confusion, or how, indeed, could they know when to act at all? (Hutchison Stirling 1885: 63)

That Kant had not answered Hume on the key issue of the necessity involved in causality undermined the whole Kantian schema, and, indeed, undermined the whole German tradition in philosophy:

In a word, to Kant metaphysic itself, to us the *Kritik of Pure Reason*, nay, German philosophy as a whole, has absolute foundation in the *whence* or *why* of *necessary connexion.* Such necessary connexion exhibited itself, in the course of the reflections of Kant, not as confined to causality alone, but as common (and, at the same time, peculiar) to all the propositions that collectively constituted what science there was of metaphysic proper. (Hutchison Stirling 1885: 48)

That the German answer to Hume was inadequate left it in no better position than that "of Reid, Beattie, Oswald, and all the rest" (Hutchison Stirling 1885: 71) – no better than, in other words, the answers of Scottish critics by whom Kant was first inspired – and, for our purposes, leaves the whole neo-Kantian edifice of postmodernity without foundations. If Kant has not answered Hume then the transcendental argument which locks us into the world as produced by the categories of our own consciousnesses – the structures of our own language, the narrative forms of history writing and so on – is deprived of its authority. The whole edifice is an illusion, its fundamental presupposition about the mind's construction of the external world – and the sublime which allows it to escape from those constructions – is invalidated. Postmodernism – in the philosophical sense – is the endless repetition of Kant's failure to address Hume's question about the necessity involved in causation.

3.

Hutchison Stirling's insight into Kant's "cold sweats" over his inability to overcome the Humean challenge was to radically re-open the ways in which Scottish philosophy was understood in the late nineteenth century. The most significant figure in this reinterpretation was Andrew Seth (later A.S. Pringle-Pattison), whose book on *Scottish Philosophy*, published in 1890, is subtitled *A Comparison of the Scottish and German Answers to Hume.* Seth presents Hume's philosophy as the *reductio ad absurdum* of the philosophical principles introduced by Locke and developed by Berkeley, which substitute the "ideas" of things as intermediaries between consciousness and the things of which it is conscious. These "ideas" lead inevitably to doubt about whether they adequately or appropriately represent the real world to which they give us access. Hume's escape from this dilemma is to abolish objects altogether, and to insist that we are never in contact with anything but "impressions" and "ideas", a metaphysical position which cannot be integrated with the ordinary business of life, as Hume himself seems to acknowledge:

> I dine, I play a game of backgammon, I converse and am merry with my friends; and when, after three or four hours' amusement, I would return to these speculations, they appear so cold, and strained, and ridiculous, that I cannot find in my heart to enter into them any further. (Hume 1888: 269; Seth 1890: 70)

For Seth, this famous passage is Hume's acknowledgment that his philosophy is its own "self-refutation" (Seth 1890: 66), and that Hume was unable to find any way beyond the impasse he had created.

Kant's philosophy appeared to provide an escape from Hume's dilemma, but if Kant has indeed not answered Hume then, argues Seth, the focus of attention must turn to the other major response to Hume, that of Thomas Reid, and Reid's demolition of the theory of Representative Perception upon which, he claims, Locke, Berkeley and Hume based their philosophies. Seth's recuperation of Reid's realism, which maintains our unmediated access to the world against the subjective idealism implied in the theory of Representative Perception, provides Scottish philosophy with an alternative to simply following in the footsteps of Kant, even if the key issues on which Reid alights – such as that the basis of knowledge is not a sensation or an idea but a unit of judgment (Seth 1890: 96) – are precisely those on which Kant also focused. The outcome in the two philosophies, however, is very different, since for Kant, as for Hume, "we cannot by any conceivable possibility tell how the world of knowledge – […] the phenomenal world – stands related to the world of reality" (Seth 1890: 136), and so "instead, of, like Reid, abandoning 'the ideal system', [Kant] elaborately reconstructed it, endeavouring to give it a more rational and tenable form" (Seth 1890: 149). Scottish philosophy, on the other hand,

> was fortunate enough […] to escape this danger, by taking up the broad position that, while the principles in question are referable to the constitution of our nature, our nature is, in respect of them, in complete harmony with the nature of things – so that they may, with equal truth, be spoken of as perceived or recognised in things. (Seth 1890: 161)

What Reid's analysis underlines, according to Seth, is that "all principles of explanation [...] are derived, and must be derived, from the nature of the explaining Self; they are transcripts, so to speak, of its constitution" (Seth 1890: 109). The nature of the "Self" becomes, for Seth, the touchstone against which both Hume's original arguments and the neo-Kantian and Hegelian philosophies of the late nineteenth century must be tested, since "the mere particular and the mere universal are alike abstractions of the mind; what exists is *the individual*" (Seth 1890: 174). *Hegelianism and Personality* (1887) measured Hegel's shortcomings with reference to his presentation of the "personality" of both God and Man. For Seth, Hegel's mode of argument "confounds" logic with ontology or metaphysics and "ends by offering us *a logic as a metaphysic*" (Seth 1887: 104), thus reducing the existential self to a set of logical rather than real relations:

The result of Hegel's procedure would really be to sweep "existential reality" off the board altogether, under the persuasion, apparently, that a full statement of all the thought-relations that constitute our knowledge of the thing is equivalent to the existent thing itself. On the contrary, it may be confidently asserted that there is no more identity of Knowing and Being with an infinity of such relations than there was without one. (Seth 1887: 126)

Seth insists against Hegel's logical system that

the meanest thing that exists has a life of its own, absolutely unique and individual, which we can partly *understand* by terms borrowed from our own experience, but which is no more identical with, or in any way like, the description we give of it, than our own inner life is identical with the description we give of it in a book of philosophy. (Seth 1887: 126)

For Seth, acknowledgment of the limits of our modes of knowing and thinking – logic, psychology, ontology – is the real insight of the Kantian argument, and it is crucial not to confuse the outcomes of one mode of understanding with the possibilities of another. For psychology, the data of sensation in their subjectivity are the basis of understanding: their truth to the external world is not an issue. But this does not mean that their truth to the world is unfounded – any more, in terms of later theories, than we can say that Saussure's deliberate exclusion of "reference" from the domain of linguistics, as a discipline, means that language has no referent. The grounding exclusion which makes one form of knowledge possible must not be taken to be equivalent to a metaphysical truth about the nature of the real. Hegel's procedure, for Seth, involves precisely such a transfer from the abstract conceptions of logic to the ontological requirements of our real existence:

we have abundantly seen the impossibility of reaching a real existence by such means. "The concrete Idea" remains abstract, and unites God and man only by eviscerating the real content of both. Both disappear or are sublimated into it, but simply because it represents what is common to both, the notion of intelligence as such. They disappear, not indeed in a pantheistic substance, but in a logical concept. If we scrutinise the system narrowly, we find Spirit or the Absolute doing duty at one time for God, and another time for man; but when we have hold of the divine we have lost our grasp of the human and *vice versa*. We have never the two together. (Seth 1887: 155-56)

Hegel's Absolute is a logical conception of self-consciousness, "not an account of any real process or real existence" and is therefore no more an account of a real God than it is an account of real human beings, since "finite selves are wiped out, and nature, deprived of any life of its own, becomes as it were, the still mirror in which the one Self-consciousness contemplates itself" (Seth 1887: 162). "What other result", Seth asks, "could we expect than that both God and man, as real beings, would vanish back into their source, leaving us with the logical Idea as the sole reality" (Seth 1887: 191).

The Idealism of the neo-Kantians and the Hegelians is, for Seth, a denial of the true meaning of personality, for "if we take away from Idealism personality, and the ideals that belong to personality, it ceases to be Idealism" (Seth 1887: 193). In a later series of lectures,[5] Seth proposes the overthrow of Idealism by a Transcendental Realism. The latter will combine at an epistemological level the Natural Realism of the Scottish tradition, stemming from Reid, with a transcendentalism that acknowledges the operation of the Kantian

---

[5] Seth's books two major books, *Scottish Philosophy* and *Hegelianism and Personality* were first delivered under the auspices of the Balfour Lectures – funded by the later Prime Minister, Arthur Balfour, himself a philosopher – at the University of Edinburgh. The third lecture series was not published until after Seth's death in 1931 as *The Balfour Lectures on Realism*.

categories as the very means by which we escape from the confines of the self-enclosed phenomenal world into which Kant plunged us – "a kind of speculative nightmare [...which] had been preparing all through the modern period" (Seth Pringle-Pattison 1933: 255). The cause of the nightmare is to mistake the conditions of knowledge for the nature of reality, to mistake epistemology for metaphysics:

> The problem of knowledge, when it comes into the foreground, inevitably tends to separate the knowing subject from the whole world of objective reality. The philosophical antithesis is no longer between the whole and the part, between the permanent unity and its dependent manifestations, as it is when the line of thought is metaphysical or ontological. The antithesis is now between the subjective consciousness and the world of real things. The subject is therefore placed upon one side and the whole trans-subjective universe upon the other, and a chasm is made between them. The knower is practically extruded from the real universe: he is treated as if he did not belong to it, as if he came to inspect it like a stranger from afar. His forms of thought come thus to be regarded as an alien product with no inherent fitness to express the nature of things. Things are rather conceived as in themselves independent of these forms, so that the forms, when applied, are treated as an unauthorised gloss, a distorting medium. A little reflection, however, tells us that to conceive matters thus is to convert the necessary duality or opposition which knowledge involves into a real or metaphysical dualism for which there is no kind of warrant. We are the victims of metaphor, if we allow ourselves to think of the individual knower as standing outside the universe in this way. (Seth Pringle-Pattison 1933: 255)

The impasse of the modern requires that we escape the "speculative nightmare" by starting from a different point from that of the isolated knower, who is the abstraction of an independent and isolated witness to the world rather than a participant in it. The thoughts of the self-enclosed Cartesian ego may be the foundation of modernity but it is not the *actual* foundation on which our *real* world is built:

> all through the modern period philosophers have been turning the subjectivity of knowledge against its objectivity, and in the last resort converting the very notion of knowledge into an argument against the possibility of knowledge. (Seth Pringle-Pattison 1933: 184-85)

The consequence is that "since the time of Hume and Kant" philosophy "has largely created the difficulties which it finds it so hard to surmount" (Seth Pringle-Pattison 1933: 185). Seth, in other words, identifies precisely the contradictions of the modern which would have to be surmounted if we were ever to be able to reach the "post-modern", but in doing so reveals how deeply rooted is our contemporary "postmodernism" in the very crises and contradictions of the "modern". Far from being truly *post*-modern, postmodernism is modernism caught in a repetitive loop in which Kant and Hume continually undermine both one another and our connection with the real.

Although Seth did not develop a post-modern philosophy of his own, much was achieved by his critical account of the philosophy of the previous two hundred years. His testing of the Kantian tradition against the Scottish tradition, was a clearing of the ground, a breaking free from the Representative Theory of Perception and all its consequences. Four key suggestions are made by Seth as providing an alternative starting point for a philosophy which will enable it to escape the contradictions of the modern. The first is that we must not conceive the Self as an isolated knower, but as a being among others:

If a mere individual, as we are often told, would be a being without consciousness of its own limitations – a being therefore, which could not know itself as an individual – then no Self is a mere individual. We may even safely say that the mere individual is a fiction of philosophic thought. There could be no interaction between individuals unless they were all embraced within one Reality; still less could there be any knowledge by one individual of others, if they did not all form parts of one system of things. (Seth 1887: 215-16)

The Self, for Seth, is both a "unique existence, which is perfectly impervious [...] to other selves" (Seth 1887: 216) and, at the same time, dependent on the otherness of other selves to know itself as a Self. The second is that the Self is a personality and that personality is related to the will rather than to self-conscious knowledge:

I have a centre of my own – a will of my own – which no one shares with me or can share – a centre which I maintain even in my dealings with God Himself. For it is eminently false to say that I put off, or can put off my personality here. The religious consciousness lends no countenance whatever to the representation of the human soul as a mere mode or efflux of the divine. On the contrary, only in a person, in a relatively independent or self-centred being is religious approach to God possible. (Seth 1887: 218-19)

Furthermore, since will is the fundamental characteristic of the Self as personality, the third suggestion is that the Self is not known primarily through its *consciousness of* the world – not, in other words, through reflective *knowledge* – but through action:

It is in action that we have the surest clue to the early stages of the animal and the human consciousness. Knowledge in such creatures exists simply in a practical reference. Consciousness would be a useless luxury unless as putting them in relation to the surrounding world. (Seth Pringle-Pattison 1933: 189)

And it is as action, fourthly, that we should think of knowledge itself. Instead of the world presenting itself to a passive consciousness, or presenting itself in the necessary forms of the Kantian categories, the world is known only in and through action:

Knowledge means nothing if it does not mean the relation of two factors, knowledge *of* an object *by* a subject. But knowledge is not an entity stretching across, as it were, from subject to object, and uniting them; still less is knowledge the one reality of which subject and object are two sides or aspects. Knowledge is an activity, an activo-passive experience of the subject, whereby it becomes aware of what is not itself. (Seth Pringle-Pattison 1933: 193)

The establishment of a philosophy of the Self as a Personality which knows itself in action rather than in contemplation, which understands itself as part of the world rather than set over against it, and which discovers its unique individual identity through the will rather than through the universal and empty *cogito*, is, for Seth, the basis for transcending the contradictions of the modern and, therefore, from our later perspective, the basis for a properly *post*-modern philosophy.

Seth's return to Scottish traditions and his critique of the Kantian-Hegelian tradition prefigure the most important Scottish philosopher of the twentieth century, John Macmurray, who set himself the task of overturning the whole tradition of modern philosophy:

Modern philosophy is characteristically *egocentric*. I mean no more than this: that firstly, it takes the Self as its starting-point, and not God, or the world or the community; and that, secondly, the Self is an individual in isolation. This is shown by the fact that there can arise the question, "How does the Self know that other selves exist?" Further, the Self so premised is a thinker in search of knowledge. It is conceived as the Subject; the correlate in experience of the object presented for cognition. (Macmurray 1957: 31)

The answer to the "speculative nightmare" of modernity – for it is Kant whom Macmurray identifies as "the most adequate of modern philosophies" (Macmurray 1957: 39) – must reverse the "Copernican revolution" by which Kant had made the world depend upon the knower:

> If we make the "I think" the primary postulate of philosophy, then not merely do we institute a dualism between theoretical and practical experience, but we make action logically inconceivable – a mystery, as Kant so rightly concludes, in which we necessarily believe, but which we can never comprehend. (Macmurray 1957: 73)

A truly post-modern philosophy will be one that starts from the entirely different basis that the Self is first an agent rather than a thinker, and that this agent inhabits a social world of persons rather than a mechanical world of objects or a dynamic world of organisms. The failure of modern philosophy from Hume to Kant and to Hegel lies in the inadequacy of its conception of the human *person* rather than simply the human being or the human thinker:

> Any "self" – that is to say, any agent – is an existing being, a person [...] The idea of an isolated agent is self-contradictory. Any agent is necessarily in relation to the Other. Apart from this essential relation he does not exist. But, further, the Other in this constitutive relation must itself be personal. Persons, therefore, are constituted by their mutual relation to one another. "I" exist only as one element in the complex "You and I". We have to discover how this ultimate fact can be adequately thought, that is to say, symbolized in reflection. (Macmurray 1961: 24)

The extent to which Macmurray's philosophy succeeded in fulfilling its ambition of transcending the modern may be open to debate, but it proposes a post-modernism radically different from the postmodernisms that remain within the Kantian frame. The question of agency is precisely the issue that postmodern theory either negates or sidesteps, since there is neither a place for an encounter with the "real" in postmodern theories nor a conception of a human individual who can exert purchase upon that reality. As Fitzhugh and Leckie have argued, there is no way out of "the relentless logic of the postmodern's incompatibility with any attempt to reconcile it with agency" (Fitzhugh and Leckie 2001: 76). Macmurray's philosophy of the "self as agent" opposes postmodernism precisely by providing a means of going beyond the modern and therefore of fulfilling a real post-modernity. It is Macmurray's form of the post-modern, I suggest, that we find "symbolized in reflection" in the works of Scottish postmodernists, rather than the Kantian postmodernism of Lyotard or any of the varieties of poststructuralism to which such postmodernisms are usually attached.

Indeed, uncovering the "You and I"[6] in the isolated individual of modernity has been the driving force of precisely those Scottish writers who are most often associated with the stylistic gestures of postmodernism, from Muriel Spark and Alasdair Gray to A.L. Kennedy, Janice Galloway and Iain Banks. One quote from James Kelman, however, will have to suffice as illustration of Scottish novelists' concern with this issue:

Fuck it man he switched on the radio, lifted out the cassette. Sometimes the voices drowned ye out. The incredible lives being led elsewhere in this poxy country, like a fucking fairy story. Ye couldnay believe yer ears at some of the stuff ye heard. Ye go about yer business, eating yer dinner and all that, washing the dishes; and ye listen to these voices. Ye think fucking christ almighty what the fuck's going on. Sammy couldnay even see. He couldnay fucking see man know what I'm talking about, and he still had to listen to them, these fucking bampot bastards. (Kelman 1994: 119)

First, second and third person pronouns are involved in a dance of substitution in passages such as this, with the narrative voice hovering between that of the character and that of the narrator. The sentence, "Ye couldnay believe yer ears at some of the stuff ye heard" is suspended between the narrator's commentary on what we, the readers, are hearing and Sammy's reflections on the world around him, a shift made more complex by the switch from "Sammy couldnay see" – which *might* either be Sammy referring to himself in the third person or a third person narrative voice – to "know what I'm talking about", where the "I" may be Sammy or may be the narrator/author. The self-referring "ye" underlines that Sammy's self-consciousness – despite his apparent isolation in the narrative – is in fact the product of a "self" which can only know itself in relation to a "you", and in the

---

[6] For a discussion of the sources of Macmurray's concept, see Kirkpatrick 1986.

lack of an external "you" creates itself as the internal correlate of that relationship. The isolation of Kelman's character, in other words, replicates the isolation of the Cartesian/Kantian ego, but <u>the linguistic structure and its invocation of "you" implies an entirely different conception of the self as always in relation with the Other. Kelman's novel, like Gray's *Lanark* or Spark's *The Driver's Seat*, dramatises the ways in which the isolated self of modernity is unsustainable, and points towards the ways in which an alternative sense of the self might begin to be acknowledged.</u> *but Craig gives no definite criteria relating to what this 'alternative sense of the self' might be, beyond some 'heterocentric' model — a postmodern utopia: idea rather than possibility*

4.

In the conclusion to *The Postmodern Condition*, Lyotard challenges one of the most influential alternatives to postmodernist and post-structuralist thought – Habermas's conception of "communicative reason". Refusing to accept that the Enlightenment's trust in truth and justice was misplaced, Habermas presents communicative reason as an escape from the "subject-centred" rationality of past philosophy, and a means of giving new impetus to the "unfinished project of modernity".[7] Lyotard, however, finds in Habermas's argument only the continuation of the notion of humanity as a universal subject to which we are each, as individuals, necessarily subordinated. It is against what he sees as the totalitarianism of Habermas's revitalised Kantian rationality that Lyotard invokes the Kantian "sublime" as that which must always escape from the dictates of reason. The argument between them, in other words, is carried out entirely within the framework of a Kantian philosophy, making it inevitable that the "modern" (the Enlightenment as the development of a rational conception of human history) and the postmodern (the anti-Enlightenment refusal of any such metanarrative) represent neither a specific historical development, nor an intellectual opposition, but rather a continual dialectic, oscillating between two sides of the same philosophical schema. The emphasis swings from the unknowable Kantian "thing-

---

[7] For a discussion of Habermas's relation to poststructuralist and postmodernist thinkers, see Norris 2000.

in-itself" to the universal Kantian rationality and back again, but the centrality of reason is never in doubt. In salvaging from Hume's critique the necessity involved in causation, Kant was salvaging the significance of reason itself as our means to the discovery of truth, and Lyotard and Habermas follow in his footsteps. For Lyotard, scientific rationality provides the model for social rationality, since in scientific rationality "consensus is a horizon that is never reached" (Lyotard 1984: 61); for Habermas, social rationality provides the model for scientific rationality, since "reason is by its very nature incarnated in contexts of communicative action and in structures of the lifeworld" (Habermas 1987: 322).

Kantian rationality is central to our conception of the Enlightenment (as well as to the anti-Enlightenment of postmodernity), and yet is built on the failed foundations of Kant's response to Hume. We might wonder if the nomenclature of the "Scottish Enlightenment" is misleading, for the real challenge that Hume laid down was not simply the dissolution of our notions of causality but the radical assertion that far from being the sovereign power of the human mind, "reason is and ought to be the slave of the passions, and can never pretend to any other office than to serve and obey them" (Hume 1888: 415). If we take Hume to be the central figure of eighteenth-century Scottish thought, it would, given its refusal of the power of reason, perhaps make more sense to describe this intellectual movement as "Scottish romanticism"[8] – the whole opposition between Enlightenment and Romantic, as between modern and postmodern, is one which cannot be mapped onto the Scottish context. Hume's *Treatise* corresponds to traditional conceptions of Enlightenment rationality to the extent that he adopts the scientific model of Newton's physics and seeks to apply it to the workings of the human mind: what he discovers, however, is that the reason by which he investigates the mind is undone by what he discovers *about* the mind – that the mind does not work on rational principles but by "irrational" associative processes and on the basis of unverifiable natural beliefs. If we identify "Enlightenment" with the rationalism of the Kantian tradition then, in the earliest stages of the Enlightenment, Hume's philosophy undoes its fundamental concept.

---

[8] This is a point made by Norman Kemp Smith.

To nineteenth-century Kantian interpreters of Hume, such as the English Idealist T.H. Green, this Hume was invisible: Green represents Hume as having reduced psychological experience to impossible atomic units which only the categories of Kantian philosophy could reconstruct into a valid conception of the human mind. But it was to Hume's insistence on reason's "slavish" role that Norman Kemp Smith reverted in his 1941 study of *The Philosophy of David Hume*. Kemp Smith, who was Seth Pringle-Pattison's successor at Edinburgh University, and Macmurray's predecessor, and who was a distinguished translator of Kant, applied to Hume the lesson of Seth's rereading of Scottish philosophy and located Hume not in relation to Locke and Berkeley but in relation to Francis Hutcheson, from whom, Smith claimed, Hume learned that "judgments of moral approval and disapproval, and indeed judgments of *value* of whatever type, are based not on rational thought or on evidence, but solely on feeling" (Kemp Smith 1966: 13). Hume's radical move was to apply this insight to all forms of knowledge not purely axiological:

what is central in his teaching is not Locke or Berkeley's "ideal" theory and the negative consequences, important as these are for Hume, which follow from it, but the doctrine that the determining influence in human, as in other forms of animal life, is feeling, not reason or understanding, i.e. not evidence whether *a priori* or empirical, and therefore also not ideas – at least not "ideas" as hitherto understood. "Passion" is Hume's most general title for instincts, propensities, feelings, emotions and sentiments, as well as for the passions ordinarily so-called; and belief, he teaches, is a passion. Accordingly the maxim which is central to his ethics – "Reason is and ought to be the slave of the passions" – is no less central to his theory of knowledge, being there the maxim: "Reason is and ought to be subordinate to our natural beliefs". (Kemp Smith 1966: 11)

The crisis of the *Treatise*, when Hume seems to despair of his own metaphysical speculations at the end of Book 1, is not, therefore, the *reductio ad absurdum* of Hume's philosophy – as Seth believed – but Hume's dramatisation of the necessary failure of reason to be able to address the issues with which it is confronted. The isolated rational consciousness is incapable of making sense of the world because the sense of the world lies in human – and animal – passion, rather than in reason. Kant's critical philosophy, as an effort to establish the appropriate limits of reason while leaving open the needs of faith, is, from a

Humean point of view, entirely misguided: the real issue is to establish the ways in which reason must subordinate itself to feeling and to establish the consequences for our conceptions of knowledge that flow from that subordination. Hume, in other words, displaces Enlightenment rationality as effectively as the Romantics sought to do and subverts it as radically as Nietzsche claimed to do.[9] Hume, we might say, is already post- or anti-Enlightenment insofar as Enlightenment is identified with the rationalism of the Cartesian and Kantian traditions; or, alternatively, Hume and those thinkers of the "Scottish Enlightenment" closest to him, such as Adam Smith, propose such a different conception of Enlightenment that it leads beyond modernity rather than towards it, and therefore prefigures a different kind of "postmodernity". Beyond the isolated *cogito*, beyond the reasoning self, what Hume insists upon is the self as fundamentally *social*. The distressed philosopher must learn that "since reason is incapable of dispelling these clouds" produced by metaphysical speculation, he must trust to nature and be determined not to "seclude myself [...] from the commerce and society of men, which is so agreeable" (Hume 1888: 269-70). It is in our interaction with other human selves that our passions come into play, and the reason that "is and ought to be the slave of the passions" mistakes its own role when it seeks to separate itself from that passional existence, when it reduces the self to a thinking thing instead of a social agent. As Hume puts it in the *Treatise*, "reason alone can never produce any action or give rise to volition" and therefore "nothing can oppose or retard the impulse of passion, but a contrary impulse" (Hume 1888: 414, 415): the reasoning self is a constricted, limited creature which seeks to ignore the fact that the real self is the passional self, and since the passions require will and action, the real self is the self as agent.

When Macmurray, in his broadcast talks on *Reason and Emotion*, published in 1935, argued that "every activity must have an adequate motive, and all motives are emotional" because they "belong to our feeling, not to our thoughts" (Macmurray 1935: 23), he cited Plato, rather than Hume, as the only major philosopher who believed that "reason is primarily an affair of emotion, and that the rationality

---

[9] For certain strands of postmodernism, Nietzsche is the key formative influence, see, for instance, Megill 1985.

of thought is the derivative and secondary one" (Macmurray 1935: 26). It may be, then, that Kemp Smith's re-reading of Hume was itself a response to the "personalist" philosophies of Seth and Macmurray, but it makes Hume the precursor of the effort to get beyond the contemplative reason of the thinking ego and to reach a post-modern rationality based in the emotions. No "affection", Hume argued "can be call'd unreasonable" except "when a passion, such as hope or fear, grief or joy, despair or security, is founded on the supposition of the existence of objects, which really do not exist" (Hume 1888: 416). Macmurray takes this to be the "rationality" of the emotions. Reason, he argues is "the capacity to behave consciously in terms of the nature of what is not ourselves [...] to behave in terms of the nature of the object" (Macmurray 1935: 19); it is therefore equally possible to distinguish between rational and irrational emotions in terms of their adequacy to their object, a distinction which does not depend on reason precisely because reason is necessarily subordinate to the passions:

The emotional life is not simply a part or an aspect of human life. It is not, as we so often think, subordinate, or subsidiary to the mind. It is the core and essence of human life. The intellect arises out of it, is rooted in it, draws its nourishment and sustenance from it, and is the subordinate partner in the human economy. (Macmurray 1935: 75)

Rationality, therefore, for Macmurray must arise not out of the Cartesian-Kantian thinking ego but out of the emotions themselves:

The rationality that appears in thought is itself the reflection of a rationality that belongs to the motives of action. It follows that none of our activities, not even the activities of thinking, can express our reason unless the emotions which produce and sustain them are rational emotions. (Macmurray 1935: 23-24)

For Macmurray, as for Hume, the quality of our social life is dependent not on the development of "reason", nor on our submission to some Kantian universal law, but on the education of the emotions, an education that begins with the recognition that our emotions bind us into a world which is not the world of cause and effect describable by scientific rationality but a world of human intentions. It is the world of "intentions" that Macmurray describes as the "personal" world, as opposed to the mechanical or organic worlds of physics and biology. The isolated ego of the Cartesian-Kantian tradition treats itself as though it were independent of the world – or, at least, as though the world is dependent upon it. Macmurray, on the other hand, insists on the self as "dependent" (Macmurray 1961: 42) – dependent in infancy in ways which are quite different from the dependence of other creatures, and dependent in adulthood not only on the whole network of society but on the existence of others through whom it achieves and maintains the significance of being a person. As Kemp Smith declares of Hume, it is *sympathy* – the "propensity we have to receive by communication [the] inclinations and sentiments" of others (Kemp Smith 1966: 170) – which is the "universal influence" that "renders man the specific type of creature he is, namely, a creature so essentially social that even in his most self-regarding passions sympathy keeps others no less than the self constantly before the mind" (Kemp Smith 1966: 175). As Macmurray puts it,

the form of the child's experience is dependence on a personal Other; and [...] this form of experience is never outgrown, but provides the ground plan of all personal experience, which is constituted from start to finish by relation to the Other and communication with the Other. (Macmurray 1961: 154)

If Macmurray's philosophy is truly post-modern precisely because it challenges both the modern and postmodern of the Cartesian-Kantian tradition, it does so by following – or by running in parallel with – the Hume who is given to us by Kemp Smith, a Hume whose philosophy has to be read not in terms of the metaphysical isolation of the thinker of Book 1 of the *Treatise* – on which earlier commentary had focused – but on the "sympathetic" self of Books 2 and 3. By revealing how "dependent" that isolated consciousness is in its real social relations, Hume subverted in advance the Kantian rational ego just as effectively as his theory of causation subverts the Kantian categories. He thereby paved the way for a "post-modernism" in Scotland that went beyond those limitations of the modern upon which late twentieth-century postmodernism has remained impaled. This tradition of Scottish ideas emerges in contemporary debate in the thought of Alasdair MacIntyre, much of whose best work has focused on the consequences of Enlightenment. For MacIntyre, human beings are "dependent rational animals" (MacIntyre 1999),[10] their rationality limited and bracketed by their "dependence" and by their "animality", their passional existence. As a critic of "modernity" MacIntyre is often included in anthologies of the "postmodern", but as someone who believes that a return to Aquinas is the true route for contemporary moral thinking, his postmodernity is, like Macmurray's, a "postmodernity", one for which, as for a whole tradition of Scottish thought from Hume to Seth, "the mere individual is a fiction of philosophic thought" (Seth 1887: 216), or, as Macmurray puts it, "human behaviour is comprehensible only in terms of a dynamic social reference; the isolated, purely individual self is a fiction" (Macmurray 1961: 38). If Scottish literary fiction shows all the marks of stylistic postmodernism it is perhaps because, from the very inauguration of the modern, Scottish thought was searching for an alternative to that "purely individual self" based on the independent, rational consciousness. Hume's crisis – "we have, therefore, no choice left but betwixt a false reason and none at all" (Hume 1888: 268) – and the self-negating structure of his *Treatise* prefigure the characteristic traits of a literature that is committed to going beyond reason in order to escape from the madness to which the isolated rational consciousness – like Hogg's Robert Wringhim or Stevenson's Dr Jekyll – inevitably leads.

---

[10] In his preface, MacIntyre underscores that "the positions I have taken involve a rejection of Lockean accounts of personal identity, of Kantian or quasi-Kantian views of perception" (MacIntyre 1999: xii), and, like Macmurray, argues that "neither the modern nation-state nor the modern family can supply the kind of political and social association that is needed" (MacIntyre 1999: 9).

Bibliography

Alison, Archibald. 1811. *An Essay on Taste*. Edinburgh: Archibald Constable.

Anderson, Benedict. 1991. *Imagined Communities: Reflections on the Origin and Spread of Nationalism*. London: Verso.

Barthes, Roland. 1977. "From Work to Text" in Heath, Stephen (ed.) *Image—Music—Text*. London: Fontana. 155-64.

Baudrillard, Jean. 1993. *Symbolic Exchange and Death* (tr. Iain H. Grant). London: Sage.

Clunas, Alex. 1982. "Stevenson: a Precursor of the Post-Moderns?" in *Cencrastus* 6: 9-11.

Craig, Cairns. 1982. "The Body in the Kit-Bag" in *Cencrastus* 1: 18-22.

—. 1983. "Peripheries" in *Cencrastus* 9: 3-9.

—. 1996. *Out of History: Narrative Paradigms in English and Scottish Culture*. Edinburgh: Polygon.

Ermarth, Elizabeth Deeds. 1992. *Sequel to History*. Princeton: Princeton University Press.

—. 2001. "Agency in the Discursive Condition" in Shaw, David Gary (ed.) *History and Theory: Studies in the Philosophy of History* 40(4): 34-58.

Fitzhugh, Michael L. and William H. Leckie, Jr. 2001. "Agency, Postmodernism, and the Cause of Change" in Shaw, David Gary (ed.) *History and Theory: Studies in the Philosophy of History* 40(4): 59-81.

Foucault, Michel. 1970. *The Order of Things*. London: Tavistock.

—. 1977. "Nietzsche, Genealogy, History" in Bouchard, Donald F. (ed.) *Language, Counter-Memory, Practice: Selected Essays and Interviews*. Oxford: Basil Blackwell. 139-64.

Gifford, Douglas. 1988. "Myth, Parody and Dissociation" in Gifford, Douglas (ed.) *The History of Scottish Literature, Volume 3*. Aberdeen: Aberdeen University Press. 217-58.

Graham, W.S. 1979. *Collected Poems 1942-1977*. London: Faber and Faber.

Habermas, Jürgen. 1987. "An Alternative Way out of the Philosophy of the Subject: Communicative versus Subject-Centred Reason" in Habermas, Jürgen *The Philosophical Discourse of Modernity*. Cambridge, Mass.: MIT Press. 294-326.

Herman, Arthur. 2002. *The Scottish Enlightenment: the Scots' Invention of the Modern World*. London: Fourth Estate.

Hume, David. 1888. *A Treatise of Human Nature*. Oxford: Clarendon Press.

Hutcheon, Linda. 1988. *A Poetics of Postmodernism: History, Theory, Fiction*. London: Routledge.

—. 1989. *The Politics of Postmodernism*. London: Routledge.

Hutchison Stirling, J. 1865. *The Secret of Hegel*. London: Longman, Green, et al.

—. 1884, 1885. "Kant has not Answered Hume" in *Mind* 36: 531-547, and 37: 45-72.

Jameson, Fredric. 1991. *Postmodernism, or, the Cultural Logic of Late Capitalism*. London: Verso. 4-5.

Kelman, James. 1994. *How late it was, how late*. London: Secker and Warburg.

Kemp Smith, Norman. 1966. *The Philosophy of David Hume: A Critical Study of its Origins and Central Doctrines*. London: Macmillan.

Kidd, Colin. 1993. *Subverting Scotland's Past*. Cambridge: Cambridge University Press.

Kirkpatrick, Frank G. 1986. *Community: a Trinity of Models*. Washington, DC: Georgetown University Press.

Kuehn, Manfred. 1983. "Kant's Conception of Hume's Problem" in *Journal of the History of Philosophy* 21: 175-93.

—. 1987. *Scottish Common Sense in Germany, 1768—1800*. Kingston and Montreal: McGill-Queen's University Press.

Lovejoy, Arthur. 1924. "On the Discrimination of Romanticisms" in *Publications of the Modern Languages Association of America* 39: 229-53.

Lukacs, Georg. 1969. *The Historical Novel*. London: Merlin.

Lyotard, Jean-Francois. 1984. *The Postmodern Condition: A Report on Knowledge* (tr. Geoffrey Bennington and Brian Massumi). Manchester: Manchester University Press.

—. 1989. "The Sign of History" in Benjamin, Andrew (ed.) *A Lyotard Reader*. Oxford: Basil Blackwell. 393-411.

MacDiarmid, Hugh. 1955. *In Memoriam James Joyce*. Glasgow: William MacLellan, 1955.

McGann, Jerome. 1999. "Scotland and Romanticism". Paper presented at *International Scott Conference* (University of Oregon, 21-25 July 1999).

—. (forthcoming). "Scotland and Romanticism". To appear in Duncan, Ian, Leith Davis and Janet Sorenson (eds) *Scotland and the Borders of Romanticism*.

McHale, Brian. 1987. *Postmodernist Fiction*. London: Methuen.

MacIntyre, Alasdair. 1999. *Dependent Rational Animals: Why Human Beings Need the Virtues*. London: Duckworth.

Macmurray, John. 1935. *Reason and Emotion*. London: Faber and Faber.

—. 1957. *The Self as Agent*. London: Faber and Faber.

—. 1961 *Persons in Relation*. London: Faber and Faber.

Megill, Allan. 1985. *Prophets of Extremity: Nietzsche, Heidegger, Foucault, Derrida*. Berkeley and Los Angeles: University of California Press.

Miller, Karl. 1985. *Doubles*. Oxford: Oxford University Press.

Nairn, Tom. 1981. *The Break-Up of Britain*. London: Verso.

Norris, Christopher. 2000. *Deconstruction and "the Unfinished Project of Modernity"*. London: Athlone Press.

Seth, Andrew. 1887. *Hegelianism and Personality: Balfour Philosophical Lectures, University of Edinburgh*. Edinburgh: William Blackwood and Sons.

—. 1890. *Scottish Philosophy: A Comparison of the Scottish and German Answers to Hume*. Edinburgh: William Blackwood and Sons.

Seth Pringle-Pattison, A. 1933. *The Balfour Lectures on Realism* (ed. G.F. Barbour). Edinburgh: William Blackwood and Sons.

Spark, Muriel. 1963. *The Comforters*. Harmondsworth: Penguin.

Stewart, Dugald. 1980. "Account of the Life and Writings of Adam Smith, LL.D." in Wightman, W.P.D. and J.C. Bryce (eds) *Adam Smith, Essays on Philosophical Subjects, with Dugald Stewart's Account of Adam Smith*. Oxford: Clarendon Press.

White, Hayden. 1973. *Metahistory: the Historical Imagination in Nineteenth-Century Europe*. Baltimore: Johns Hopkins University Press.

Index of Names